EXAMINING THE CATHOLIC INTELLECTUAL TRADITION

EXAMINING THE CATHOLIC
INTELLECTUAL TRADITION

Edited by
Anthony J. Cernera
and
Oliver J. Morgan

SACRED HEART UNIVERSITY PRESS
FAIRFIELD, CONNECTICUT

Library of Congress Cataloging-in-Publication Data

Examining the Catholic intellectual tradition / edited by
    Anthony J. Cernera and Oliver J. Morgan
        p. cm.
    Includes bibliographical references and index.
    ISBN 1-888112-04-2 (hardcover)
    1. Catholics—Intellectual life. 2. Catholic learning and
scholarship. 3. Catholic universities and colleges—Philosophy.
I. Cernera, Anthony J., 1950- II. Morgan, Oliver J.

BX1795.I57 E83 2000
282—dc21   99-087071

CONTENTS

PREFACE

I n 1997, as the two of us walked the countryside surrounding Mount Saviour Monastery in Elmira, New York, we came to the conclusion that a project needed to be undertaken. Both of us had worked in Catholic higher education for a number of years and been engaged in efforts to articulate and reclaim the Catholic identity of our institutions. Both of us had been schooled in the philosophical and theological underpinnings of the Catholic intellectual tradition, and in its potential integrating applications across several other disciplines, in our undergraduate days at Fordham University. Now, several decades later, we had come to believe that a number of contemporary writings about the Catholic identity of colleges and universities were correct in asserting the need to lift up, transmit, and develop the Catholic intellectual tradition as central to the task of Catholic higher education.

As we walked, it seemed clear to us that one way to proceed would be to develop a resource book for discussion among faculty and staff at our universities. Many of our colleagues—good and hard-working people, willing to make their contribution to the overall good of the institution—were ignorant about the Catholic intellectual tradition. They would be open, we felt, to discussion and even self-education about the "tradition." However, it seemed to us that not much had been written about the tradition in a contemporary vein that was both clear and engaging. The landscape delimited by the term "Catholic intellectual tradition" seemed vague at best, or was addressed in a variety of places and in language that was not accessible to a number of our colleagues.

Some persons with whom we discussed the idea of a published resource in this area wondered who the representative authors might be; others suggested a variety of representative titles; still others spoke about a particularly Catholic "sensibility," noteworthy qualities of a "Catholic imagination," or a unique approach to education. The variety of responses to our initial idea indicated the need for such a project.

These were the beginnings of the book you hold. It is intended to lay out some of the content behind the term "Catholic intellectual tradition." As Monika Hellwig suggests in her initial essay, the "tradition" is both a "heritage," that is, a treasury of classic and more contemporary works, including intellectual, religious and aesthetic products by a variety of creative persons, and a "way of doing things" borne of experience, prayer, and critical reflection. Another volume, lengthier and more detailed, is planned and will investigate the relationship of the Catholic intellectual tradition to a number of different intellectual pursuits and disciplines.

A special word of thanks is due to two members of the Sacred Heart University community, Sidney Gottlieb, Professor of English, and Michelle Quinn, editorial assistant in the President's office, for their extraordinary efforts in bringing this volume to completion.

Anthony J. Cernera and Oliver J. Morgan

CHAPTER ONE

The Catholic Intellectual Tradition in the Catholic University

Monika K. Hellwig

We are in an age of increasing ecumenical activity in scholarship and in university circles. For example, Scripture scholarship has become almost totally inter-denominational. Traditions in sacred music have continuously borrowed from one another, as have conventional representations in the visual arts. Catholic programs in philosophy now have on their required reading lists books that were formerly listed in the Index of Forbidden Books and therefore inaccessible to Catholic students through normal channels. Recent trends in the study of literature have tended to abandon any claim to a canon of required classics. The study of history and of religion now addresses many cultures and languages.

In the midst of this, several questions arise. First of all, is depth of knowledge being sacrificed for the sake of breadth? In university studies, especially at the undergraduate level, this is no idle question. Secondly, are we abandoning efforts towards the integration of knowledge? Thirdly, are we in danger of losing our distinctive identity? Catholic universities and colleges, responsible more than any other body for the care and continuity of the Catholic intellectual tradition, are particularly challenged by these three questions.

The first of these questions, about the risk of losing depth, has exercised educators in the broader higher education field for some time. The extension of post-secondary education to a much larger proportion of the population has meant in many cases lowered expectations and less personal intellectual exchange between professors and students. While this may be quite efficient in technical fields, it impoverishes study in the humanities. It may be reducing higher education simply to longer schooling. Because religiously motivated schools of all traditions are concerned with assimilation of culture and critical discernment about values, this trend to the less personal in favor of the more technically efficient is damaging to the essential fabric of religious higher education.

The question about sacrificing depth for breadth is closely related to the second question, namely, whether we are achieving any integration in higher education. It has been fashionable, even in Catholic circles, to say that integration of studies is no longer possible in a pluralistic society, that each student must find some sort of personal balance or integration, but that it cannot be found in the planning of programs and curricula. Clearly, this is not a problem if education is seen as a matter of acquiring certain specialized skills and the means of access to information. If education is seen as preparation for life and for societal responsibilities, the lack of integration is disastrous because there is no foundation for making serious decisions about lifestyle, social participation, career goals, and so forth. Religiously sponsored institutions cannot surrender the task of integration.

The third question is whether we are in danger of forgetting and losing our identity. This risk is built into the pattern of contemporary developments in communication technology. It is caused in part by rapid sequences of change in the economy, upsetting employment patterns, calling for quick retraining of large numbers of the newly unemployable. It is a function of the political restlessness and reshaping of the world's alliances and balance of power with consequent shifting of what needs to be known for practical purposes. It is part of the culture, with its unquestioning favoring of the new over the already tested and the consequent changing relationships between the generations. All these are but a few of the external factors that tend to erode both the integration of higher education and the identity of religiously sponsored institutions. Erosion of identity is not a matter of any conscious decision to abandon the particular religious identity of an institution, but rather a combination of many new demands and the subtle influence of the secular expectations of the wider academy.

All these forces contribute to a situation in which a Catholic university or college cannot take its Catholic identity for granted in the way we might have done in the earlier decades of the twentieth century. It is not by anyone's failure or fault that U.S. Catholic colleges and universities had in many cases moved unnoticed towards secularization in the seventies and early eighties, to discover with a jolt in the late eighties that without taking thought and action they would not retain their distinctive identities. Such action had to address hiring policies, public statements of the institutions about their identity, leadership of the central administration, departments of theology and philosophy, the focus of university-sponsored research, structure and formation of boards, continuing bonds with the sponsoring religious community or diocese, student recruitment, campus ministry and much else. But most basic to the whole enterprise is the institution's respect and care for the Catholic intellectual heritage.

This paper discusses two topics: what defines the Catholic intellectual tradition; and how we can expect it to be present in the life of a university or college.

The Catholic Intellectual Tradition: Content

Our tradition is alive and growing in the present while greatly enriched and supported by many texts, objects, architectural structures, customs and rituals, modes of thought, expression and action, and relationships and organizations from the past. Because it is alive, it cannot be reduced to a treasury of deposits from the past, though it certainly contains such a treasury. Perhaps the most fruitful way of thinking about the Catholic intellectual tradition is in terms of two aspects: the classic treasures to be cherished, studied, and handed on; and the way of doing things that is the outcome of centuries of experience, prayer, action, and critical reflection.

The classic treasures are like crystallized deposits precipitated out of the living stream. If we reach far back into our history, they include the Scriptures, some primitive formulations of Christian faith and prayer, the rudiments of the rituals of Eucharist and baptism, the most basic elements of church and Christian calendar, and so forth. But based on Scripture, and growing with the centuries, are commentaries on Scripture and elaboration of biblical themes in further expressions, both those that are explicitly religious and those that are more generally exercises of the Christian imagination in art and literature. Based on the primitive formulations of faith, we see through the centuries the elaboration of catechesis, theology, religious drama, fiction, and poetry, and vast systems of Christian philosophy. Based on the primitive formulations of Christian prayer, we can trace whole systems of spirituality with their texts and commentaries, their Rules for living, and their exhortations, their hagiography, devotions, pilgrimages, shrines, and much else. Based on the rudimentary forms of Eucharist and baptism, we see the elaboration through the centuries of a complex sacramental system, whole traditions of liturgy and of sacred music, of church and monastic architecture, of the symbolism of incense, gestures, processions, bells, and vestments.

In the course of time, certain formulations became classic, not to prevent later developments but to form a touchstone against which later developments were to be seen and judged. These certainly include the pronouncements and explanatory texts handed down to us from the great church councils of antiquity, and in a broader sense the whole body of patristic writings, followed by the medieval and modern councils and the writings of the medieval doctors and certain modern theologians. These become classic by being habitually affirmed in retrospect by the discerning Christian community.

Certain figures in history became classic elements of the Christian story and heritage: Helena and Constantine, Macrina and Basil, Monica and Augustine, Benedict and Scholastica, Francis and Clare, Albertus Magnus and Thomas Aquinas, Catherine of Sienna and Teresa of Avila, to mention but a few whose personal stories are closely interwoven with the history of the Christian people. These are stories not to be forgotten or neglected. They come out of the memory and understanding of generations of believers who resonated with their lives, actions, or teachings.

Likewise, certain texts in literature became classics, throwing light on the Christian journey through history, on Christian faith and life and understanding of the big issues. Immediately coming to mind are: *Piers Plowman*, *The Divine Comedy*, *The Canterbury Tales*, and such modern classics as *Murder in the Cathedral*, *A Man for All Seasons*, and *Four Quartets*. Nor should we exclude from the treasury great Protestant and Orthodox classics like *Paradise Lost*, *The Pilgrim's Progress*, and *The Brothers Karamazov*. The treasures of Christian lyric poetry and hymnody are too many to list.

Much can be said, and more is yet to be discovered, about the treasures of Christian art and architecture, both the explicitly religious and the wider expression in decorative and representative art, in the building of hospitals, pilgrim shelters, schools, and universities, in the structuring of cities, towns, and villages among believers, expressing their hierarchy of values and their vision of reality. There is much to be studied and treasured in music, both sacred and profane, that expresses the Christian consciousness, whether in orchestral, operatic, choral, or chamber music, whether medieval plainchant, Baroque polyphony or modern classical and folk styles. Of course much of this is studied in art history or musicology, but by contemporary academic conventions it tends to be stripped of its religious relevance and studied only from a technical perspective. When these things are appreciated as part of the Christian intellectual heritage, they are studied in a way that tends to integrate the disciplines by relating everything to the meaning of human life in its relationship to the transcendent.

Something similar can be said of the development of experimental science and of technology. We have a heritage in which the development of the printing press, for instance, and the earliest discoveries in genetics were seen in their relationship to the meaning of human life and its ultimate destiny. The very notoriety and conflict generated by Galileo's demonstration of the Copernican hypothesis or Darwin's demonstration of the tenability of the evolutionary thesis testify to the relevance that the natural sciences have had to the integration of human life and knowledge with a spiritual focus.

We have, then, a treasury of many components in the Catholic intellectual tradition that should not be left hidden or unexplored because of the pressure of contemporary busy-ness. It should not be left unexplored. It is enriching, supportive, inspirational, and full of insight and wisdom for present and future generations of Catholic people. There is a further reason for keeping this treasury available and engaged with contemporary reality: it is wealth that the Catholic community holds in trust for the whole human community, whom it may profit in many ways.

Catholic Intellectual Tradition: Our Approach to Knowledge

All of the foregoing, however, is only one aspect of the Catholic intellectual tradition. The other aspect is the way we have learned to deal with experience and knowledge in order to acquire true wisdom, live well, and build good societies, laws and customs. Central to this are values and assumptions that we share with all religious traditions. These include the conviction that human life has meaning and that the meaning can be known. Further, they include the understanding that the basic principles of moral right and wrong are given and not humanly invented. Beyond this we hold in common with all religious traditions the deliberately fostered yearning for communion with the ultimately transcendent, and the understanding that in some way this is connected with the way we relate to one another.

These are foundational principles that we usually treat as presuppositions and therefore do not even examine. They are seldom called into question by ordinary people. Yet the drift of modern philosophies, especially since the end of the Second World War, suggests that it is urgent that some of us in scholarly circles reflect seriously on these underlying principles and their consequences at the levels at which contemporary science and technology, contemporary analysis in the humanities, and contemporary philosophy and social sciences influence the shaping of our society.

Beyond the common base that we share with all religious traditions there is, of course, a Christian core that we share with our fellow Christians. At its simplest, this is the conviction that in the person of Jesus of Nazareth we have an utterly trustworthy interpretation of the meaning and destiny of human life, of human relationship with God, and of what constitutes a good life. From this simple beginning, the Christian community over the centuries has elaborated ways of worship, structures of society, beliefs, and expectations, all of which go to make up a way of proceeding. Among Christian communities, however, some characteristic emphases and understandings are more particularly Catholic. In this essay, I would like to point to some that have direct implications for Catholic higher education and scholarship. These are: commitment to the continuity between faith and reason; respect for the cumulative wisdom of the past; an anti-elitist bent; attention to the community dimension of all human behavior; concern for integration of goals and objectives; and keen awareness of the sacramental principle.

The first of these, the continuity of faith and reason, leads Catholic universities and colleges to include philosophy and theology as essential components of the liberal arts core of undergraduate education, and to offer public lectures on current issues in public, professional and private life, to address these issues from a faith perspective. In contrast to some strands of Christian tradition, the Catholic tradition has strongly emphasized the need to think through the coherence of the faith and to face challenges to it from secular events and knowledge. We see this as a practice of faith, not a rejection of it. And this has led Catholic universities to develop philosophical traditions that train the mind to think clearly about the implications of the faith. The fact that the Scholastic tradition as it was passed on earlier in the twentieth century no longer serves this need adequately does not mean that we should abandon the project, but rather that we must find new philosophical vehicles to pursue it.

The second characteristic emphasis that I have singled out is that of respect for the cumulative wisdom of the past. In contrast to the position of some Christian communities which look for Christian wisdom only in Scripture or only in the legacy of the pre-Constantinian era, the Catholic community has set great store by knowledge of the cumulative wisdom of all the Christian centuries. Indeed, we have inherited and preserved the attitude of the second-century Greek apologists for Christianity in appreciating even the wisdom of pagan traditions as seen and adapted in the light of the faith. Catholic universities, therefore, have typically had strong programs in the humanities and often outstanding programs in classics at a time when others have tended to abandon the classical languages and deal with classical literature and mythology only very lightly.

The third characteristic mentioned above is the anti-elitist bent. This is another way of expressing that mark of the church that we used to call universality. Salvation and all other human goods are intended by the creator for all. All human beings and all peoples and nations are precious to God, who is at all times self-revealing to them. There is, therefore, a certain intellectual humility required in Catholic scholars and Catholic institutions, as well as a certain sense of responsibility for the conduct and use of scholarship, time, and resources. Non-elitism means responsibility to the whole community for what we choose to research and write, for the resources we use up in doing it, and for the way we use time when the labor of others indirectly makes possible our leisure for study and scholarly work. But non-elitism also means writing in a style that is accessible to non-specialists and teaching in a way that is helpful to all students. It means making strenuous efforts to include the underprivileged or excluded from society. It also means treating respectfully cultures and customs alien from our own.

The fourth characteristic is closely related to this. Attention to the community dimension of all human actions means that there cannot be a pursuit of any and all kinds of research or teaching simply out of the intrinsic interest of the subject, as though it were all a game without consequences. Critical discernment must be exercised as to the impact of releasing certain kinds of information into the society, as with increasingly powerful weaponry, or the effect of using resources for one kind of research that are badly needed for another kind that addresses urgent human need. Similarly, to say that there is a community dimension to all human actions also implies that teaching can never be without reference to the impact on the students and, through them, on their society. This applies, for instance, to the kinds of questions that are unfolded in relation to the maturity of the students to deal with such questions. And it applies to the kind of literature that is read in relation to the ability of the students to be discerning about the values expressed or implied, and about the behavior described. Moreover, the community dimension means that everything that is taught is placed in the context of what the students will do with their knowledge and the impact on their community.

This relates in turn to a fifth characteristic, namely, the concern to integrate knowledge as a basis for true wisdom in the living of one's life. Perhaps one of the most troubling aspects of rapid change and technical development in our times is that people of all ages have to learn so much so fast. They have to master so much instrumental knowledge and skill at such speed of assimilation that the more significant questions of meaning and purpose are often crowded out. The integration of learning in a coherent worldview or philosophy of life is a necessary basis for living a good, productive, well-directed life. It is necessary, though not sufficient, for setting proper priorities, for attaining a proper hierarchy of values, and even for attaining an appropriate intellectual humility in work and career, and in relations with other people.

A sixth characteristic, the final one mentioned here, is the experience and understanding that modern Catholics have come to name the sacramental principle. This refers not only to the seven sacraments that are central to Catholic worship, but to a broader experience that has to do with the way human beings use their memory and imagination. Our perception of reality is never in terms of raw experience, but is always arranged, interpreted, focused by the active mind of the perceiver. How we do this depends in large part on what we have experienced in the past, how those about us interpreted the experiences in which we shared, the representational art about us, the stories we heard, the way space and society had already been organized for us, and so forth. Two faculties play a role in this: memory which records what has been, and imagination which arranges the elements of experience in a meaningful pattern. An insight that Catholics particularly inherited from their Jewish or Hebrew past is that this is the way a people shapes its culture, and likewise the way the culture shapes the people. It can happen almost by default, a real risk in a pluralistic rapidly changing society like ours, or it can be the outcome of focused contemplation and critical reflection.

It has been a continuing practice of the Catholic community to build on religious memories by story and image, in literature and art, in music and architecture, in the liturgy and in extra-liturgical devotions, and in the elaboration of symbols of all kinds. The purpose of this is to shape the memories and the imagination of succeeding generations of believers so that they will interpret all their experiences in terms of the pervasive presence of the sacred and in terms of a history of salvation. The value that this gives to the education of the imagination is a precious heritage with implications for all education and in a special way for higher education. It demands a foundation in the liberal arts, a style of education that fosters contemplation, and a respect for works of scholarship that take a long time. This is all rather counter-cultural in our times.

The Role of the Catholic University

Some of the most significant contributions to Catholic culture, and to culture in any tradition, have been made by individuals working in relative isolation. Some important Catholic scholarship of our times comes from professors in large secular institutions and from independent scholars not employed by universities. But the Catholic universities are the normal trustees of Catholic learning, and the whole intellectual heritage would be greatly impoverished in their absence. In light of all that has been said above, some desirable components and aspects of a Catholic university emerge.

As we all know, at the minimum a Catholic university should be a true university in the accepted sense, and it should maintain a lively familiarity with the treasures of the tradition and the way of proceeding in the tradition. But this still leaves many questions: who, where, when and how? It may be well to begin in the library. It is not only a question of library holdings, but also of the welcoming atmosphere, style of architecture and interior decoration, works of art displayed, and most of all the placing of the collection. The significance of this last point is that what is most central to the character and purpose of the university should be most accessible, most attractively arranged, and offer the best possibilities for browsing and for sitting comfortably to read.

What has been said about the library could be said about the entire campus. Once a campus exists, its basic architectural pattern is established. However, at any opportunity to reshape the campus, the principle might be kept in mind that the very layout of the buildings ought to express the priorities and the relationship among the various activities of the campus, and that utility or efficiency need not mean ugliness. That may seem to some a trivial consideration in relation to the construction of curricula, the choice of programs, and so forth, but in the context of the sacramental principle, the visual-kinesthetic impact of the campus sets an important tone even before any activity is engaged. Of particular interest, of course, is the placing and design of the university's main chapel, whether it is the focus to which the eye and the steps are naturally drawn as to the center, or whether it is hidden away to be discovered only by devotees. Again in terms of the sacramental principle, the quality, character, and placement of statuary and other art about the campus is significant.

What can be said about space can also be said about time. In these days of external and financial pressures for maximum efficiency and maximal use of buildings, there are great temptations for weekend programs to spill into Sunday, even Sunday morning, for spring break to replace Holy Week and Easter, and for weekday feasts and holy days to disappear. Much is conveyed by the cessation of routine activities on special occasions that would never be communicated in the reading of books about it. The regular tolling of a bell for a daily celebration of Eucharist becomes part of consciousness even for those who do not darken the chapel door. The solemn celebrations of Eucharist at the beginning of the academic year, at graduation, on the occasion of faculty or student deaths, and at other special occasions, similarly help to constitute the character of the school even for those who do not participate. In aid of efficiency and conformity to more general academic expectations, there is pressure to eliminate all the particular Catholic markers in space and time that constitute the particularity of the environment. It is important that we resist this pressure in order to maintain our own particular identity.

The role of campus ministry, which has developed in the universities and colleges of the United States as the presence of the sponsoring communities has dwindled in numbers, could be defined as something more than individual care of souls. Given appropriate appointments, it could be the focal point of scholarly interdisciplinary conversations in which the encounter of faith and culture could take place in some depth and with some continuity. With an investment in occasional significant outside speakers, the participation of top administrators, and perhaps an occasional formal reception, this could become the intellectual focus of the school.

The seriousness and focus of the curriculum, especially for undergraduates, begin with the manner and style of recruitment of students. A university or college that states its identity and character clearly in its literature, and takes care that admission personnel understand and support this statement, will certainly attract both faculty and students who are attuned to the institution's expectations. That being so, it will be easier to maintain in the structure of the curriculum the components of the Catholic intellectual tradition. It may be important to note in passing that the Catholic colleges and universities of the United States are almost alone among the Catholic universities of the world in offering all students a liberal arts foundation including an introduction to philosophy and theology. Elsewhere, students entering the university begin immediately to concentrate in their specialized field, though they may have had a more extensive and intensive secondary education before they come.

The foundation in the liberal arts is important in developing both a more effective use of the imagination in creative approaches to personal, technical, professional, and societal challenges, and better honed skills in critical thinking and evaluation. In our society, it is rapidly becoming counter-cultural to spend time in the undergraduate years on laying this foundation rather than going directly into professional preparation. Moreover, even where liberal arts programs remain, they are often so dissipated into unrelated elective offerings, each focusing rather narrowly in its own field, that the benefits of a truly liberal education are lost. Those benefits ought to include the integration of learning, the realization of the community dimension, increasing experience of the continuity of faith and reason, a deepening respect for and appreciation of the cumulative wisdom of the past, progressive transcending of facile and unexamined prejudices and, of course, the integration of life and learning.

Both philosophy and theology play a central role in such a liberal education. It is a role that is little appreciated in our culture. It is thrown in question by the prevailing interpretation of the constitutional separation of church and state, an interpretation followed even by some of the large private foundations on whose financial assistance private higher education has become steadily more dependent for its very survival. For Catholics this role of philosophy and theology is central to our intellectual tradition. It follows from the need to integrate one's life and activities with a focus on ultimate ends. This clearly requires the development of analytical and critical skills, and is immensely helped by acquaintance with the great thinkers of the past, the questions they raised, the ways in which they worked towards answers, the kinds of answers they found satisfactory or unsatisfactory. That is the function of philosophy, and it involves the foundational questions for the natural and social sciences, for the appreciation of art, music, and literature, for an approach to history, a grasp of languages and mathematical reasoning, and much else.

It has been the custom in Catholic higher education in the past to teach an introduction to the branches of philosophy according to later presentations of Thomistic thought. In our time, when so much has changed and is constantly changing, it may be more consistent with the Catholic intellectual tradition to teach an introduction to philosophy through a tracing of the history of philosophy. Our tradition cherishes the cumulative wisdom of the past. In philosophy this retracing of the past is a particularly apt introduction to the main lines of thought of the great thinkers, each developing further what had been handed on through the centuries of Western thought. If there were unlimited time, one might look at the traditions of India and China. Given the time constraints of the undergraduate years, it seems more relevant to the project of Catholic higher education to furnish our students with a common memory of the development of the great questions in their own tradition. On the whole, that is what is sadly lacking for most educated people of our culture and society. In providing a certain breadth, their education has often failed to give them either solid cultural roots of their own or a common memory shared with others in their milieu. This last is so important for meaningful conversation because it offers a common vocabulary understood in a common sense, as well as providing reference points, assumptions, accepted modes of argumentation, and such like.

As mentioned above, the teaching of theology to all students in Catholic higher education is a very important contribution to the passing on of the Catholic intellectual tradition. This much is clear. What is less clear, even now more than four decades after the Second Vatican Council, is just what should be the content of theology for an educated laity. It is clear that to go back to a popularization of traditional seminary formation misses the mark. It is equally clear that the trend of recent decades does not fulfill the need. The recent tendency has been to offer some introduction to critical Scripture scholarship, some discussion of foundational questions concerning the nature of faith and religious language, concerning traditional efforts to demonstrate the existence of God, what is meant by claims of revelation, and other questions common to all traditions. Sometimes even these are not required, and each student can make a personal selection of courses from a slate of electives. This seems to fall far short of the role that theology should play in the education of students in Catholic undergraduate programs.

If theology is really to play an integrating and focusing role, our programs probably need to declare themselves boldly and devote more time to the theological sequence. To achieve the essential purpose, we need minimally to offer students an introduction both to the understanding of Scripture in their own culture and intellectual environment, and to a coherent, well-informed, and intelligent grasp of their own faith tradition with its creedal content. Moreover, we need to engage faculty and graduate students in the difficult questions about their own tradition.

At the same time, it is evident that the whole burden of a Catholic focus and integration of the curriculum cannot simply be carried by the theology and philosophy departments. That burden must be shared by all departments in ways appropriate to their disciplines, but in a special way by literature, history, fine arts, and some components of psychology, sociology, and political theory. It is a question of relating everything to the greater whole, to human destiny, responsibility for society and culture, stewardship of the resources of creation, and so forth. It is also a question of knowing, taking seriously, and engaging the wisdom of our tradition in the questions that arise. And it is a question of treating the material learned in the student's major field not only as a matter of technical competence but as a matter of wisdom for life.

The character and identity of a Catholic university need to be evident not only in undergraduate education but also in the graduate and professional programs and in the original scholarly work and research of the faculty. This is even more difficult to achieve in the present climate of higher education and scholarship worldwide. The university world is still firmly rooted in the Enlightenment with its secularizing tendencies and its disregard for the particular in favor of the universal and whatever can be broadly standardized. The claim that a particular tradition such as the Catholic has something of value to contribute to research in politics, economics, psychology, and so forth is still suspect in most circles. The idea that a religiously based ethics should be part of the curriculum of professional schools seems quite absurd to many of our colleagues. But a counter-cultural stance on these issues belongs to the very core of the Catholic university's task in the world. It is there that the wisdom of our tradition meets those who make the decisions for society, and it is there that the engagement of the Catholic intellectual tradition with the culture can effectively happen.

The requirements for realizing this are exacting. We need competent scientists, social scientists, and scholars in all fields who are sufficiently formed in the Catholic intellectual tradition themselves to bring their graduate students and already qualified practitioners to an understanding, appreciation, and critique of the issues that arise. Almost all of the professors in various fields in our universities and colleges have themselves been educated at the doctoral level in the large state university graduate schools under the post-Enlightenment secularizing and specializing influences. If they have had a formation in the Catholic intellectual tradition, this will at best have been at the undergraduate level, but for many will have ended at the secondary level or with parish instruction for the sacrament of confirmation. That is a very fragile foundation on which to provide their graduate students with serious faith-based analysis of issues in their fields. It is clear that in order to realize the potential of a Catholic university in some fullness, continuing education or self-education of the faculty is an indispensable prerequisite. This can be done with reading circles guided by competent people, with public lectures, faculty-run seminars and colloquia, summer institutes attended by invitation, and other such initiatives. It can engage good theology and philosophy faculties with their colleagues as well as with their students.

The other side of this is the selection, focus, and conduct of research. It has become customary on the university campuses for research of some kind to be required for promotion and tenure, but for the nature of that research to be entirely at the discretion of each individual professor. The endeavor of the International Federation of Catholic Universities, on the other hand, is to build connections among Catholic universities so that joint major research projects can be undertaken which relate to such problems as world hunger, development of Third World cities and economies, the international illegal drug trade and the agricultural economies integrated into it, development of legal systems in emergent nations, conflict resolution over major land claims, armaments control mechanisms, world literacy, and other peace, justice, and development issues. Clearly, the ideal Catholic university would have a focus in research and scholarship that would further the Catholic intellectual tradition in bringing both the classic treasures and the way of proceeding into play in relation to contemporary culture and society. This requires rather a bold stand on the part of the institution to assert its research priorities and to hire and give grants by the criteria of those priorities.

There is, of course, nothing in the inner logic of our intellectual tradition that would require that we hire only Catholic professors or admit only Catholic students. The requirement is rather the contrary, namely, that it is important for a Catholic university to have both faculty and student participants of other traditions. Being open to the cumulative wisdom not only of our own but of other traditions happens more readily when we meet them in their living representatives. Moreover, an authentic dialogue of faith and culture is more likely to happen where other perspectives are represented. And again, while it is good that students get a firm grounding in their own tradition, being segregated from others in their intellectually formative years does not prepare them to live in a pluralistic society and in an ecumenical age. Complementarity and ecumenical exchanges are an important aspect of scholarship for the faculty and of education for the students.

At the same time, it is becoming increasingly clear that a critical mass of faculty, administrators, and staff really committed to the Catholic mission of the institution is essential if the character of the institution is to survive. It is a matter requiring careful attention in our time. Much could be taken for granted in the past when the sponsoring religious congregations were a strong presence on each campus and guaranteed continuity in the spirit of the foundation. These were men and women with a solid formation in Catholic experience, worship, and thought, as it was mediated through a particular congregational spirituality and apostolate. Moreover, it was accepted without dispute that the founding congregation's vision and philosophy was the criterion by which all things were judged in the conduct of the institution. Such is no longer the case on most campuses, where the faculty at large is the arbiter in many matters. If that faculty does not share the ideals of the founders, those ideals will not remain the philosophy and spirit of the institution.

There is, of course, a further consideration: the character of the board of directors. Boards have largely assumed the guiding function of the sponsoring congregations. They select the president and make major decisions concerning property, financing, and priorities. It is critical that trustees be selected not only for their contacts and skills but also for their commitment to the Catholic identity, character, and ideals of the institution. In the long run, it is the board that sets the direction in which the institution will grow. Board members are likely to be in the same position as the faculty in relation to the Catholic intellectual tradition. They are likely to have had their last education in the tradition in the undergraduate years at most, but perhaps only at the secondary level, or only in parish preparation for confirmation. If the Catholic universities are to realize their potential as participants in the shaping and the handing on of the intellectual tradition, there also need to be ongoing programs of board formation in order to support the spirit and focus of the institution.

Conclusion

We are the heirs and trustees of a great intellectual and cultural tradition founded on Christian faith and enhanced by grace and by many centuries of testing for fidelity and authenticity. It is a trust not only for the benefit of the Church but also for the benefit of the world. The Catholic universities play a key role in bearing this trust with its treasury of classic deposits and its long-developed approach to life and learning. The conditions for fidelity to our trust have changed a good deal in the twentieth century. If we are still moving experimentally and are not always clear and successful in what we are doing, that is not from ill will or unconcern, but due to the uncharted nature of our situation. On the other hand, we cannot afford to let the future of our universities take their course without careful attention, reflection, and planning. In this planning the characteristic contribution that the Catholic universities can make must be not one criterion among others but the guiding principle of the whole project. And in this the Catholic universities and colleges of the United States have a particular role to play because of the unique character of their undergraduate programs, because of their sheer numbers among the Catholic universities of the world, and because of their excellent academic standing among the universities of the continent.

CHAPTER TWO

On the Task and Vocation
of the Catholic College

LOUIS DUPRÉ

We all know the original purpose of education: to incorporate the young into the group by acquainting them with its customs, practices, and beliefs. Early on in our culture, a more universal purpose was added to that particular one. Socrates in his conversations may well have been the first to formulate it when he exhorted his disciples not only to obey the laws of Athens, but also to pursue a wisdom common to Greeks and barbarians alike. This universal ideal, both theoretical and practical, was further articulated by Plato, Aristotle, and the Stoics. Christians did not hesitate to adopt its basic principles. Once education in the early Middle Ages took the form of schooling, the universal and the particular became well-nigh indistinguishable. Since the *res publica christiana* under Pope and Emperor extended beyond cities, counties, and duchies, the initiation into a Christian culture prepared for public office as well as for personal perfection.[1] Together with the superior Muslim and Jewish centers of learning in Baghdad and Spain, those Christian schools and, later, the universities laid the foundations of what we have come to call Western culture.

The political and religious crises of the fifteenth and sixteenth centuries threatened to tear apart what had barely gelled into a fragile unity. The rise of the autonomous nation-state as well as the split of the Reformation ended the era of a more or less homogeneous education in a culturally united Europe. Theology, which had functioned as the unifying discipline, now became the dividing one. In the polemics, it lost its ultimate authority. The sciences followed an independent course; philosophy desisted from being the handmaid of theology; literature and the arts went their own untheological ways. What did not change, however, even after Europe's culture lost its Christian character, was the idea that education should lead to universal wisdom. But theology's loss of a central position as well as the emancipation of the various branches of knowledge inevitably transformed that universal goal into a pragmatic one. The pursuit of wisdom ceased to be an end in itself. As Francis Bacon put it, learning should stop being sterile and pursued for its own sake; it should bear fruit for the human race.

The two educational ideals of Greek theoretical knowledge and Hebrew practical wisdom became united in Western culture and were rarely challenged. Those few who did question the Greek ideal in principle, such as Tertullian and Jerome, remained faithful to that ideal in practice. Even today the Church has not abandoned it, as we may learn from the Second Vatican Council's definition of the Catholic school: "a synthesis of culture and faith, a synthesis of faith and life: the first reached by integrating all the different aspects of human knowledge through the subjects taught, in the light of the Gospel; the second in the growth of the values characteristic of the Christian." In fact, however, that ideal but seldom directs the actual course of Catholic college education, despite our repeated profession of loyalty to it.

Having received its last major impulse in the *studia humanitatis* of early Italian humanism, by the time of the Renaissance the idea of *humanitas* began to degenerate into an artificial superstructure presented as *Lebenskunst*.[2] The late-eighteenth-century ideal of *Bildung* may well have been the final attempt to revive the idea of an integral humanism. What von Humboldt, Goethe, and Schiller advocated was the most ambitious educational project ever devised—a grandiose moral, aesthetic, and intellectual synthesis destined to bring the entire human potential to harmonious and full development. Did it, at last, bring the early humanist dream to fulfillment? No! The Christian humanists, Dante, Salutati, Landino, even Ficino, had still conceived of *culture* primarily as developing a divinely given nature, in accordance with the Latin root of *colere* (to foster). The German classicists, however, interpreted educating as assisting a person to shape his or her life itself into a work of art. As the architectural terminology suggests, *Bildung* consists essentially in what one "makes" of oneself, not in how one fosters a given nature.

To be sure, there had been genuine attempts to steer the process of education back to nature. Herder's organic concept of culture clearly moved in that direction. So did Schiller's theory of the aesthetic education of man. We must first *receive* nature before we can start nurturing it. The entire aesthetic education, model of all pedagogical activity, consists in balancing the active with the passive functions of the mind. "The material of activity . . . man has first to *receive*; and he does in fact receive it, by way of perception, as something existing outside of him in space, and as something changing within him in time."[3] But this happy "naturalism" characteristic of Herder, Schiller, and the young Goethe would soon give way to a Promethean self-assertiveness. Life was to be *construed*: nature would provide no more than the building blocks.

What links this drive toward self-assertion (Theodor Litt has called it *Selbstbehauptung*) to the present functional approach to education?[4] We have lost the naively optimistic faith in the unlimited potential of human nature and appear to have settled for the modest task of adapting a person to the needs of a technological society. But on a fundamental level, both conceptions may be traced back to the same attitude defined by the idea that the person shapes his/her destiny and that consists in self-achievement. It needs no repeating that this attitude, though technically and economically successful, has also caused some serious problems.

The idea of an uninhibited creative freedom that first inspired the Renaissance ideal also stimulated the unrestricted technological development of the last two centuries. It now seems to have become trammeled in its own creations. Technology has begun to escape human control; the ideal of self-realization is rending the social fabric apart. The urgency of these problems forces us to rethink the goals of education. This is no easy task. The school today has no choice but to adapt its programs and, indeed, its overall orientation, to the functional society within which its students are destined to make a living. Catholic colleges have, perhaps more than others, attempted to preserve at least the ideal of a Christian liberal education, as formulated in the sixteenth and seventeenth centuries. Yet confronted with the practical realities of the present age, many have reduced its realization to offering a few courses on religion, ethics, and a smattering of philosophy in an otherwise wholly pragmatically oriented curriculum. The complexity of a technological society imposes an unprecedented number of secular demands on a university which its graduates must be prepared to meet if they hope to occupy a useful position in it. To be sure, the college cannot be held responsible for equipping students with the kind of expert knowledge required for highly specialized tasks. But it must at least train their capacity for learning principles and for applying them. For that purpose, the distinction between a religious and a secular school hardly seems to matter.

Do the educational conditions imposed by the contemporary world, then, leave Catholic institutions of higher learning any possibility of maintaining a Catholic identity in anything more than the name? What are the conditions for preserving this identity? Speaking in most general terms, we might state, as the Papal *nuncio* Cardinal Pio Laghi did in a recent address on John Paul II's Apostolic Constitution, *Ex Corde Ecclesiae*, that the identity of the Catholic university consists, first and foremost, in an institutional link with the Church. Stated negatively, that implies, I presume, that neither teachers nor administrators should publicly embrace principles clearly in conflict with the doctrinal principles taught by the Church. Of course, it does not deny them the right to question precisely what those principles imply or how they must be applied. They may publicly disagree with a particular interpretation of them, even one issued by some member or members of the hierarchy. Nor does it deprive teachers of the right to err in their attempts to determine what a still developing tradition involves on a given point—as the rector of the Catholic university of Louvain eloquently claimed in his welcoming address to Pope John Paul II at the occasion of his visit there. Leo O'Donovan, S.J., the current rector of Georgetown University, in a letter to students and alumni, touches on the delicate subject of academic autonomy in a university that professes an allegiance to the Catholic Church:

> The University needs a legitimate institutional autonomy in order to fulfill its mission, which is to create and transmit ideas. It needs space, an arena of free discussion and exploration, if it is to serve the fundamental purposes of a university dedicated to the pursuit of truth and to the intellectual and moral development of its students. The norms of institutional self-governance and autonomy in American universities constitute one dimension of this space; . . . protections of free inquiry and discussion [another]. Conceiving "space" this way suggests the room for error, within the constraints of civilized discussion, that is appropriate in an intellectual community. The Catholic university does not flourish or serve the Church well, nor does it prepare its students for the conflicts and dilemmas of contemporary American life, by avoiding difficult discussions or by silencing thought.

More difficult to define is the positive task incumbent upon the Catholic university, namely, that its teaching ought to be inspired by Christian principles. A first and obvious way of fulfilling this task consists in including courses in philosophy and theology in the curriculum. As experience has proven, this is by no means sufficient for conveying an adequate idea of what the Christian way of thinking and acting implies. Indeed, if poorly taught, as they have often been, they tend to have a more negative effect than no courses in that field at all. Nonetheless, they remain an essential condition for providing students with a basis of Catholic thought. They may, and if successful, they will convey a perspective on the entire educational program. Theology and philosophy unite what otherwise remains a fragmentation of unrelated disciplines. In the words of the late Timothy Healy, President of Georgetown University, they "bring into the preoccupation with immediacy that is so much a part of a modern American university her habit and understanding of contemplation as a self-justifying enterprise."[5] Indeed they ought to have a direct bearing upon all disciplines. The fact that theology and philosophy yield no tangible results does not imply that the university can dispense with them. Newman forcefully insisted on the primacy of disinterested, universal knowledge that had given shape to Western education, while, nonetheless, fully allowing for specialized and even pragmatic learning:

> Knowledge is capable of being its own end. Such is the constitution of the human mind, that any kind of knowledge, if it be really such, is its own reward. And if this is true of all knowledge, it is true also of that special Philosophy which I have made to consist in a comprehensive view of truth in all its branches.[6]

Precisely such a disinterested knowledge is what allows us to call a college education "liberal," that is, according to Aristotle (*Rhetoric* I, 4 and 5), appropriate for the free man, as opposed to technical training required for mechanical skill.

For both Newman and Healy, then, the Catholic university, and for that matter any university which grants theology a place of honor, represents most fully the ancient ideal of learning. Their emphasis on the need for disinterested, universal wisdom is supported by Whitehead, himself a pioneer in the highly specialized field of mathematical logic: "Though knowledge is one chief aim of intellectual education, there is another ingredient, vaguer but greater, and more dominating in its importance. The ancients called it wisdom."[7] In the rhythm of the mind's development, the ultimate motive power consists in a sense of value, and in conveying that theology plays a crucial role: "No part of education has more to gain from attention to the rhythmic law of growth than has moral and religious education."[8]

But can the principles of theology and philosophy still penetrate a curriculum dictated by technical demands and a functional orientation? From theology in particular, this requires that it be more than class instruction. For the believing student, even for one less than totally committed to his or her faith, theology must fulfill a different task and follow a different method than other academic disciplines. It is expected to initiate into a mystery that touches on all aspects of human existence. One might consider it one of the main objectives of the Catholic school to extend a religious vision to all areas of life. Theological education should invite exploration of reality in all aspects— scientific, philosophical, and aesthetic—rather than setting limits to it, as it all too often has done. It should assist the young learner in raising questions before presenting answers. In no case should it be satisfied with providing religious "information" about sacred history, dogma, and morals without rendering that information *meaningful*, that is, fit to in*form* all of life.

In raising the capacity for a religious view of life, the aesthetic education plays a significant part. More than any other approach, the perception of beauty opens up a dimension of depth beyond the reality we all too readily take for granted. Aesthetic perceptiveness unlocks the sense of wonder which an objective culture has systematically dulled in our daily lives. Poetic word and artistic symbol, more than rational reflection, prepare the young person for discovering the meaning of transcendence. Without them, theological instruction tends to become factual information with little chance of conveying a genuine sense of otherness. Unfortunately, today courses of literature and art all too often are taught as if they were part of scientific, objective learning, a branch of the "human sciences" that takes its place beside political and social history. Even in this reduced format, the "humanities" everywhere are losing ground. Catholic schools should consider it their particular duty to put up a firm resistance to this general rout. Nor should we restrict the aesthetic education to acquainting its pupils with specifically "religious" art and literature. *All* beauty, by its very nature, opens up the space of wonder, which alone allows the divine to *reveal*.

One part of the aesthetic initiation that deserves special emphasis consists in restoring the student's linguistic sensitivity. Christianity is rightly named the religion of the Word. Continuing the Hebrew tradition, it interprets, preserves, and transmits God's revealing events through sacred language. Everywhere the Christian *kerygma* affirms the primacy of the Word. Everywhere, except from the pulpit in Catholic school and church. In both places, the sacredness of the word has become seriously threatened by the invading vulgarization of contemporary discourse. In our day, language serves as the principal instrument for pursuing the functional, technical aims of an objectivist culture. Never before was the word so deprived of its innermost dignity and its ability to express and to shape from within. Instead of respecting that dignity, we have lowered language to the role of an instrument, empty of meaning, devoid of poetic resonance, replete with technical neologisms.

The shorthand language in which technicians communicate and which workers speak at office, shop, or factory is gradually becoming also the language of the school, and even of the church. With its unique concern for functional simplicity and its disdain of spiritual subtlety, this language grinds everything into cultural pulp. Far from resisting this universal profanation of the word, the school actively cooperates in the degrading of speech. To some extent, this has become inevitable. If we train people for "functioning" in a functional world, we are forced to teach them the language to do so. But this necessity renders a revaluation through poetry all the more imperative. For without an authentic language, no culture can preserve its identity, nor can religion continue to "reveal." All the problems confronting faith in a flat, one-dimensional culture perpetuate themselves through corrupted and corruptive speech. One of the most urgent tasks for the young student consists in relearning a respect for language, not merely, and not primarily, for religious language. If our cultural situation requires a new sense of depth, the rediscovery of language becomes an essential condition. When a conversion of culture itself is needed, theology should relate to all aspects of culture—including the ones that lie far outside its disciplinary boundaries.

Religious education includes practice as well as theory. Ever since Pope John XXIII, the Church's *Magisterium* has repeatedly insisted that social justice holds a primary place in Christian ethics. This implies, as the Medellin episcopal conference in the presence of Paul VI concluded, that the Catholic university should foster in its students "a healthy sense of criticism of the social situation and a vocation to service." This means not that the Catholic university must engage in revolutionary activity even when conditions of grave social injustice prevail—such activity forms no part of its educational task and can only obstruct an effective performance of it—but that the Christian university has nevertheless the right and the duty, on the basis of social research and ethical principles, to make what the former rector of the University of Central America, Fr. Ellacuria, S.J. (one of the six Jesuits murdered in San Salvador), called "social projections" about the state of society.[9] Without attempting to draw the fine line between theoretical conclusions and principles for action, we may nevertheless safely conclude that, even if one remains within the theoretical model, as I do, courses in theology and Christian ethics alone do not suffice to render a college "Catholic." The university ought to create an environment that renders it possible to convert ethical principles into voluntary, extra-curricular service. At the very minimum, this requires the availability of such service activities as have been traditionally connected with Catholic education and social action in the United States.[10]

It also implies that theology must be embodied in symbols and liturgical action as well as in formal instruction.[11] Enough has been said about poetry and the arts as effective catalysts for conveying the kind of symbolic perceptiveness needed for a sacramental view of life essential to Catholicism. Yet equally important is the central presence on campus of a properly performed liturgical practice such as a Catholic university is uniquely capable of providing. I remember with some nostalgia how during my Georgetown years at the heart of the ancient campus in Dahlgren Chapel, in the quiet of dawn, at noon break, or at special occasions joyful or sad, few or many gathered for Eucharistic services. There we met, students and teachers, of chemistry and of philosophy, of literature and languages. These precious moments of recollection somehow shed a different light on the rest of the day's activities. If education implies a cultivation of the spirit, then these exercises are as much part of it as the academic curriculum.

Next, a word should be said about the moral education that ought to distinguish a Catholic college. It is generally known that today's parents hesitate to enforce the moral rules and instill the religious principles which they unquestionably accepted from the previous generation. Understandably so, since many have not been able to withstand responsible criticism. But the result has been a moral and religious vacuum. A strong moral and theological education in college may try to fill this vacuum with a few critically resistant principles. Nor do colleges need to apologize for a tradition based on the idea that the good life is the virtuous one. But a serious moral initiation requires more than what it all too often has become at the hands of timid teachers, a sociological presentation of the choices people actually make and of their theoretical attempts to rationalize them. By its very nature, the Catholic college has already declared its commitment to certain ideals of perfection and to specific norms for distinguishing good from evil. I believe that for a college to maintain its Catholic moral identity requires teachers to be unambiguous about what clearly agrees and what certainly conflicts with those fundamental principles.

A choice of values fails to be practically effective, however, unless that choice itself is grounded in an absolute that orders and integrates all values. Without a transcendent foundation, values lose their ultimate basis. This is not to say that ethics cannot survive without a belief in God. It does mean, however, that only a transcendent absolute adequately integrates values and prevents any single one of them from becoming an absolute in its own right. At this point, however, we often encounter a serious misunderstanding. Catholic educators often take the foundation of values to be itself a value. Because the school's curriculum includes theology, they pride themselves on teaching values. This claim is at least ambiguous. For what is a value? Is it more than what I or what we "value?" It remains, despite all intentions to the contrary, an inherently subjective concept. Applied to God, it symptomatizes the fundamental heresy of modern culture, namely, that *all*, including God, is a projection of the human mind, subject to human valuation. When Nietzsche declared Being itself to be a value, he subjected the meaning of reality itself ultimately to a human choice. This move completed the modern turn to the subject as sole source of meaning in the ethical field.[12] While previously value had been the *effect* of the real, henceforth *Being* itself would be recognized only in terms of value. Even to describe God himself as eminently "valuable" (ie., valuable in and for himself) as Max Scheler did when he defined the exclusively divine attribute of holiness as a value category, seems misleading.[13] Quite logically, then, religion, the foundation of all values, becomes itself the supreme value, and a religious education becomes reduced to an integral value education.

Unfortunately, such a view merely multiplies the pitfalls which a Catholic education tries to avoid. Nor can Catholics claim to hold a monopoly in "value education." All educational systems today are value oriented. So-called "valueless" theories merely posit scientific objectivity (or some derivative from it) as the one and only value of all formal education. Precisely their monolithic character results in the strongest possible affirmation of the value mentality: only what can be formulated objectively possesses the kind of value that justifies us in considering it meaningful. Religious believers rightly consider such subjectively rooted values unstable and ultimately fragmentary. Hence they look for an absolute beyond the subject, both to support and to integrate all values. Christians identify this absolute foundation of value with a single, transcendent principle. Referring to this absolute principle itself as a value merely perpetuates the subjective slant of modern culture. As long as a Christian education persists in accepting such a subjectivist perspective, it cannot claim to present a serious alternative, and its education toward values, far from solving the problems of modern culture, may aggravate them.

The qualities described thus far may be considered directly linked to the Catholic identity of a college or university. There is still another factor, less exclusively connected yet almost as indispensable for maintaining that identity as any of the preceding ones. Regretfully, far from being a distinctive property of Catholic learning, we now find it more carefully preserved by eminent non-Catholic schools, including the one at which I teach. I am, of course, referring to the maintenance of the link with tradition. Actively to participate in the life of a culture requires acquainting oneself with its past accomplishments that have shaped its present and must continue to provide guidance for its future. Initially, the classical segment of that past—the Latin and Greek literature—was considered to hold the essence of all that mattered in that tradition. These days are, of course, long gone—in America even longer than in Western Europe. But what has remained, and what the American College has probably better preserved than the increasingly specialized and professionalized European university, is the concept of a liberal—and that is the opposite of a practical—education as the most appropriate basis not only for a life of learning, but also for a professional career, or one in civil service, business, or any other occupation. In our era of intensified communication, an abundance of news media impresses upon the mind an inflated urgency of the immediate. The idols of the marketplace have also begun to invade the Academy. To their worshippers, the patient and often tedious quest for truth must yield to what arouses today's attention, causes controversy, or evokes discussion, even if it flies in the face of well-established principles and of common sense. Only a vital continuity with the past creates the distance needed for assessing the true significance of the present. The living presence of a tested tradition protects the mind against the intrusion of the immediate. In a country where the future tends to elbow out the past, Catholic colleges have always shouldered the unfashionable burden of keeping tradition alive.

Ironically, today when the need to maintain a vital continuity with the past has begun to be universally recognized as indispensable for understanding the present, more and more Catholic schools appear tempted to drive the past into a corner of specialized historical studies. In yielding to that temptation, they abandon their Catholic identity as well as their particular attractiveness. A few years ago, at a symposium on Catholic education organized by Georgetown University, one of the speakers, a Jewish alumnus, stated: "In 1966, Catholic philosophers were just about the only academics philosophically interested in the perennial question of natural law, the question that lies at the heart of all ethical, political, and legal philosophy." What he claimed for philosophy is no less true for literature. The poetry of Homer, Virgil, Horace, and Dante constitutes an indispensable sounding board for perceiving the echoes and resonances of poems of a later age. In many secular schools, teachers of literature nowadays face the almost impossible task of having to explain the multiple and multi-leveled allusions to Scripture, scholastic philosophy, and medieval culture that have become entirely lost to their students.

To conclude, it is not the task of the Catholic college or university to convert its students to a religious life, nor is it competent to do so. But it can awaken and nurture religious perceptiveness. Its teaching ought to lead toward an intellectual openness capable of integrating from a transcendent perspective the variety of tasks and disciplines that modern civilization imposes upon us. The school cannot teach virtue, but it can show virtue to be the vocation of the noble soul and establish a moral environment that measures the person against a higher standard than what promises immediate rewards. The most fundamental task of the Catholic university, to which all others must remain subservient, is that of preserving, nurturing, and developing the *spirit*. The highest predicate ever granted human nature is that of being spiritual. That one attribute contains all the powers active in *homo sapiens:* artistic and literary creativity, scientific inventiveness, technical skill. It also includes the moral creativity of those who, by placing their lives at the service of their fellow humans, or even sacrificing them altogether, again and again raise human dignity to new summits. At the core of all spiritual creativity, however, lies the mysterious desire to respond to a transcendent summons that calls us humans to move beyond its present limits. One of the major accomplishments of our past culture consisted in having recognized, named, and honored this spiritual Eros as originating in a divine source.

In our own time, however, that recognition is in jeopardy. The awareness of a transcendent presence at the heart of human activity has gradually disappeared from culture and morality. Our very existence as spiritual beings has thereby come into crisis. Religion has withdrawn into isolation, protecting itself against the secular onslaught in a sterilized environment of its own. Culture and morality, on the other side, having mostly lost their awareness of a transcendent Eros, have become impoverished. Without the religious dimension, culture and morality become hollowed out, formalistic, shallow; without culture, religion loses what it most seriously needs, namely, an embodiment in moral practice and cultural symbols. The vocation of the Catholic university in our time is, against all odds, to keep the disparate elements of our culture together within an integrating transcendent perspective. In the past, it has not always succeeded well in achieving that goal; often it has failed altogether, sacrificing religion to the idol of culture or culture to the idol of religion. But its lasting merit lies in having kept alive the awareness, crucial for our spiritual survival, that a synthesis is needed. The dehumanizing utilitarianism to which Western society has descended, the collapse of public morality, combined with an unprecedented technical power, raises even in the secular mind alarming concerns about the future. Nietzsche wrote that modern man has a small soul. But enormous power in the hands of persons with small souls constitutes a great danger. Matthew Arnold foresaw what we witness today:

> We went after the blind guides and followed the false direction, and the actual civilization of England and America is the result. A civilization with many virtues, but without lucidity of mind and without largeness of temper. And now we English, at any rate, have to acquire them, and to learn the necessity for us, "to live (as Emerson says) from a greater depth of being."[14]

To alert the young to that necessity may well be the principal task of the Catholic college in a time of spiritual need.

Notes

1. Glenn W. Olsen, "Deconstructing the University," *Communio*, 19, no. 2 (1992), 226-53.

2. See August Buck, "Die Krise des humanistischen Menschenbildes bei Machiavelli," *Archiv für das Studium der neueren Sprachen*, 189 (1953): 304-17.

3. Friedrich von Schiller, *On the Aesthetic Education of Man*, trans. Elizabeth M. Wilkinson and L.A. Willoughby (Oxford: Clarendon Press, 1967), Letter XI, 6, p. 75.

4. Theodor Litt, *Das Bildungsideal der deutschen Klassik und die moderne Arbeitswelt* (Bonn: Bundeszentrale für Heimatdienst, 1955), 108.

5. Timothy Healy, "Probity and Freedom on the Border: Learning and Belief in the Catholic University," *America*, 163, no. 1 (July 7, 1990), 6.

6. John Henry Newman, "Knowledge Its Own End," in *The Idea of a University* (1854), discourse 5, §2.

7. Alfred North Whitehead, *The Aims of Education* (1929; rpt. New York: New American Library, 1954), 46.

8. Whitehead, *The Aims of Education*, 50.

9. Ignacio Ellacuria, "The Task of a Christian University," translated in Jon Sobrino, *Companions of Jesus: The Jesuit Martyrs of El Salvador* (Maryknoll, NY: Orbis Books, 1990). See the excellent discussion of the different interpretations of the university's ethical role in Richard Antall, "Evangelization and the Catholic University" *Listening: Journal of Religion and Culture*, 30, no. 2 (Spring 1995): 104-20.

10. Michael J. Lavelle, "What Is Meant by a Catholic University," *America*, Feb. 5, 1994, 4.

11. Christopher Dawson, *Understanding Europe* (New York: Sheed and Ward, 1952), 242-44.

12. Cf. Martin Heidegger: "Nietzsche's Word: God Is Dead," *The Question of Technology* (New York: Harper and Row, 1997), 102. The moral consequences are, of course, equally significant, since the entire relation between ends and means becomes wholly relative where a conflict between rival values cannot be rationally settled. See Alasdair MacIntyre, *After Virtue* (South Bend: Notre Dame University Press, 1981), 26.

13. Max Scheler, *On the Eternal in Man* (New York: Harper Brothers, 1960), 169. Rudolf Otto qualifies this position but basically adopts it himself when defining the "holy" as what is valuable *in itself*. See *The Idea of the Holy* (New York: Oxford University Press, 1958), 50-53.

14. Matthew Arnold, Preface to *Irish Essays* (1882).

CHAPTER THREE

Spirituality and Philosophy: The Ideal of the Catholic Mind

GERALD A. McCOOL

S ome time ago, a promising young theologian gave a sermon before a university audience in Paris which caused quite a stir. It was blunt and incisive in its assessment of contemporary intellectual confusion. Three great evils, the young preacher said, had caused disarray in the modern university. The first was the intellectual pride of professors who invented new theories simply to call attention to themselves. The second evil was provoked by the first. Ceaseless battles, in which truth was the first victim, went on between factions on the faculty grouped around rival professors. Given the first two evils, the third and worst became inevitable. The students gave up all hope of finding the truth. And so the university, by driving its students into agnosticism through intellectual despair, finally robbed them of their Catholic faith.

The only cure for these three evils, the preacher continued, was a return of the university to Christ. There were plenty of poets, scientists, philosophers, and theologians in the world of higher education; but Christ, the Word of God, was the only teacher of truth to be found there: Christ, the Word, Pre-existent and Incarnate, the universal master of every student—*Christus omnium magister*. For, without the light, natural and supernatural, which flows into the human mind from the Word of God, no thinker's mind can hope to find the truth. Saint Augustine had seen that centuries ago, and none of us can afford to forget it. But professors do, and, by cutting themselves off from the light of Christ, they make their own human minds the ultimate norm of truth. When that happens, the result is confusion and disarray in education.

As I said, that sermon was preached some time ago—quite some time ago—about seven hundred years ago, to be exact. The preacher was St. Bonaventure, theologian, mystic, educator, and administrator, friar of the new order of St. Francis, professor of the new University of Paris, and soon to be elected General of his order. What he was urging, even as he was teaching in a new way in what was then a new type of school, was retention of the tradition of Catholic education which he had inherited from the Fathers of the Church—the same tradition, by the way, in which many of you, like me, were educated. Develop that tradition by all means, even transform it, as he himself was doing at the University of Paris, St. Bonaventure urged, but never abandon it. Otherwise the result will be intellectual confusion in which both our faith and the truth slip away from us.

It is about this patristic tradition of Catholic education that I would like to speak to you tonight. It was already an old tradition when St. Bonaventure helped to bring about one of its great renewals. As a philosophical theology of culture, education, and spirituality, it reached back, through Augustine, to the great theologians of Alexandria, Clement, and Origen. The thirteenth-century crisis in theology, religious life, and education, provoked by the rediscovery of Aristotle, the establishment of radically new kinds of religious orders, and the displacement of the monastic and cathedral school by the university as the center of higher education, had shaken its foundations. Rising to that challenge, the great theologians and spiritual writers of the thirteenth century, especially St. Bonaventure and St. Thomas, both of them university professors and members of the new religious orders, brought about its restoration and development. Challenged once again by the Reformers and the Humanists of the sixteenth century, this patristic philosophy of education, theology and spirituality took on new life in the Catholic renewal after Trent. It showed itself in the restoration of Catholic theology and social thought and in the re-flowering of spirituality among the Carmelites, the Jesuits, and the priests and religious of the French School. In education it took on new life by adapting itself to the age of the baroque in the curriculum of the new Jesuit colleges. Almost buried in the Enlightenment, the patristic tradition came back to life once more and adapted itself to the modern age in the great Catholic Renaissance of the nineteenth and early twentieth centuries. Our system of Catholic schools, the growth of teaching congregations, and the social teaching of our popes from Leo XIII to Pius XI are memorials of that last reincarnation of the tradition to which a number of us owe our intellectual formation.

Essential to this tradition, which seems to survive through constant transformation, is the conviction, based on both faith and reason, that the world makes sense and that the human mind has the power to understand it. That understanding can be brought about if the liberal arts, science, and philosophy are unified by a sound and believing mind under the light of faith. Once human knowledge has been integrated by a coherent education, it will enable the believing mind to understand God's revealed word. More than that, it can lead a prayerful and reflective mind through the meaning which it finds in God's creation to knowledge and love of God himself. Inspired by that tradition, in its sixteenth- and seventeenth-century form, my own intellectual ancestors, the old Jesuit schoolmasters, could cheerfully spend their life in the classroom. For what they were doing was forming minds which, in the beautiful Ignatian formula, "could find God in all things."

But to assign an aim like that to our own classroom work today would strike a lot of us as a charming but outmoded ideal. For, whether we look at the world from the point of view of culture, philosophy, or theology, the very possibility of that type of integration of experience has become extremely questionable. And with good reason. For the philosophical attack on the foundations of our traditional philosophy of Catholic education goes deeper today than it has done at any time in the past. And even those who, like myself, are unwilling to concede that a long-lived tradition has reached at last the moment of its death, must admit in all honesty that contemporary philosophy and culture have brought it to an hour of crisis. We know that, if this time around, we hope to contribute to another renewal of our inherited tradition through our philosophical reflection, we will have our work cut out for us.

We must refresh our memory of the philosophical and theological tradition from which our schools have come; we must honestly assess the difficulties which are now brought against its intellectual foundations; and only then can we determine whether our educational tradition can be renewed once more without losing its continuity with its past. Should that renewal prove impossible—and it may—then a completely new aim will have to be found for Catholic education, and its future history will be one of rupture, of radical discontinuity, with its past.

Intrinsic to the spirituality of the Church Fathers as it was to their theology was a view of man, human knowledge, and human freedom which can be summed up in what I will call the ideal of the Catholic mind. The same ideal structured the Fathers' philosophy of education, the tradition of Catholic education which we have inherited from them. That ideal was once as familiar to Catholic teachers, who knew their Newman, as it was to the Fathers of the Church, but in the last few decades it has been practically forgotten. This lapse in our Catholic memory is significant, as I hope to show you. For the crisis in Catholic education is due to our present uncertainty as to whether our inherited ideal of the Catholic mind can continue to serve as a viable aim for Catholic education.

Let me then speak first about the ideal of the Catholic mind, its history, its pervasive place in the tradition of Catholic education, its possibilities for development, its philosophical and theological foundations. This I will do at some length and with great affection. Then I will outline the serious intellectual difficulties brought against the viability of this ideal today. This I will try to do honestly and soberly. Finally, I will assess the prospects of this ideal passing in our time through another moment of continuity through transformation. This I will do tentatively and with great caution.

The Ideal of the Catholic Mind

When, at the turn of the century, a group of American Jesuits decided to found a review of Catholic intellectual interest, the name which they decided to give it was *The Catholic Mind*. Their choice is quite understandable. By the turn of the century, the

Catholic intellectual revival was well under way. Cardinal Newman had published his *Essay on the Development of Doctrine*, his *Grammar of Assent*, and *The Idea of a University*. Leo XIII had recommended the philosophy and theology of St. Thomas as the structuring element of a Catholic liberal education in his landmark encyclical, *Aeterni Patris*. In the United States, the Catholic University of America had been established, and a thriving system of Jesuit higher education was coming into being. In their defense of the uniqueness, breadth, and excellence of Catholic education, its defenders usually pointed to its integration of the arts and sciences by the believing mind under the guiding light of theology. This was, of course, the ideal of Catholic education proposed by Cardinal Newman. Papal support for that ideal and some practical hints for its realization could be found in *Aeterni Patris*, the encyclical of Leo XIII, who had made Newman a cardinal at the outset of his pontificate. Jesuit educators claimed the authority of these great prelates for their own educational endeavors.

Catholic education was unique and successful because the philosophy of man and the knowledge which guided it promoted both the unity of knowledge and the proper distinction and independence of the individual disciplines. Integration of the disciplines, rather than the imperialism of a single type of knowledge or a single scientific method, was the key to a humanistic education. Because the distinctions between faith and reason, theoretical and practical intellect, conceptual science and artistic imagination, defended by both Newman and the scholastics, were properly appreciated in the Catholic school, philosophy and theology, scientific and literary experience could be progressively integrated in the individual's mind in the course of his liberal education.

Since the living mind, oriented by nature and grace to intuitive knowledge of God, progressively prepared itself for the culminating experience through its response in knowledge and love to God's whole creation, visible and invisible, the goal of Catholic education, which Newman described as the development of the integrative habit of mind, could rightly be called the cultivation of the Catholic mind.[1]

The cultivation of the Catholic mind was the directive ideal of Catholic education during the first half of this century. It is the ideal of Christian education proposed by Pius XI in his encyclical *On the Christian Education of Youth.* Jacques Maritain presented a brilliant theoretical justification of this ideal in his Thomistic philosophy of man and knowledge. Maritain's major work, as you recall, was *The Degrees of Knowledge,* sub-titled *Distinguish to Unite.*[2] It should not surprise us then that the turn of the century team of Jesuit editors chose *The Catholic Mind* as the title for their intellectual review. In choosing it, they echoed the common conviction that Catholic uniqueness and Catholic universality were reconciled through the integrative habit of mind developed by a Catholic liberal education. A centuries-old tradition in Catholic philosophy, theology, and spirituality could be drawn upon in support of this contention.

The Jesuit review is no longer in existence. It died because, in a market place crowded with competitors, it could no longer rally enough support to stay alive. The same, I am afraid, could be said of the Catholic mind as an ideal of Catholic education. In the latter half of our century, the idea no longer stirs the interest which it provoked a quarter century ago.

There are good reasons, of course, for the current decline in interest in the idea. Nevertheless, the decline represents a loss. For it can be argued that the idea of the Catholic mind is one of those notions whose life and interest put it in the category of what Cardinal Newman called "leading ideas." A leading idea not only proposes a thematic view of some important aspects of human reality; it also tends to organize around itself institutional forms of social realization, schools, societies, and religious orders, for example.[3] This has surely been the case with the idea of the Catholic mind.

Among the institutional forms of social organization to whose constitution this idea has contributed significantly since its emergence in the Alexandria of Clement and Origen are great religious orders. Among these we can surely count the Benedictines, Augustinians, Franciscans, Dominicans, and Jesuits, whose contribution to the history of education is significant. Through their schools and their educational tradition, these orders have notably influenced the development of Catholic education. Other forms of the idea's social realization have been the classic works on Christian education whose abiding influence on Catholic schools extended over many centuries. Among these classics we might mention Clement of Alexandria's *Paedagogus*, Augustine's *De Doctrina Christiana*, Bonaventure's *Itinerarium Mentis in Deum* and *Reductio Artium ad Theologiam* and, on a much lower literary level, the various editions of the Jesuit *Ratio Studiorum*.[4]

An idea which has remained alive for a millennium and a half and incorporated itself in a variety of concrete realizations in the course of its history is also what Newman would call a "developmental idea." An understanding of the idea of the Catholic mind as a developmental idea could provide a key to a proper appreciation of the continuity in Catholic education. The idea of the Catholic mind has incorporated itself in the Alexandrian catechetical school of Clement and Origen, the Benedictine monastery school, the Franciscan and Dominican *studia generalia* at the medieval universities, the Jesuit college of the Catholic Reformation, and Newman's Oratory School in the nineteenth century.[5]

Developmental ideas have a history of continuity through diversity. They are personal and historical realities. They are neither Hegelian ideas nor elements in a deductive system. Because developmental ideas incarnate themselves in the concrete historical world, they constantly provoke us to a fresh contemplation of their object. This means that they are successively interpreted and clarified over a period of time. They die in one incarnation only to come to life in another. They unfold their virtualities through change.

The variety of concrete educational projects which the idea of the Catholic mind has inspired and directed in diverse cultural epochs from Clement's Alexandria to Newman's Birmingham makes it reasonable to anticipate that the virtualities of this idea have not been exhausted. If, as some would argue, the idea is no longer effective in the concrete form it took in the Catholic college and school of the first half of our century, there may be reason to believe that it will reemerge in a new and more effective form. Such has been its history of continuity through change in the past, and it is probable that its history of development will continue in the future. In any case, it might pay the philosopher, the theologian and the educator to remain alert to this possibility.

It might be worth our while, therefore, to look a little more closely at this educational ideal which Catholic philosophers, theologians, and educators found so attractive at the beginning of our century. Its history shows us that, although the idea of the Catholic mind is not compatible with every system of philosophy, it is by no means restrictive in the variety of philosophies through which it can be expressed, and by no means narrow in the range of cultures in which it can incorporate itself. Its first great proponents were the Alexandrian theologians, Clement and Origen. Augustine carried the idea to the Benedictines of the Middle Ages. The Franciscan and Dominican scholastic doctors picked it up and passed it on both to the Anglican Church of Andrewes and Laud and to the Jesuit educators of the Catholic Reformation.[6] That is why both Newman and the Benedictines—neither of whom found Jesuits or scholasticism particularly congenial—shared the Jesuit commitment to the ideal of the Catholic mind and to its educational significance.

What, then, in the broad patristic tradition, shared by Augustine, the scholastic doctors, and Newman, despite their significant philosophical differences, was meant by the Catholic mind? Before we consider its catholicity, we will have to examine the patristic notion of the mind itself. In the patristic tradition, the thinking mind is always a concrete, spiritual reality. The human mind is distinguished from its objective content. Unlike many post-Cartesian philosophers, the Fathers of the Church never confused the living personal mind with an idea or a complex of ideas. St. Thomas never confused the ideal system of the *Summa Theologiae* with the concrete subject who reasoned, made moral decisions, and submitted himself to God's personal influence in prayer. Abstract concepts have no history. Personal minds do. The Platonic and the Christian elements in the patristic tradition both support its conviction that the conquest of truth is the result of an interior conversion of the mind and will, and that self-transformation through the moral and intellectual virtues is the necessary condition for human growth and the integration of knowledge. Conversion and self-transformation is the path to contemplation of the truth.

Truth was the fruit of personal activity. Nevertheless, the activity of the human mind, ordered to truth by its very nature, was a participation in the light of truth communicated by the Word of God himself. For Clement, the Word was the Universal

Pedagogue. For Augustine, Christ, the Word, was the interior master dwelling in every mind. Growth in truth was always both teaching and learning, the interpersonal cooperation of the human person and the Word of God. Learning was conversion, the progressive transformation of the student into the likeness of the Eternal Word.

In this conception of the human mind, illuminated by God himself, we find the reason for the sacred character of the work of teaching—any teaching whose goal is the truth—in the patristic tradition. To teach is to share in the work of the Interior Master, the Divine Pedagogue. In the eyes of Newman, whose theology was formed by the Alexandrian Fathers, teaching the arts and sciences was a sacred ministry.[7] As the Interior Master taught by shedding his own light, the human teacher taught by his personal influence. Both teachers, human and divine, taught by sharing with their students what they were. Teaching—any genuine teaching—was a holy and highly personal activity. It was never a job like another. Once you hold the patristic conception of the human mind, that conclusion follows.

If growth in learning is a process of self-transformation, we are far from the world of abstract impersonal reason drawing conclusions from universal principles. As a good Aristotelian, St. Thomas placed great stress in his moral and religious teaching on prudence, the virtue of the practical intellect which enables the mind to judge correctly in individual cases. As a disciple of the Fathers, however, he placed equal weight on *synderesis*, the moral sensitivity of a well-developed conscience, and upon *connaturality*, the "feel" of the religiously or aesthetically cultivated mind for definite areas of experience, a "feel" developed only through lived experience, personal history, and good moral habits acquired through the exercise of proper moral choice.

Their common commitment to the patristic tradition of learning as the interior transformation of the personal intellect, will, and imagination through the acquisition of good cognitive and moral habits explains why both Newman and Maritain, two of the great defenders of the Catholic mind, insist on the need for literary and artistic as well as scientific education in the formation of the cultivated mind. If learning is conversion in the full sense of the word, theoretical education cannot be divorced from moral education. On the other hand, the proper distinction of the intellectual disciplines demanded by a coherent philosophy of knowledge requires that the individual teacher observe the demands and follow the proper method of his own subject. Integration is not confusion. Systematic schooling in the arts and sciences, and the personal influence of a community of educators, not all of them classroom teachers, must work together to develop the integrative habit of mind. The school as a community of personal influence is all-important in the patristic tradition of the Catholic mind.[8]

Our consideration of the mind in the patristic tradition up to now has been largely philosophical. But the mind is not only catholic in the universal sense. It is also Catholic in the specific sense attributed to a mind illuminated by the Catholic faith and elevated and strengthened by the power of supernatural grace. In the patristic tradition, the Word of God is not only the creator and supreme exemplar "through whom all things are made," the normative truth whom all reality imitates. He is Christ, the Word Incarnate, the Redeemer who restores fallen nature to a new life of grace. In the spirituality of all the great religious orders who have influenced the history of Catholic education, Christ, the Creator and Redeemer, is the key to the meaning of nature and human history. The goal of human development achieved through a liberal education can be properly appreciated only through the light of faith.

It follows, then, that a theoretical education which in principle divorces itself from the truths of Christian revelation formulated in the Church's theology and a moral education which in principle denies the need and efficacy of grace and prayer will fail to develop the integrative habit of mind. Neglect of Christian truth does not mean simply that a significant element in liberal education has been omitted. The meaning of the whole of knowledge, in the light of which each of the liberal disciplines and their relationship to one another must be interpreted, has been fundamentally misunderstood.[9]

Within that whole of meaning, created nature and human history can be understood, and the concrete world, to which each one of us must respond through the history of his life, makes sense. Created and redeemed by the Word of God, who is Wisdom and Truth, created nature is neither corrupt nor meaningless. Visible creation has its own intrinsic intelligibility, autonomy, and order. The theology of the hypostatic union and the theology of grace and nature, by proclaiming the intelligible autonomy and goodness of God's restored creation, grant to every art and science its own independent status.

In the patristic tradition, however, visible nature points beyond itself. In Newman's theology of the economies and in St. Thomas' metaphysics of man and being, subordinated to his theology, visible nature is sacramental.[10] It is a sign leading the reflective mind to the invisible God. Only through the gift of faith, however, can the sacramental sign of nature and history be understood in the light of what it signifies. To the believer, therefore, Christian revelation is not an intruder in the field of liberal education. Christian revelation makes possible the interpretative whole of meaning within which the arts and sciences can be properly appreciated.

The Contemporary Challenge

Such was the ideal of the Catholic mind which directed Catholic education in the first half of our century. Given its coherence, its attractiveness, its perdurance through the history of Catholic education, why has it so suddenly and dramatically dropped from view?

There are serious reasons for its disappearance. Some are practical problems of application. The expansion and diversification of Catholic education, the increased variety of the curriculum, the demands of university research, and the growing specialization of graduate education make practical application of the ideal across the board difficult and ambiguous. Catholic education has many more tasks today and serves a more varied clientele than it did at the turn of the century when it confined its efforts largely to academic high schools and liberal arts colleges. These problems of interpretation and application, however, formidable though they are, are not the profound intellectual challenges which today threaten the very life of the Catholic mind as a directing principle in Catholic education.

The intellectual validity of the ideal itself has been called into serious question within the Catholic community. There are Catholic theologians and philosophers today who would deny any probability to the claim that the idea of the Catholic mind could be called a leading idea in Newman's sense of the term. The idea of the Catholic mind, they believe, can no longer provide a sound thematic view of man or education. Far from being able to inspire Catholic enterprises as it did in the past, the idea of the Catholic mind is superannuated, and it can only hurt educational institutions which still cling to it. A new and different ideal must inspire Catholic education today.

The challenge to the old ideal, which has reached crisis proportions, is due to the radically different approach to culture, theology, and philosophy in the Catholic community in the quarter century after the Second Vatican Council. The ideal of culture regnant in the Catholic Church before that time was essentially the normative classicist culture of Greece and Rome. This was the conception of culture which shaped Leo XIII's view of education, and it dominates the educational writing of Cardinal Newman. Its norm of taste was dictated by classical literature. Its universal person, we are now told, was no more than Aristotle's ideal of human nature. Greek philosophy determined its norms of thought and truth. This culture's universal man, in other words, was the Christianized Greek man of Hellenistic society, Clement of Alexandria's educated man.[11]

The supposed universality of the culture was really a sign of its great deficiency, its ignorance of history and of empirical social science. History and the social sciences have taught us that there are and have been many cultures. There is no such thing as a single universal culture based on human nature. There are many cultures, Eastern and Western. All are historical creations. All are culturally conditioned. Each enjoys its own cultural autonomy, sets its own norms, proposes its own view of man.

If the Catholic Church wishes to be truly universal, it must abandon its alliance with an outmoded classical culture, venerable though that culture may have been. The Church can no longer afford to tie her theology, her spirituality, her preaching, and her ideal of education to the pseudo-universality of an outmoded classicist culture. So runs the first challenge to the idea of the Catholic mind today.

The second challenge comes from a radically changed approach to theology in the Catholic Church since the Second Vatican Council. It is no secret that Catholic theologians, as a whole, are no longer devoted to Scholastic philosophy. Increasingly biblical and historical in their approach, and deeply concerned with the ecumenical dialogue, contemporary Catholic theologians are chary of metaphysics, and of Greek metaphysics in particular.

One consequence of this change is that the affection for the Greek Fathers which nourished Newman's thought is not the distinguishing trait of contemporary Catholic theology. Yet the idea of the Catholic mind is clearly part of our patristic inheritance. Born in the Greek East, it has come down from the Alexandrian Fathers, through Augustine, to the Latin West. The patristic inheritance is too deeply embedded in the Church's tradition both in doctrine and in spirituality for it to remain long out of the center of theological concern. For the moment, however, the metaphysical theology of the Fathers is a source of problems rather than of inspiration for contemporary theologians. The project of defending the patristic heritage of the Catholic mind does not attract them.

Two other serious challenges to the idea of the Catholic mind come from contemporary philosophy, where the influence of Hume and Kant is still felt. Contemporary analytic philosophers would question the philosophical evidence for the existence of a personal mind clearly distinguished from its objective content. They would question the existence of a spiritual mind associated with a power of free choice and a sensibility. They would ask for evidence that there really is a person, known through immediate self-consciousness, whose capacity to integrate his knowledge and judge soundly in ethics and aesthetics can be developed through the experience of a life and a history of personal choices. As we indicated earlier, a philosophy of knowledge and a philosophy of the human person are implied in the idea of the Catholic mind. A number of contemporary philosophers would question them.

The second difficulty which contemporary philosophers would raise is whether any philosophy, even aided by theology, can validate a worldview, an integrative interpretation of the whole of knowledge, which, even in principle, could lay claim to universality. The vastness of the universe, the limited nature and uncertainty of human knowledge, the partial and historical character of every viewpoint make any universal worldview philosophically impossible. Each one of us must view the world from his or her own limited point of view. Within that limited viewpoint, we determine our scale of values, set our definition of humanity, decide what we mean by human development and the means to achieve it. Universal agreement, even in principle, on the fundamental meaning of the world and the basic value of human life is quite impossible. All that we can do is to talk to one another across our fundamental disagreements and try to solve our immediate common problems in a reasonable and decent way.[12] Ideals, based on catholicity as universality, like the integrative habit of mind or the Catholic mind, are chimeras. They can do no good. All they can do is breed intolerance and block discussion.

We can begin to understand the malaise that affects both Catholic religious orders and Catholic institutions of education when we appreciate the pervasiveness of the idea of the Catholic mind in Catholic spirituality and education. From the time of Clement of Alexandria to the present day, the history of Catholic spirituality and Catholic education have been intertwined. It is easy to see why. Implied in both is a philosophy of personal development through response to the world in knowledge and love. Every crisis in culture provokes a crisis and a reaction in Catholic spirituality and Catholic education.

None of these crises, however, has been as intense or widespread as the cultural crisis which we face today. The malaise which many of us feel today arises from the perception, clearly seen or dimly felt, that the ideal of the Catholic mind, which has structured spirituality and education for centuries, and whose foundations are under attack today, may not survive.

If the idea of the Catholic mind is a genuine developmental idea, which preserves its identity through change, then Catholic philosophers and theologians should be able to reexamine the idea, modify, and develop it in the light of the serious difficulties which have been brought against it. Should they succeed in their endeavor, a developed idea of the Catholic mind might continue to inspire Catholic education and structure a reinvigorated Catholic spirituality. Continuity would be preserved through change.

If, however, the idea has been thoroughly invalidated, continuity has become impossible. A new model of Catholic spirituality and education must be found. Otherwise both will lose their identity and disappear. But when the new model emerges, it will be in radical discontinuity with the past.

At the moment, Catholic philosophers and theologians are divided over which of these alternatives represents the sound Catholic option for the future. Hence the crisis in the Catholic philosophy and theology of education and the malaise in Catholic education which it has provoked.

Prospects for Survival

Is it likely that the idea of the Catholic mind will survive the attacks directed against it today? Does it still have a future as a valid ideal for Catholic education? I am not a prophet. Still, I am not convinced that the time has come yet to count the idea out.

In the first place, the idea of the Catholic mind, even if we grant it only plausibility as an ideal, justifies a number of values in Catholic education which many of us are convinced are sound. Among these are the focus of education on the formation of the total person, the ideal of the integration and distinction of the disciplines, the emphasis on personal influence in teaching and the demands which it places on the teacher, the sacredness of the teacher's work, and the appreciation of the school as a community of personal influence.

The ideal of the integrative mind, even if we take it as an asymptote, preserves education from a number of distortions. Faith in the presence in the world of a creating and redeeming God is a protection against a narrow, this-worldly secularism or a despairing resignation to an unintelligible universe. Conviction that the human person has a divine call to wholeness is a defense against a narrow professionalism in education or the tyranny of a single discipline or a single method. Interdisciplinary cooperation is neither a sacrilege nor an imposition. Fidelity to an old and coherent tradition frees the educator from slavery to the present or to the immediate future.

Nevertheless, are the difficulties against the idea of the Catholic mind from the contemporary understanding of culture and from contemporary philosophy so great that they are unanswerable? They are formidable, I admit, but I remain convinced that they can be handled. It would take more time than we have at our disposal to do more than drop a few brief hints to indicate why I believe that my hopes are not without foundation.

Implied in the idea of the Catholic mind was a philosophy of the person as a spiritual knower associated with a power of choice and ordered to self-development through his grasp of a variety of distinct disciplines, each with its own proper method. The path to self-development was through intellectual and moral conversion under the illumination and attraction of the Supreme Truth present through his causality in the human spirit. In Maritain's *Degree of Knowledge*, the philosophy of the person was the philosophy of St. Thomas. Newman's original philosophy of the person was inspired to a great extent by the metaphysics of the Alexandrian Fathers and the ethics of Aristotle.

In his major works, *Insight* and *Method in Theology*, however, a contemporary philosophical theologian, Father Bernard Lonergan, has developed a philosophy of knowledge and of the human person through which I am convinced the great values of the idea of the Catholic mind can be defended.[13] Yet Lonergan's philosophy of the person is not a Greek philosophy. It is not bound to Greek metaphysics or to the Aristotelian conception of human nature. It is a contemporary philosophy which presents evidence for its assertions which contemporary philosophers can understand.

Father Lonergan is well aware of the distinction between the classicist and contemporary notions of culture. He too is convinced that what he calls classicist culture is dead. If, however, the human person, who is the author and reviser of cultures, transcends culture, as Lonergan claims he does, then an idea of the Catholic mind and its integration of knowledge based on a philosophy of the transcultural person need not perish with the classicist ideal of culture. The ideal of the Catholic mind may have to be transformed but it need not die. In other words, it may turn out to be one of Newman's developmental ideas.

Finally, if the mind's self-development is ordered to the vision of God, whose Second Person is the Word, then we know, if only by faith, that the world which came from Unity and Truth is an intelligible whole. If matter has been assumed by God himself, it is an autonomous, intelligible sacramental sign, sound in itself, yet pointing beyond itself. Trying to make sense of it in its own reality and in its status as a sacramental sign is the way in which we prepare ourselves to contemplate the Truth. For continuity goes beyond the grave. Life is changed, not ended.

Therefore the drive to integrate our knowledge, which philosophy of knowledge reveals at work within us, is not a drive to frustration. The drive makes sense. It should be fostered, even if total integration, in our modern world, must remain an asymptote. The philosophy of the person and the Catholic theology of the Word as Creator and Redeemer, as Karl Rahner, one of our great contemporary theologians, has pointed out in his *Foundations of Christian Faith*, make marvelous sense out of the experience and aspirations of contemporary man.[14] Why should they not provide an antidote to much of contemporary philosophy's despair of finding meaning in the world in a contemporary idea of the Catholic mind?

It would seem, then, from what has been said about the philosophical theologies of Rahner and Lonergan, that one of the great intellectual traditions in Catholicism at least, the tradition of St. Thomas, can be transformed and developed sufficiently to cope with the contemporary problems of knowledge and culture which threaten the viability of the ideal of the Catholic mind. The ideal itself, however, is older than St. Thomas, and, as our consideration of Bonaventure and Newman showed, it can be defended by philosophers other than the Angelic Doctor. Catholic educators should remember nonetheless that not every philosophy is capable of bearing the weight of the Catholic ideal of the integration of culture. Nor is every theology capable of doing justice to the Catholic tradition of created and redeemed human nature. The Catholic mind cannot be just *any* mind formed by *any* philosophy or theology. Nor can the Catholic school be just *any* sort of school which a group of Catholics decides to attend or support. Its intellectual justification has to be more than "birds of a feather flock together."

Conclusion

The crisis of Catholic education today, I have argued, is due to its inability to define and defend the basic purpose of its work. Up to now, I have also argued, its traditional purpose has been defined through the ideal of the Catholic mind, an ideal now subject to serious intellectual attack. Can a Catholic philosopher, or group of philosophers, be found capable of doing justice to that traditional ideal aim of Catholic education in our contemporary climate of cognitional and cultural pluralism? If they are to make the attempt with any hope of success, they will need a theory of knowledge capable of dealing with both nature and history, and a philosophy of being which can lead the mind from the created world to its personal creator. I have not given up my hope that in our Catholic tradition and in the community of philosophers and theologians formed in our Catholic schools we have the resources to create that contemporary philosophical theology. But I dearly wish that more of our philosophers and theologians would show some interest in the project; for with some notable exceptions, few of them have made any move in that direction. Should they do so, Catholic education, along with Catholic spirituality and Catholic education, should wish them well. For what is at stake today is our intellectual continuity with our past, the continuity through change which is found in every living tradition. Will the ideal of the Catholic mind survive through renewal as it did in the time of St. Bonaventure with whose sermon our talk began? We cannot be complacent, but we can hope. And I, for one, still do.

Notes

This essay was previously published in *Continuity and Plurality in Catholic Theology: Essays in Honor of Gerald A. McCool, S.J.*, ed. Anthony J. Cernera (Fairfield, CT: Sacred Heart University Press, 1998), 215-33.

1. For an excellent exposition of Newman's theory of liberal education, see Vincent F. Blehl, *The Essential Newman* (New York: New American Library, 1963), 156-60. For the influence of the Alexandrian Fathers on Newman's philosophy of education, see Vincent F. Blehl, "Newman, the Fathers and Education," *Thought* 45 (1970): 196-212.

2. Jacques Maritain, *The Degrees of Knowledge: Distinguish to Unite* (New York: Charles Scribner's Sons, 1959).

3. See James Collins, *Philosophical Readings in Cardinal Newman* (Chicago: Henry Regnery Company, 1961), 251-59.

4. One of the finest introductions to the thought of St. Bonaventure remains Etienne Gilson, *The Philosophy of St. Bonaventure* (New York: Sheed and Ward, 1938).

5. For the Benedictine humanism of the Middle Ages, see Jean Leclercq, *The Love of Learning and the Desire of God: A Study of Monastic Culture* (New York: Fordham University Press, 1974). For medieval education in general, see David Knowles, *The Evolution of Medieval Thought* (New York: Random House, 1964).

6. Laud's greatest educational achievement was the statutes which still governed Oxford in Newman's early days at the University. See H.R. Trevor-Roper, *Archbishop Laud* (London: Macmillan, 1963), 271-94.

7. Louis Bouyer, *Newman* (New York: Meridian Books, 1958), 74-95.

8. Blehl, *The Essential Newman*, 167-70.

9. Blehl, *The Essential Newman*, 171-76; Pius XI, *On the Christian Education of Youth* (Washington: National Catholic Welfare Conference, 1936), 29-31.

10. Blehl, "Newman, the Fathers and Education," 210-12.

11. For a clear exposition of the difference between the classical and the contemporary conception of culture, see Bernard J.F. Lonergan, "The Transition from a Classicist World-View to Historical Mindedness," in *A Second Collection* (Philadelphia: Westminster Press, 1974), 1-9.

12. A powerful expression of this approach to philosophy can be found in Richard Rorty, *Philosophy and the Mirror of Nature* (Princeton: Princeton University Press, 1979).

13. Bernard J.F. Lonergan, *Insight* (New York: Philosophical Library, 1958); *Method in Theology* (New York: Herder and Herder, 1972).

14. Karl Rahner, *Foundations of Christian Faith* (New York: Seabury Press, 1978).

CHAPTER FOUR

Monastic Culture and the Catholic Intellectual Tradition

Jeremy Driscoll

The winter night is cold and clear. I finish singing *Compline* with my monastic community and step out into the garden where, far from city lights, I look up to the sky and see the million stars. Verses from the Psalms still move in me: "He who dwells in the shelter of the Most High" (Psalm 91); "the Lord who made heaven and earth" (Psalm 134); "I will lie down in peace" (Psalm 4). In the stars I see moving fast among them a jet plane and think with love of its cargo of passengers. I am able to imagine from my own experience how different the same moment is for them. They speed along somewhere, probably a little cramped and uncomfortable; and yet for all that, what they are doing is amazing. They travel at great speed to a desired faraway destination. And given the circumstances, there is relative comfort. The terrible cold is shut out, as well as the night. They can listen to music, watch a movie, drink wines from another continent, do remarkable calculations and other work on their computers.

I would like this image to serve as an emblem for the reflections I hope to unfold here. In this series of reflections on the Catholic intellectual tradition, I have been invited to participate as a representative of the monastic tradition and also as one whose academic training is in patristic theology. As a Benedictine monk, I am privileged to live a tradition that is 1500 years old, but I am not living in another time different from my own. This is my century too. I travel in planes, see the movies, use a computer. So, what I want to reflect upon here is how a monk might think *today*, with what heritage, with what intellectual tradition.

The monastic environment offers unique advantages for thinking in a particular way. This environment and these advantages are certainly linked to a tradition, indeed to a very old one. And yet at the same time, the one thinking is also a product of and a player in his own times. That is, he is involved in the kind of world of which jet travel may serve as an emblem. So like any other person living in our times, the monk is potentially a partner and player in a cultural dialogue. He is not disqualified by the ancient traditions to which he adheres. In this fact, among other things, we have in monastic life a clear example of how any tradition works. Traditions are not lived for their own sake. They are valued and lived when they are thought to contain a wisdom still useful for our present and future. I am willing to live according to the 1500-year-old *Rule of St. Benedict* (hereafter abbreviated *RB*) because I believe it contains a wisdom useful not only for me but for my companions, my race, with whom I live this present period of human history.

Monasticism adds a further useful dimension to the idea of what it looks like to live from an intellectual tradition. It definitely has an intellectual tradition, but this is only a dimension of a much bigger something; namely, a way of living. Monasticism suggests that an intellectual tradition springs up from and flourishes within a larger context: concrete practices, an environment, sets of relationships, an atmosphere. An intellectual tradition is able to reflect on all these and thus promote and protect them; but more than that, all these cause a way of thinking to come about, with its own prevalent themes, its characteristic tones.

These observations, which so far might be valid for any community that has existed long enough to have what eventually rather spontaneously comes to be identified as a tradition, could be applied to a quite specific embodiment in 1500 years of Benedictine monastic life. And yet history need not be reviewed here, for it has been amply studied and reflected upon elsewhere. But one observation drawn from that history can show the kind of intellectual tradition upon which a contemporary monastic thinker relies—or could, or should.

Rather unconsciously, it would seem, the way of life that St. Benedict created by his Holy Rule made it possible for the first generations of his followers to insert themselves deeply within a tradition (including the intellectual but not limited to that) which was seriously threatened by historical circumstances in the sixth and seventh centuries. The golden age of patristic literature had already produced its treasures by the time Benedict appears on the scene. And the comparatively short-lived ideal of a Christian Empire and Imperial Church in which Christian mysteries were grasped ever more deeply with the tools of Greco-Roman culture and learning was already broken apart, especially in Italy, by wave after wave of barbarian invasions.

Yet Benedict in his Rule had the genius of somehow designing a way of life that could pass on the best of the patristic heritage even to the new invaders and in their very midst. Whether intentional or not, this was the effect. Gregory the Great especially understood this and promoted both the Rule and a cult of St. Benedict. Later Charlemagne, led by the monk Alcuin, will do something similar.

All this is known, but it suggests something about how *The Rule of St. Benedict* can function today in the part of the Catholic intellectual tradition that I would like to reflect upon here, in which I attempt to participate personally. Monks today do not live in historical times characterized by barbarian invasions. Nonetheless, they do live in a culture—and I repeat, they are also products of this culture and players in it—which in many ways greatly threatens, or at the very least overlooks, some of the greatest and still valid wisdom of the patristic tradition. Still, in a world very different from the fourth and fifth centuries (the "golden age"), contemporary Benedictine monasticism in fact can turn out to be an actual way of living in which, among other things, this ancient intellectual tradition is practiced, not as a curious and quaint anachronism, but as a font of wisdom for people accustomed to travel by jet and all the rest of which this serves as emblem.

In what follows, I would like to describe and reflect upon monastic attitudes and practices which form the larger context in which a specific intellectual tradition can flourish. My reflections can be developed in two major steps. First, I will try to be descriptive of situations both in culture and in theology which indicate that there is such a thing as a specifically monastic culture and a specifically monastic theology and intellectual tradition, even if one is hard-pressed to say precisely what these are. Secondly, I will attempt to ask and give some answer to the question of what it is about monastic traditions, practices, and ethos which can account for at least some sense that we have that there does exist a monastic culture and a monastic intellectual tradition. My emphasis first falls on "con-text." In monastic life, this greatly affects the "text" of the intellectual tradition. I hope to suggest ways in which something very old might produce something very new: fresh ways of living, fresh ways of thinking.

Situations Which Indicate the Existence of Something Specifically Monastic

Many elements in the culture today contrast strongly with attitudes and practices that monks have always identified as constitutive of their way of life. The relation between a monastery and the prevailing culture is first always one of tension, often though not always fruitful. Cultural values can also threaten monastic values. Yet despite the tension and the threat—actually, through the tension and threat—specifically monastic values emerge for all that.

For example, the monastic attitude toward time—slow, measured, expressive of qualitative differences and nuanced rhythms—contrasts often very strongly with the world's speedy pace, its capacity to travel great distances quickly, to accomplish much (especially in business) in a short span of time, to have near instant access to vast amounts of information of all kinds, to be quickly impatient of whatever requires slow maturation.

These days the monastic reverence toward the word, expressed also by silence, can appear simply incomprehensible to contemporary culture. Words are cheap in the world, and they are many. And if not words, then images, which have progressively supplanted words in culture. And images too are cheap and many, delivered with overwhelming velocity one after another. Monks, on the other hand, attempt to practice silence and be careful when they speak. They sing words which they reverence as the very Word of God, and they let this word form some few images slowly in their hearts.

What about the attitudes of the general culture toward personal relations and sexuality? Here liberality is the norm. Expression of oneself sexually is *de facto* one of the highest values of our times, an expression not to be bound by traditional frameworks of marriage, by exclusivity or permanence of partners, by the complementarity of the sexes. Those who are not beautiful perhaps are not even worth relating to. This can contrast sharply with today's monk who devotes himself to celibate chastity and relationships in which one strives "to show the pure love of brothers" and "support with the greatest patience one another's weaknesses" (*RB* 72).

Differences like these could be mounted. The non-achievement of community on so many levels of society will contrast with the wisdom of the monastic *cenobium*, which more often than not patiently builds and achieves real community. So also will post-enlightenment ideas of *liberté* be very different from what monks mean by the same word; namely, the freedom of the children of God, a freedom established by obedience. So also will the concept of work conjure up major differences in the two cultures. In the one, work tends to be about money, pleasure, excessive gain; in the other, work is a sacred undertaking, a privileged and real cooperation with God in his purposes for the world.

These comparisons are sufficient perhaps at least to say that monastic life is certainly a "something," a something not like the general culture that surrounds it, a something that could perhaps be described as a different culture in its own right. But if, as I am suggesting, the monastic experience can serve as an example of the dynamics of how any intellectual tradition is lived, then the following observation is especially important; namely, the monk, a product of his own culture, is himself the point of tension between this culture and the monastic culture he would more and more make his own. Before attempting to account for where the deepest roots of the monastic culture lie, which provoke these contrasts, I would like first to turn to the description of a different set of contrasts, this time contrasts within the household of the faith. I refer to a difference which seems to exist between what we may call the broad theological community that functions in the life of the Church and the kind of theology that arises in monastic settings. In observing this difference, we are drawing closer to the theme of a specific *intellectual* tradition.

I would offer as evidence that there is a difference—without trying to say what exactly it is—the following examples. Monks who do formal theology in a monastic setting undertake it differently and produce a different vision from those who do theology in other settings, the most striking contrast probably being the theology of high powered academic settings. But there is also considerable contrast between the theology that the monastic setting produces and that produced by, say, those directly concerned with pastoral care, with the establishment of base communities in impoverished lands, with evangelization in cultures which have not yet heard the Gospel.

Another kind of evidence for the differences is exhibited in a situation which more and more monasteries in the United States are experiencing; namely, that of diocesan priests, already formed theologically, who are joining monasteries. Unexpected difficulties can arise in developing a monastic ethos precisely because the priest-novice is already formed theologically. It is not lack of good will that makes for the difficulties but rather the profound influence of any particular theological way. The priest already has a developed theological way, and it meets, often only implicitly but also sometimes with difficulty, another theological way that, however ill-defined, is the monastic way.

In the United States, for historical reasons, a number of monasteries have long operated free-standing seminaries for the formation of diocesan priests. Bishops who choose to send students to such seminaries and priest alumni invariably express their appreciation for something specifically monastic in the training. Professors in these seminaries are generally trained and qualified in the great universities of the world, so what is this difference that they impart to their students once returned to their own monasteries?

Whatever it is, it is more complex than a style or method that could be objectively imparted in a monastic equivalent to a lecture hall or classroom. For on the one hand, there are many monks who have no critical theological training and yet who live the life profoundly and who have what we can correctly label profound theological insight. The opposite is also the case, although hopefully less often; that is, there are monks who have a well-developed theological capacity but who do not succeed in living the life well.

So, what is theology in a monastery and the intellectual tradition by which it is nourished? As with our observations about the culture in general, we have perhaps observed enough to allow us at least to say that it certainly is a something, a something different from theology produced in other settings, a theology that could perhaps be described as monastic in its own right. So far, I have meant to be descriptive of what I am calling the "con-text" of a particular intellectual tradition. In a second step, I would like to move closer to the "text" itself of this tradition, if not to its actual content then to the specific *forms* in which that content is carried. I will try to face the question of what it is about monastic traditions, practices, and ethos which can account for at least some vague sense we have that there does exist a monastic culture and a monastic intellectual tradition.

The Specifically Monastic Something

Monks who follow the Rule of St. Benedict are, at least comparatively speaking, not in doubt about what are the central values and practices of their way of life. These have long been constants of the monastic life: the *Opus Dei* (Benedict's name for the Divine Office celebrated in choral form throughout the hours of the day), *lectio divina* (a slow and prayerful reading of the Scriptures), and well-tried monastic practices and styles. It is in these very things that the specific monastic identity lies, a specific monastic identity that will stand both in contrast and in relation to the general culture, a specific monastic identity that will stand both in contrast and in relation to a broader theological community and its intellectual tradition.

Opus Dei

Surely one must look to what St. Benedict calls the *Opus Dei* for some major clues about what renders monastic culture and theology unique and peculiar. Its rhythms and demands saturate the monastic day; and day by day, hour after hour, year by year, its contents sink deeply into each monk's and each community's consciousness, more and more framing responses to what the culture at large also responds to, more and more structuring an approach to questions that the theological community at large approaches from its own perspectives. What accounts for its power to slowly create a culture in its own right, to slowly establish a tone for theology that it would not otherwise have?

In part its power lies in the Word of God itself, of which it is almost entirely composed. By their commitment to the schedule of the various offices spread throughout the day and night, monks really live out a determination to grant primacy to the Word of God in everything. But not only that. The *Opus Dei* is a living, singing, worshipping proclamation of the Word of God, "good and pleasant in the midst of brothers living in unity" (Psalm 133:1). So much is achieved in what not for nothing is called an "*opus.*" Monks come to discern the power and beauty of these divine words in comparison to all others. It slowly becomes inconceivable for them to treat the sacred scriptures as a book whose contents could somehow be grasped by isolated, individual effort as one might master the contents of some other book or body of thought. No, here is a book whose infinite wealth only unfolds for brothers worshipping in unity. Here is a book so precious and varied and layered in its meanings that its words must be uttered in sweet, peaceful and forceful chants, surrounded with adoring silence, responded to in thanksgiving and praise. Here is a book that pulls again and again through the consciousness of the monks words and images that express as types virtually every emotion and situation that human beings confront; it recounts the history of Israel and so of the world; and all this is played in its final and truest key in the presence of the risen Lord, who stands in the choir and "beginning with Moses and the prophets and the psalms explains every passage of scripture which refers to him" (Luke 24: 27, 44-45).

Whenever a monk truly yields in mind and heart to the words he is pronouncing, as St. Benedict urges him to do (*RB* 19:7), then he is through the years forever changed by this experience. His responses to culture and to what culture responds to will inevitably be marked by it. His style of theology could not fail to take account of it and include the insights which are possible only there.

Lectio Divina

Intimately connected with what happens to a monk in the regular practice of the *Opus Dei* is what happens in *lectio divina*. *Lectio* is a practice which insures that the Word of God heard in the liturgy is heard and applied in a way that is very personal to each monk. When this is done well, then on a yet deeper level, monastic consciousness is shaped and marked by the Scripture.

The tradition of *lectio* also alerts us to search for and ponder what we might call the great patterns of the Sacred Scripture. Creation and history are the fundamental categories through which Israel understood God's action in the world. In her history, and most especially in the Exodus and in the temple worship to which this eventually led, God's intentions for the whole of creation and history were to be mysteriously discerned. The Old Testament text expresses precisely this. But then that text is played in an entirely new key with the coming of Christ. He is the fulfillment of Israel's history and indeed of the whole creation. The New Testament text expresses precisely this. These are the texts that monks read, ponder, and pray over. In doing so, they are looking for and praying about the meaning of all history and creation. But the intensely personal dimension of the exercise which the whole tradition insists upon suggests to the monk that he must search his own life and the life of his community and find there the same story and patterns which the Scriptures proclaim. The monk discovers that the meaning of his personal existence and of his community's cannot be understood apart from the great patterns of the sacred text. And so monastic culture becomes the culture of particular monasteries which know they are in continuity with the particular history and relation to creation which the Scriptures proclaim.

Thus, for example, in the original creation, the whole world may be understood to be God's temple. Sin destroys our capacity to live in the world as in God's temple, but the covenant with Abraham and Moses can be viewed as moving toward the building of a temple in Jerusalem, where once again God's presence in our midst is known and celebrated. Jesus transposes the key in which the temple of his day is understood. By his death, he mysteriously destroyed it, as he had predicted. And in three days, a new temple, his risen and glorified body, is raised up. But these patterns reach all the way to us now, for as St. Paul says, we are that temple built of living stones. It is by *reading* texts and *pondering* them that I grasp this pattern in which my community and I are intimately involved. I *pray* my wonder and gratitude and beg mercy for my failings. I am taken beyond any particular text or pattern and share by *contemplation* in the dynamic of love in which, to my astonishment, I am invited to share: the pattern of love between Father, Son, and Holy Spirit.

We are looking for a specific monastic something that might explain the uniqueness of the culture of the monastery and of its approach to theology. I am suggesting that one of the principal roots of such uniqueness lies in these two fundamental Benedictine monastic practices, the *Opus Dei* and *lectio divina*, and in what they slowly and patiently accomplish in the life of a community and an individual monk. I would like now to articulate just briefly what difference these practices create between the culture at large and the monastery, between the kind of theology this produces and the kind of theology that is produced elsewhere.

I contrasted monastic and our culture's attitudes toward time. The unique monastic pace is established by the rhythms of the hours of Divine Office, by the patience and care with which its words are let to unfold in song, by the long pauses over single words or thoughts which both the Office and *lectio* promote. When the atmosphere of a monastery is pervaded by a great and solid sense of peace, sometimes inexplicable in its force, is it perhaps due in large part to what has happened there during decades and even centuries? Day by day, hour after hour, monks have opened themselves on many levels to the transforming power of the Word of God, and the community knows with a conviction that sinks deep below words that their own piece of history and their own involvement in the creation are part of the salvation story that the Scriptures proclaim. The price for the conviction of sharing in this great story is the slow and steady pace of the Office and of *lectio divina*. A world that moves too fast will never know it.

The Divine Office and *lectio divina* effectively saturate monastic life with the Word of God and the effects of that word on creation and history. This will inevitably contrast with the culture where words are cheap, half true, or not true at all. A single word from God, a single image from the history which God's Word has redeemed by becoming flesh there, will suffice to engage the monk for long hours and even days and will inevitably contrast with the culture where words and images are far too numerous, where they often attempt to seduce or drug one's consciousness.

In light of this, something can be said about the tone that would characterize a specifically monastic theology and its intellectual tradition. Monastic theology would be greatly marked by the experience of the sustained and prayerful encounter with the scriptural text which the Office and *lectio* promote. The classical struggle between monastic theology and the new scholasticism of the High Middle Ages has its relevance in our own day. Although monasticism has made its peace with the theology of the scholastics, it struggles today, and should do so, with a new version of that classical struggle; namely, the theology of the modern academy. In contrast with it, and without needing to deny its obvious values and benefits, monastic theology will want to be, to use a term taken from the original struggle, theology with unction. The formal theology in which monks are engaged at their desks has its roots in the more primary theology in which they are engaged in the choir and in their prayerful, reverent reading of the Word of God. And their formal theology will return them to these experiences with greater understanding and fervor. The monk-theologian's colleagues are not fellow professors but, say, the farmer who stands beside him in the choir and whose voice climbs together with his to savor and praise the same divine mysteries. Colleague likewise is the cook who, the monk-theologian knows, practices *lectio* alongside him and with whom he is grateful for the fruits of the earth which sustain the community in its day by day existence.

In contrast to the theology of the academy, monastic theology will employ faith and an ecclesial community as an explicit part of its method and this not for the same kinds of reasons that a scholastic theology which does the same might do. A scholastic theology would be more inclined to expose the logical necessity of these for the pursuit of theology, whereas the monastic theology is much more immediately (and urgently) connected to the faith with which his confreres pray and do *lectio*. His particular community is "sacrament" for him of that ecclesial community without which theology, as here conceived, would be impossible.

There are, of course, many theologians in the academy who practice theology with faith and an ecclesial community; but it must be admitted that for large segments of the academy, this is not a requirement; and some indeed would consider it an impediment. We have also mentioned the kind of theology produced by those directly concerned with pastoral care and evangelization. This clearly is a theology practiced within the context of faith. But for all of these, monastic theology has a unique contribution which it can make. For academics who practice without faith and an ecclesial community, it would launch a challenge; namely, that the subject matter of theology is not properly approached apart from the context of a community which with adoration and love struggles to hear anew each day God's Word and all its demands. To theologians who share the ecclesial faith of the monastic community but practice it in other settings, monastic theology can hold clearly before the greater theological community some of the essential goals and purposes of the theological enterprise: adoration and thanksgiving, contemplative union with the Word.

Monastic Practices

If I have looked to the Divine Office and *lectio divina* for the specifically monastic something in an intellectual tradition, I certainly would not want to limit my attempted explanation to these, even as central as they are. There are other dimensions of this way of life that also account for something specific about monastic culture and a monastic intellectual tradition.

Throughout the centuries, Benedictine monasticism has developed numerous practices, some of them small things but nonetheless important, which express various values articulated in the Holy Rule. Often these practices are already present in the Rule itself. It is a host of little things taken together that constitutes and expresses a culture, that gives a group its identity and sense of self, that reminds that group of its purpose.

Chapter 63 of the Holy Rule on Community Rank articulates a beautiful and delicate order of relations among the brothers:

> The younger monks must respect their seniors, and the seniors must love the juniors. When they address one another . . . the seniors call the younger monks "brother" and the younger monks call their seniors *nonnus*, which is translated "venerable father.". . . Wherever brothers meet, the junior asks his senior for a blessing. When an older monk comes by, the younger rises and offers him a seat, and does not presume to sit down unless the older bids him. In this way, they do what the words of Scripture say: *They should each try to be the first to show respect to the other* (Romans 12:10).

Whether or not the details of these particular practices are observed in a given monastery today, all monasteries have ways of expressing the ideals that St. Benedict puts before us in this chapter. It is about living together with a profound respect and courtesy, even with an affection toward one another. It articulates the "pure love of brothers" spoken of in chapter 73. In short, small as it may seem, there is a monastic way of passing each other in the hall, a glance or a gesture which says "Nonnus," a response which says "Brother," body language which asks for a blessing and the sign that grants it.

The Holy Rule is full of injunctions which promote this love and respect among the brethren, such that we may expect that this theme somehow lies toward the center of a specifically Benedictine something that we are tempted to call culture. Think of what St.

Benedict says of the sick: "Care of the sick must rank above and before all else, so that they may truly be served as Christ" (*RB* 36:1). And yet respect and courtesy are elicited from the sick too: "Let the sick on their part bear in mind that they are served out of honor for God, and let them not by their excessive demands distress their brothers who serve them" (*RB* 36:4). One of the dimensions of the practice of silence is so that the brethren may do things "without disturbing the others," as Benedict puts it concerning silence during siesta (*RB* 48:5). For the same reason, there is to be silence in the oratory "so that a brother who may wish to pray alone will not be disturbed by the insensitivity of another" (*RB* 52:3). The eleventh step of humility can be seen also as promoting the carefully calibrated relations among the brethren: "The eleventh step of humility is that a monk speaks gently and without laughter, seriously and with becoming modesty, briefly and reasonably" (*RB* 7:60). Or again, still in the category of relations, the abbot is to send brethren secretly to console a brother who may be in excessive sorrow (*RB* 27:3). All the brethren are to be called together for counsel "as often as anything important is to be done in the monastery," and it may be hoped—this is very gracious on Benedict's part—that the Lord may "reveal what is better to the younger." And, "the brothers for their part are to express their opinions with all humility, and not presume to defend their own views obstinately" (*RB* 3). In short, Benedict's monastic way has very much to do with the style and tone of the relations among the monks:

> Obedience is a blessing to be shown by all . . . If a monk gets the impression that one of his seniors is angry or disturbed with him, however slightly, he must, then and there without delay, cast himself on the ground at the other's feet to make satisfaction, and lie there until the disturbance is calmed by a blessing. (*RB* 71:1, 7-8)

If we may use the term culture for all that we are describing here, we can note that St. Benedict wants to extend this culture beyond the monastic family to the guests who come to the monastery. His instructions to the porter shimmer with a sense of joy and expectation at the arrival of anyone at the door, attitudes thoroughly shaped by immersion in the Word of God. He says, "As soon as anyone knocks, or a poor man calls out, he [the porter] replies, 'Thanks be to God' or 'Your blessing, please'; then, with all the gentleness that comes from the fear of God, he provides a prompt answer with the warmth of love" (*RB* 66:3-4). Benedict's detailed chapter on the reception of guests is surely a recipe combining many of the ingredients of a monastic culture. Guests are met with courtesy, prayer, and a kiss. A bow of the head or even a complete prostration expresses adoration of Christ in them. The Word of God, the monastery's most precious gift, is immediately read, and after that every kindness is shown the guest (*RB* 53).

Tremendous respect and courtesy for persons pervades the Holy Rule, and this surely has its roots in the whole scriptural culture promoted by the *Opus Dei* and *lectio divina*. A similar respect—and we may also call it courtesy—is also extended by St. Benedict even to things. A lucky phrase from the Rule, lucky in that it was destined to exercise tremendous influence over the way monks dealt with temporal goods, is his injunction to the cellarer: "He will regard all utensils and goods of the monastery as sacred vessels of the altar" (*RB* 31:10). With this one line, St. Benedict prevented what is perennially a temptation in monasticism; namely, despising too intensely things not immediately religious. With it he opened the door to the spiritual value of common labor and the sense of respect with which it should be done. Something similar holds good for monks in one of the places where they are likely to come into close contact with the culture that surrounds them; namely, in establishing prices for goods to be sold. This price "should always be a little lower than people outside the monastery are able to set." Why? "So that in all things God may be glorified (1 Pet 4:11)" (*RB* 57:8-9).

Perhaps a key to the difference between the kind of culture which all these practices create and the culture characterized by failure to achieve community, by difficulties in relationships and sexuality, by consumerist attitudes toward work—perhaps a key to the difference lies in nothing less than contrasting understandings of love and how it is achieved. Does the modern culture perhaps associate love too closely with a feeling, such that when the feeling is not there or goes away, one concludes that love is not required or that it has failed? The imagery of love is intense but transient.

In contrast to this, St. Benedict offers concrete things to do that will insure love in many different kinds of circumstances. The monastery is a culture, not literally a family; and monks love each other not because of blood ties but because the love of Christ enables them to do so. For love of Christ, *every* senior is to show love to *every* junior, regardless of personal attraction or feeling. *All* the sick are served, not because it is a pleasant or rewarding task, but "out of honor for God" (*RB* 36:4). *Whoever* knocks elicits a "Thanks be to God," and not just those whom one would want to knock. Benedict is strict on this, and he justifies this strictness in the prologue precisely for the sake of "safeguarding love" (*RB*, Prologue, 47) This way will seem "narrow at the outset" precisely because of a different culture from which monks come. "But as we progress in this way of life . . . our hearts overflow with the inexpressible delight of love" (*RB*, Prologue, 48-49).

Conclusion: Toward Defining a Specific Intellectual Tradition

When I came to my monastery as a novice, I immediately began to be instructed in the spirituality of the *Opus Dei*, to be taught how to do *lectio divina*, and to learn the specific little practices that characterize monastic observance in my house. Having lived this way for some twenty-five years now, and reflecting on the specific topic of this collection of essays, I realize that this was an introduction into, among other things, an intellectual tradition that has slowly become my own.

Within a monastery, one can find the interesting phenomenon of an intellectual tradition being practiced without conscious awareness. I have suggested that it is precisely this possibility that St. Benedict created in his Rule. Scholars, farmers, and cooks live side by side, and in their monastic practices they are living and thinking the riches of a tradition. Nonetheless, what may be lived unconsciously has also been consciously articulated. To focus the issue on a consciously conceived intellectual tradition, I think it is best to turn once again to how a monk might be taught to do *lectio divina*; for this is a question of one person sitting down and grappling with a text, thinking it through, and perhaps articulating in writing, speech, or art the fruits of the struggle. If we can observe a monk doing this, we are observing an intellectual tradition in action.

The tradition eventually articulated four steps in the process of lectio, which should not be understood mechanically or applied woodenly. They are rather four dimensions of a single experience, but naming and describing these dimensions help the monk to keep the experience focused and assure its dynamic movement. They are, first, *reading* itself. One reads just a verse or two of the Scriptures, makes sure it has been understood on its immediate and obvious level and then pauses for what is the second step; namely, *pondering* that text. This pondering is meant to be very personal. A meaning of the text is sought which applies to me in this very moment in which I am reading. The discovery of this meaning, however clearly or dimly grasped, gives rise naturally to the third step: *prayer.* I pray in short little prayers that come directly from the heart, that express my heart's reaction to whatever I have grasped in pondering the text. I express adoration, thanksgiving; I confess my sins; I am moved to pray for somebody or something; I beg for deeper understanding. The fourth dimension of *lectio* is on a different level from these first three. It is *contemplation.* Whereas the first three steps are in a certain sense the monk's responsibility to practice, contemplation is a gift entirely of the Spirit and is not to be considered as something that can be automatically produced by an application of the first three steps. But monks discovered that the practice of *reading, pondering,* and *praying* especially disposed them to receive the gift of *contemplation.* In contemplation they were carried above the text, left specific thoughts and formulated prayers behind, and were simply in deep communion with God.

This kind of encounter with the scriptural text was practiced by monks of every type: scholar, farmer, cook. But the monastic scholar also tended to employ it, perhaps unconsciously, in his own scholarly work such that it can in fact be identified as an actual methodology for studying—again, however, not to be woodenly applied. If one thinks of the four steps which articulate the practice of personal reading of Scripture, it is not difficult to see that in some sense the monastic intellectual tradition is an expansion of these. *Reading* expands what is read and the depth at which something is read. It will not simply be Scripture, but in the long run, anything at all since all things converge in the Christian mysteries. It would devote itself to languages, always so that more can be read and be read ever more deeply. *Pondering* is no longer simply an exercise in search of personally meaningful insight, but it becomes a sustained effort to understand at the deepest possible level all that emerges from the expanded reading. The monk will use, in the first place, the Rule of Faith of his ecclesial community as a guide in this move to the deepest possible level. But he will also employ every creative means possible and available to ponder mysteries that in themselves can ever be thought anew. *Praying* while doing this might be what most characterizes the tone of this intellectual tradition. It is a way of studying and thinking which is never far from the kinds of little prayers which suffuse the practice of personal *lectio*; namely, expressions of wonder, praise, gratitude, pleas for blessings and mercy. *Contemplation* reminds the monk-scholar that his study is not an end in itself but a means toward something which may well leave such study behind.

If I began these reflections with an image that shows both the contrast and the common ground between monasticism and contemporary culture—a jet moving among the stars observed by a monk in the quiet of the monastic garden—I can end with an image that shifts the weight of the equation: a novice coming to a monastery today. Such a novice comes from the contemporary culture, is an embodiment of it. The first task is to teach the novice to take on, however slowly, the traits of a truly venerable monastic tradition. When that happens, then the community can justifiably hope for what St. Benedict claims the Lord often does; namely, "reveal what is better to the juniors" (*RB* 3:3). In light of the present discussion, maybe we have stumbled here onto the place and the framework whereby the present cultural scene can also make its contribution to the monastery. The history and the culture of each one of us remain inextricably a part of who we are even as we become monks, and herein lies a mystery and a hope. The culture from which we came into the different culture of the monastery remains a part of us, but it is expanded, purified, redeemed, thus salvaged and transformed by the grace of Christ which is operative in the monastic culture. In this way, on a very deep—if hidden—level, monasteries are in dialogue with contemporary culture and are a place where there occurs what is meant to occur wherever Christians are found: all things brought into unity under Christ's headship.

CHAPTER FIVE

The Christian Wisdom Tradition and Enlightenment Reason

GERALD A. McCOOL

I n his latest encyclical, *Fides et Ratio*, John Paul II, writing at the end of her second millennium, reflects on the interplay between faith and reason during the course of the Church's history. The Christ of faith, he tells us, comes to individual Christians through the tradition of Church in which Christ Himself is always present.[1] Christian revelation therefore is also Christ's revelation of Himself, and it comes to individual Christians through the Gospels, which hand on to future generations the saving truth about God and the world that Christ Himself communicated to His own contemporaries. In other words, Christian revelation is historical.[2] Its reception is a free encounter between the disciple, who responds to historical revelation in faith, and the Christ who manifest Himself through it. Therefore, Christ's self-revelation must also have a personal dimension.[3]

It does not follow, however, that the Christian disciple's reception of revelation through faith is a purely individual process. For the Christ who comes to the believer through the word of Scripture is the same Christ who vivifies His Mystical Body, the Church, and since the Body of Christ is also the people of God, to whom Christ's word has been entrusted, Christ's Body, the Church, by her nature, is a community. In that community, the disciple who encounters Christ in faith is a free, responsible person, related to the fellow disciples who share his bond to

Christ and obligated, as they are, by the Master's command to transmit His saving word to the men and women with whom, as Christ's disciples, they engage in personal intercourse. In both its reception and transmission then, Christian revelation is a social process.

As the community of faith, which has been authorized to do so by her Founder, the Church cannot avoid the responsibility of passing judgment on the varying forms through which, over the centuries, historical revelation has been transmitted at different times and in different places.[4] In the first two millennia of the Church's history, the forms through which Christ's revealed word found expression were the philosophical categories and cultural symbols of classical, medieval, Renaissance, and modern Europe. In all likelihood, during the next millennium, those forms will also include the categories and symbols of non-Western philosophies and cultures, quite different, in their origin and in the course of their development, from categories and cultural symbols of Western Europe. Nevertheless, since the Christ who reveals Himself to His disciples in every place and in every age must always be the same Christ, there cannot be a plurality of irreducibly diverse Christian revelations.

No matter how diverse the forms of its expression may be, the revealed word of God contained in them must remain essentially the same.[5] Revelation, like the Church, which has judged and proclaimed its content since the age of the Apostles, is one and must be one. Therefore, the only source to which the faithful Christian can look for Christ's authentic revelation is the historically transmitted teaching of Christ's own Church. Sacred Scripture, transmitted and interpreted by the Church's authoritative tradition, is the abiding link between the contemporary Christian and the original revealing word spoken to His first disciples while the Lord was in their midst. Confidence in that link comes from the active presence of the living Christ within the Church. Because she is Christ's Body, in which His Spirit dwells, the Church has been able to preserve the unalterable truth of Christian revelation through all the vicissitudes of time and place associated with its historical transmission. The individual act of Christian faith is a uniquely personal act. Nevertheless, the truth of its object depends upon the common tradition of Christ's Church preserved from error by His Holy Spirit

Tradition and Culture in the Patristic Tradition

From the early Christian centuries, the Church has linked her official teaching of the wisdom of the Old and New Testaments to the purified secular wisdom of the world. In the Alexandria of Clement and Origen, that synthesis of revealed and human wisdom appeared to be entirely justified. The created world on which pagan philosophers reflected proclaimed the wisdom of the Word of God who had presided over its creation and who unfailingly maintained its constant order. Man's inquiring mind was the divine Word's created image. As such, it was moved by its very nature to return to God. Enlightened by the divine Word, who dwelt within it, the human mind could find the evidence of its Creator's presence in His created handwork and, using God's creation as its starting point, the mind could begin its ascent to Him. Encouraged by the example of Philo, whose Alexandrian Jewish theology had been framed in the categories of Middle Platonism, Clement and Origen incorporated the same Platonic epistemology and metaphysics into their patristic synthesis of exegesis, theology, and spirituality—a synthesis to which Newman returned in the nineteenth century.[6] Through its progressive growth in knowledge and love, the created image of God in the human mind was gradually transformed, under the influence of grace, into the state of perfect likeness to God, the state in which the mind could know God face to face. In the course of his or her religious and intellectual development, the contemplative Christian could discern, with steadily increasing facility, the presence of God in material creation, in the text of Scripture, and in his or her own spiritual reality.

In the patristic age, the Alexandrian synthesis of philosophy, secular literature, science, and Christian revelation gave rise, in both the Eastern and the Western Church, to the tradition of what can be called Christian Wisdom. In the Middle Ages, that tradition guided the Church's approach to education, exegesis, theology, spirituality, and religious life. For the medieval Christian, the created world could not fail to have an intelligible meaning, since it was being continually formed and directed, as a unitary whole, by the omniscient wisdom of God's uncreated Word. The vocation of the contemplative mind was to grasp that intelligible meaning through a disciplined integration of human knowledge by the arts and sciences. The great minds of antiquity had already shown their ability to do that, if only in a partial and imperfect way, and the fruits of their labor were still available to Christ's disciples in classical literature, philosophy, and science.

Christians, therefore, were urged to make use of the wisdom of the ancients in their own contemplative effort to see the active presence of God's Word in nature, in the human mind, in Sacred Scripture, and in the Church. Fortified by God's activity within it, man's reflective mind, through a lifetime of study and prayer, could gradually acquire the deeper knowledge of itself, the world, and God, that was the goal of medieval monastic contemplation. The interior, allegorical meaning of Scripture, greatly prized by early medieval piety, could be made more easily accessible thanks to the knowledge of God's creation which classical literature and science provided. In both the Eastern and Western Church, the praise of God, expressed through monastic architecture, art, and liturgical prayer, was nourished by that contemplative allegorical reading of Holy Scripture, and the verbal beauty of monastic poetry and prose was due in large measure their judicious use of literary forms inherited from classical antiquity.[7]

For the monk and, in the later Middle Ages, for the scholar of the Western Cathedral school, Scripture, literature, science, and philosophy were integral elements of their common Christian wisdom. In both Eastern and Western Europe, therefore, that Christian tradition remained alive, despite the turbulence caused by the fall of Rome and the rift between East and West which the establishment of Charlemagne's Western Empire had made unbridgeable. The preservation, restoration, and enhancement of the Christian wisdom tradition in Western culture and religious life became the driving force of the Carolingian Renaissance, and the ideal which inspired the Renaissance of the twelfth and thirteenth centuries. In the West, that tradition is generally thought to have reached its high point in the universities of the thirteenth century.

Nevertheless, remarkable as the achievements of the thirteenth century were in education and theology, they were counterbalanced by some significant losses in the areas of literature and exegesis.[8]

In Western Christendom's orderly world, God, as the providential orderer of the universe, conferred on both the Church and civil society their legitimate authority to direct the social order without which man could not attain his temporal and eternal end. Western civil society therefore never attempted to become a theocracy on the Old Testament model and, largely due to the influence of Augustine, the Western Church did not submit itself to imperial authority as fully as the Eastern Church had done. As a result, an unresolved dispute was carried on between the Church and the civil powers over the proper role assigned to each by God in directing the social order of what, until the Reformation, could still be considered a unified Christendom. The influence of St. Augustine in the West and the quarrels between reforming popes and civil powers increasingly jealous of their own authority exacerbated the ongoing tension between Church and state.

With the codification of civil and canon law in the twelfth century and the rediscovery of Aristotle's ethics and politics in the thirteenth, that tension led to the emergence of a late medieval political philosophy through which, it was hoped, the proper role of the Church, the state, and the individual in procuring the common good could be determined. In the nineteenth century, when the revived Christian wisdom tradition found itself in conflict with Enlightenment reason, the importance of that medieval social and political philosophy was recognized again. Modern Catholics, living in a secular liberal society, hoped that they could find in it the intellectual resources through which the freedom of the Church and the autonomy of Catholic education, the rights of the individual and of the family, and the worker's right to a just living wage could be defended.[9] In the nineteenth and twentieth centuries, St. Thomas was usually taken to be its greatest representative, and for that reason, although political philosophy had continued to flourish during the later Middle Ages, the modern Christian Wisdom tradition turned back to the tradition of St. Thomas for its social ethics.

Medieval Decline and Baroque Revival

After the thirteenth century, the Christian Wisdom tradition went into its long decline. The unity between revelation and philosophy, which St. Thomas had brought about, did not long survive his death. The synthesis between Platonic and Aristotelian metaphysics, through which St. Thomas' integration of knowledge had been accomplished, was abandoned by the anti-metaphysical nominalists on the fourteenth-century university faculties. As a result, faith and reason split into isolated and independent realms between which communication was no longer possible. In the narrow world of nominalistic theology, no place could be found for the synthesis of revelation, philosophy, and culture which had nourished the prayer and liturgy of the early medieval monasteries and justified their allegorical reading of Scripture.[10] By the time of the Renaissance, literature had explicitly declared its independence from university theology, and Renaissance textual scholars worked in conscious opposition to the theologians in their editing of patristic texts.

Conflicts between the papacy and European civil powers continued to divide the continent as kings and emperors recruited theologians and canon lawyers to plead their anti-papal case. The prestige of the papacy, already damaged when the popes were forced to abandon Rome for Avignon, was further lowered when rival claimants to the papacy denounced each other during the Western Schism. Ultimately, the conciliar movement, whose growth had been fostered by that schism, threatened to submit the Papacy to the authority of a general council. Little was left then of the earlier medieval synthesis of revelation, culture, spirituality, and Christian social theory when the Reformation, by rejecting the religious authority of the Catholic Church, brought an end to the religious and political unity of Europe.

From Baroque Catholicism and Christian Wisdom

Reform of the Church, however, was also the concern of other Christians who had no wish to separate themselves from her and, years before the outbreak of the Reformation, the revival of the Christian wisdom tradition was underway. In that revival, the strands of the earlier tradition, which had gradually fallen apart in the later Middle Ages, were drawn together again. The successful result of that endeavor was the distinctive synthesis of philosophy, theology, art, literature, and piety associated with the Catholic Baroque. In Northern Europe, the *devotio moderna*, one of whose classic expressions can be found in *The Imitation of Christ*, flourished in the Netherlands among the Brothers of the Common Life and, in the work of scholars like St. Thomas More and Erasmus, a new form of Renaissance Christian humanism made its appearance. The *devotio moderna*, one of whose distinguished representatives at the University of Paris was John Gerson, found a home there in the Collège de Montaigu and influenced St. Ignatius Loyola, the founder of the Society of Jesus, when he was student there. In Paris, Ignatius was also impressed by the orderly system of liberal education which Montaigu's Christian humanists had taken over. Many years later, Ignatius would make that system the model to be followed in Jesuit education.

At the University of Paris, Ignatius also came into fruitful contact with a very different strand of the revived Christian wisdom synthesis. This was the remarkable spiritual and intellectual revival movement among the sixteenth-century Dominicans. One of that revival's most important intellectual consequences was the systematic editing of St. Thomas' major works and the Order's decision to make the Angelic Doctor's *Summa Theologiae* the required text in Dominican teaching of theology.[11] St. Ignatius decided to follow the Dominican example in that respect and, in the Constitutions of his own Order, he made the theology of St. Thomas the norm which his Jesuits were to follow in their own teaching.

Presented in diverse and sometimes opposing ways by Jesuits and Dominicans in the sixteenth and seventeenth centuries, the theology of St. Thomas thus became a major element in their scholarly and influential Baroque scholasticism. Faithful to their own tradition, the Franciscans leaned more to the scholastic theology of Duns Scotus than they did to Thomas, but the reformed Carmelites were content to revive their own distinctive Thomism. As a result, in the reformed religious orders of the Baroque period, spirituality and theology were able to regain their former unity. The breach between the mysticism of Pseudo-Dionysius and the theology of St. Thomas, which had opened for a while among late medieval Dominicans, was definitely closed in Baroque Dominican spirituality. John of the Cross, the greatest of the Carmelite mystics, was a highly competent Thomist theologian, and his Carmelite brethren saw no conflict between John's Dionysian dark night mysticism and the clarity of their Carmelite Thomist theology. In the colleges and universities of the Society of Jesus, the literary humanism of the Renaissance was joined to Ignatius' *Spiritual Exercises* and integrated with a Jesuit theology inspired, in its main lines, by the Angelic Doctor. The Baroque art and architecture of Jesuit Churches, in conscious opposition to the Reformation's more pessimistic theology, affirmed the beauty of God's redeemed creation and manifested God's sacramental presence within it.

In Baroque Catholicism, it appeared for a while that the old Christian wisdom tradition had come back to life again in a new and vital form. For, although much in Baroque spirituality and theology was medieval in its origins, there were other elements in the Baroque synthesis, such as the *devotio moderna*, favored by the Brothers of the Common Life and by the Jesuits, the literary humanism of Baroque education, and the style of Baroque art and architecture that clearly owed their origin to the Renaissance. On closer inspection, moreover, even Baroque theology, medieval though it might appear to be in form, differed in its spirit from the theology of the high Middle Ages. Catholic theology was required to be defensive in its opposition both to the attacks of the Reformers and to the increasing secularism of Europe's absolute monarchies, and it was also challenged by a new set of moral problems arising from Europe's overseas expansion and the birth of modern capitalism. Baroque theology, therefore, had to be more problem conscious and controversial in its approach than medieval theology had been, and its intellectual horizon was restricted by the immediate needs of an embattled Church. Writing in the sixteenth and seventeenth centuries, before the development of scientific history, Baroque scholastic theologians were not yet ready to deal in a lastingly satisfactory way with the new historical problems which faced the post-Reformation Church. Those deficiencies of Baroque theology have frequently been noted.[12] They should not cause us, however, to overlook the importance of the Baroque period in the history of the Christian wisdom tradition. Among the lasting contributions which it made to Christianity were the ecclesiology, moral theology, and political philosophy of the Baroque Dominican and Jesuit theologians. Vitoria, Soto, Bellarmine, Molina, Suarez, and Lessius are still great names. The work of those theologians proved to be of invaluable worth in the revival of Catholic theology and social thought during the last two centuries. Even to this day, the possibilities of their Baroque theology for further development in the areas of just war theory, social justice, and international law have not yet been exhausted.

The Impact of Modern Enlightenment Reason

Baroque Christian wisdom remained a vital force in European culture for the first three decades of the seventeenth century. After that, however, its own diminishing vigor and an increasingly hostile cultural climate led to its decline. By mid-century, the Peace of Westphalia had shown that the long campaign to restore the religious unity of Europe by force had not succeeded, and, from that time forward, Europe took a secular approach to statecraft. The legitimate role of the Church in the direction of secular society, which the medieval Emperors had never denied to her, was now rejected or progressively curtailed. Although the Empire itself managed to survive in a weakened state, it had lost its sacred character. In modern Europe, therefore, Church and state could no longer play the roles which the medieval Christian wisdom tradition had granted them and which, in its Baroque revival, Christian wisdom had still assigned to them.

The mechanist physics of Galileo and Newton was not reconcilable with the older Greek philosophy of form and finality on which the Christian wisdom tradition had relied to justify its ascent from the world to God.[13] The modern philosophy represented by Descartes and his rationalist or empiricist successors, to which the seventeenth-century mechanist science looked for justification, required the rigid separation of Christian revelation from natural knowledge of the world through philosophy and science. Intentionally or not, therefore, the gulf between Christian revelation and critical natural reason, which modern philosophy had created, fostered the growth of agnosticism and deism in the seventeenth and eighteenth centuries.[14]

The secularization of culture was also encouraged by the modern philosophy of mind and body, which post-Cartesian epistemology required. The isolated, impersonal reason of the post-Cartesian subject had no intrinsic bond to the extra-mental world or to the bodily machine with which it found itself contingently united. Unlike the intellect of Aristotle, which was both speculative and practical in its operation, modern post-Cartesian reason was purely speculative. Furthermore, unlike the intellect of both Plato and Aristotle, post-Cartesian reason was claimed to function equally well in every subject. The soundness of modern reason's judgment, therefore, was unaffected by the moral conduct or social history of its possessor. In principle, therefore, contrary to the ethics of both Plato and Aristotle, any possessor of modern reason was equally competent to pass judgment on moral or religious issues, since the presence or absence of moral virtues in the judging subject in no way influenced the soundness of his moral judgment. This meant that the purely abstract reason of moral philosophy was a totally abstract reason, divorced from the concrete life of virtue. It was also an unhistorical, individual reason, independent of any social context or concrete cultural history. In the course of the eighteenth century, this abstract, isolated, lifeless, unhistorical reason became the reason of Enlightenment philosophy, politics, and culture.[15]

Obviously, that type of modern reason could not be reconciled with the patristic understanding of the human mind as the living, developing, dynamic image of God. For the patristic theology of the mind, as we recall, was inspired by an older conception of man which belonged to the classical philosophy of knowledge, man, and nature which the new post-Cartesian epistemology and the purely mechanical world of seventeenth-century science could no longer accommodate. Conflict between the modern seventeenth-century worldview and the classical Christian wisdom tradition, therefore, was inevitable. For without the theology of man as the image of God and the metaphysics of man and nature which justified it, Christian spirituality could never have been integrated with philosophy and science in the medieval synthesis of knowledge which the Baroque revival of Christian wisdom had brought to life again. Furthermore, once modern philosophy had severed the link between its disembodied thinking mind and the extra-mental world of material reality and once modern science had excluded intrinsic finality from its mechanical world of nature, both philosophy and science worked together in undermining the Platonic and Aristotelian foundations of medieval political philosophy, the philosophy which the Baroque revival of Christian wisdom had taken over, modernized, and extended in its own social thought. Once those foundations had been destroyed, the ground had been cleared for the construction of the very different sort of political philosophy, the new political theory which post-Cartesian epistemology and metaphysics made necessary, and in that political philosophy the relation between the individual and society would differ radically from what their relationship had been in the classical philosophy of the Christian wisdom tradition.[16]

In the eighteenth century, Enlightenment reason set the tone for culture in Europe and, largely because of that, the deism and agnosticism which Enlightenment reason fostered became widespread among the educated classes. Christian revelation, which modern reason systematically excluded from its consideration, could then be more easily dismissed as an outmoded superstition. In the natural world of Enlightenment reason, even the laws of society had to be mechanical and so, like all mechanical laws, they were timeless and impersonal. Nothing, therefore, like social or religious tradition had any claim to rational consideration. Society, like any other artifact, could be no more than a contingent assemblage of individual elements put together by human reason. The political philosophies of Locke and Rousseau were intended to explain how individual consent or an implicit social contract could perform that task, while Hume, perhaps more realistically, justified the legitimacy of society through reason's recognition of its utility. By the end of the century, when the leaders of republican and Napoleonic France overturned the thrones and altars of Europe, rewrote its laws, and transformed its educational system, modern scientific reason would be given as the justification for their revolutionary action. Nineteenth-century anti-clerical liberalism, the lay state, and the lay school of nineteenth-century Europe would later be justified in the same way.

Faithful Catholics were dismayed and demoralized by the triumph of Enlightenment reason and the hold which it had acquired on the governments and educated class of Europe. In order to meet its challenge, early in the eighteenth century, some Catholic theologians replaced their inherited Baroque scholasticism with the modern theology inspired by the French Oratorian, Nicholas Malbranche. That theology was to survive the French Revolution and reappear in the nineteenth century under the form of Ontologism. Modifying the epistemology of the self-enclosed Cartesian subject by linking it to an Augustinian intuition of the divine ideas, eighteenth-century Ontologism could not avoid the mind-body dualism of Descartes, and its finite extra-mental world was also the mechanical natural world of Cartesian physics. That meant, of course, that in eighteenth-century Ontologism, the world-view of the Christian wisdom tradition had already been abandoned.

As the century wore on, other theologians began to lose their faith in it as well. This was true even of Jesuit theologians. For, although Jesuits were still devoted to Baroque literary humanism in their international network of colleges, Jesuit theologians no longer maintained the same fidelity to the scholastic theology of their great Baroque predecessors. Sometimes under government pressure, as in Austria, and sometimes due to their own failure of nerve, Jesuit theologians also began to come to terms with Enlightenment reason. The outcome of their effort to compromise with it was an attempted synthesis of traditional scholasticism and modern rationalist philosophy, an unstable amalgam which, lacking conviction and coherence, was bound to be short-lived. Eventually a number of Jesuits simply gave up scholasticism entirely. Bendict Stattler, for example, the last great Jesuit theologian to teach in Austria before the suppression of his order in 1773, made no pretence of remaining faithful to the Baroque Christian wisdom tradition.[17] The Christian wisdom tradition was not killed by the French Revolution, as we might suppose. It was already dead before the Revolution, and the reason for its demise was its failure, in the eighteenth century, to weather the assault of Enlightenment reason.

The Nineteenth-Century Revival

With the rise of the Romantic movement in nineteenth-century Europe, however, a reaction set in against the Enlightenment reason of the eighteenth century, and, in a scattered, piecemeal way, the Christian wisdom tradition slowly returned to life. Among its first great representatives were the German theologians of the Catholic Tübingen School and the French Traditionalists, especially Joseph de Maistre, whose philosophy, like the philosophy of the Tübingen theologians, had been shaped by German idealism.[18] The German theologians had no interest in returning to Baroque scholasticism. Instead, they looked for inspiration to the early philosophy of Schelling. Like Schelling, they hoped to escape confinement in Kant's finite world of discursive consciousness through an immediate intuitive contact with the Infinite Absolute and, for them, Schelling's Absolute was also the God of Christian revelation. The God who created the finite universe revealed His vital presence through the dynamic finality of nature and through the history of the diverse communities, to one or other of which each individual belonged by nature. Unlike the mechanical, unhistorical world of Enlightenment reason, the world of the Tübingen theologians, therefore, was a living historical world. Its evolution was actively directed by its Provident Creator and, for that reason, the vital presence of His formative divine ideas could be discerned in it. Far from being the contingent product of a social contract, society, in the world of the Tübingen theologians, was a natural community, whose culture, history, and tradition were needed for the emergence and development of individual reason. Consequently, the autonomous isolated reason of the Enlightenment was an illusion, since no individual mind could begin to function on its own until it had been stirred to life through communication with another human mind in the inherited language of their shared historical community.

Yet, in order for that language and community to come into existence at the start of human history, the first human beings must have experienced an immediate intuitive contact with God's Infinite Intelligence in what, for Traditionalism, constituted God's "primitive revelation" to the human race.

In both the German and the less philosophically grounded French forms, Traditionalism became an important movement in early nineteenth-century Catholicism. Thanks to its influence, the notions of revelation, the presence of God in dynamic nature, history, tradition, inherited culture, and community, which individualistic eighteenth-century reason had banished as relics of the past, were taken seriously again. Later in the century, for a number of reasons, the influence of Traditionalism diminished. In Germany, the great systems of German idealism, which had inspired it, fell out of favor. In France, the reactionary politics of Joseph de Maistre, which identified the Church with the *ancien regime*, worked against its survival. Above all, the Neo-Thomists, whose influence in Rome increased during the latter portion of the century, considered Traditionalism's "primitive revelation" incompatible with orthodox Catholic teaching on faith and reason.[19]

Nevertheless, although it was not recognized at the time, Catholic Tübingen theology had made a lasting contribution to the revival of the Christian wisdom tradition. The theology of Johann Anton Moehler, the greatest of its representatives, would be taken up again in the twentieth century by Catholic theologians Joseph Geiselmann and Yves Congar, for example, and through them, the heritage of the Catholic Tübingen school would be given its proper due in contemporary theology.[20] Post-Kantian idealism was attractive to other Catholics committed to the revival of Catholic thought. German idealism, after all, had been influenced by Neo-Platonism, and to Catholics reacting against Enlightenment individual reason, Schelling's idealism seemed to be a natural ally. Antonio Rosmini, a brilliant and saintly Italian philosopher, was one of them. Long before twentieth-century Thomists thought of it, Rosmini had seen that, in some aspects, the post-Kantian starting point and method could be reconciled with the philosophy of St. Thomas. The Jesuit disciples of St. Thomas, who were violently opposed to both, attacked Rosmini savagely for that, and eventually secured the Church's condemnation of his teaching. In *Fides et Ratio*, John Paul gave Rosmini the recognition which the failure of his opponents to understand him had denied him but, because of them, the contribution which Rosmini could have made to Catholic thought could not be given at that time.[21]

In England, however, John Henry Newman made his own distinctive contribution to that revival. Newman was an independent thinker with no links either to German idealism or to Baroque scholasticism. His own theology had been shaped by his knowledge of the Greek Fathers, English philosophy, and Aristotelian ethics, and his approach to education had been influenced by his personal experience of Oxford's transition from the older Anglican community of scholars to a modern secular institution whose ideal was the autonomous reason of the Enlightenment. Newman's own opposition to Enlightenment reason was due to his patristic conception of the world as a sacramental universe in which God's presence revealed itself. It also came from his conviction that history was an evolutionary process in which the implications of what Newman called living ideas worked themselves out. It was fostered as well by his firm conviction that God's presence in the human mind manifested itself in man's moral judgments. Unlike his more rationalistic scholastic contemporaries, Newman showed an appreciation of the role of probability and of insight in the reaching of concrete conclusions, a role for which impersonal, abstract Enlightenment reason could find no place.

In the nineteenth century, Newman was generally praised for his English style, and his talent as a Catholic apologete was thoroughly appreciated. By showing the place of Christian revelation in an integral liberal education and by his defense of the Catholic university as a community of believing scholars, Newman's *The Idea of a University* made a powerful case for the schools and universities through which the Church hoped to compete with the secular educational system of the anti-Catholic liberal state. These were extremely valuable contributions to the Catholic intellectual revival, and for them Newman's co-religionists were genuinely grateful. Nevertheless, the power and depth of Newman's theology was not yet fully understood. Neither was the affinity of Newman's thought to the historical theology of the Tübingen school and to important aspects of St. Thomas' philosophy. That would not be properly appreciated until the twentieth century.[22] During the nineteenth century, Newman was destined to remain an isolated thinker. He was not always properly understood and, at times, he was unjustly distrusted by fellow Catholics whose knowledge of their own tradition was not as broad and extensive as Newman's knowledge of it.

In the nineteenth century, the religious orders, which had suffered seriously during the French Revolution, regained their vitality, and although the liberal anti-clerical governments of Europe made life difficult for them, their numbers and influence increased. In France, Prosper Guéranger established the Benedictines, and his monastery at Solesme became the fountainhead of an international Benedictine movement to restore the authenticity and dignity of the Church's liturgy. Henri-Dominique Lacordaire refounded the Dominicans in France, and in a number of European countries, the Jesuits reestablished themselves. Thanks to the increase in priestly and religious vocations, the Church was able to maintain its place in education and to influence the thought and culture of Europe. Toward the end of the century, Leo XIII was anxious to increase that intellectual influence, and he was also anxious to challenge the moral basis of secularist Enlightenment liberalism in the areas of civil government and social justice. In order to do that, the Pope turned to the philosophy of St. Thomas, to which he was personally favorable.

The consequences of the Pope's decision were momentous. Leo's encyclical *Aeterni Patris* recommended that, in the education of the clergy, the philosophy and theology of St. Thomas should be followed. Leo's encyclical on the "Condition of the Working Classes," *Rerum Novarum*, laid down the principles for a just solution to the problem of capital and labor, a solution which neither individualist liberalism nor collectivist Marxism had been able to find. Those principles had been taken from the restored philosophy of St. Thomas. Decades of Catholic social teaching followed from *Rerum Novarum*, and *Aeterni Patris* inaugurated a fruitful period of textual and historical research, first in medieval and later in patristic and biblical studies. Without that research, Vatican II would never have been possible.

By the end of the nineteenth century, the restored philosophy of St. Thomas had become the principal integrating force in the Christian wisdom tradition. Thomism shaped the formation of the clergy, and it justified the integration of knowledge in Catholic liberal education. It restored coherence to Catholic thought and gave confidence to Catholics in their dialogue with contemporary philosophy and culture. Nevertheless, there were serious deficiencies in nineteenth-century Thomism. Although it believed itself to be the common philosophy of St. Thomas and the other medieval Doctors, it was in reality the revived Thomism of the Baroque theologians.[23] Nineteenth-century Thomists were unaware of the difference between Baroque scholasticism and the theologies of St. Thomas and the Church Fathers. Furthermore, their resolute hostility to modern philosophy blinded them to the possibilities of dialogue with it which Rosmini and Newman had held out. The same blindness cut them off from the historical theology of the Tübingen School, whose emphasis on tradition and community would later prove to be so valuable.

The nineteenth-century revival of the Christian wisdom tradition was neither mature nor complete. Its historical and theoretical foundations had not yet been fully mastered. Largely because of that, its great representatives often failed to understand each other and were often hostile to one another. More work remained to be done before the scattered pieces of the Christian wisdom tradition could be fitted together to form a whole.

Twentieth-Century Development of the Tradition

In the first half of the twentieth century, the revived Christian wisdom tradition came to maturity, the historical heritage of medieval philosophy and theology was recovered, and accurate texts of St. Thomas, St. Bonaventure, and other medieval Doctors became available. Scriptural research and study of the Church Fathers were encouraged, and the quality of that research had reached a very high level by the middle of the century. Catholic universities in Belgium, Austria, and Italy became respected centers of intellectual activity, while in the United States an extensive network of colleges and universities gave the Church an effective voice in national culture as they educated an increasing number of Catholic leaders. Vocations to religious orders and congregations flourished and, thanks to the Church's colleges and universities, the number of committed Catholics among the intellectual leaders of Europe grew. Catholic scholarly publications, especially in philosophy and theology, were published in the major European languages.

The weak and marginalized Church of the early nineteenth century had become a strong and confident one by the middle of the twentieth. Catholic scholars and artists held their own with the leaders of Europe's Enlightenment culture and expressed themselves with a courage and optimism born of intellectual confidence in what they had to say. French authors like Leon Bloy, Paul Claudel, François Mauriac, and Georges Bernanos were unabashed in the profession of their Catholicism. The same could be said of Sigrid Undset in Norway, of Gertrude von le Fort in Germany, and of G.K. Chesterton and Christopher Dawson in England. A mature Christian humanism, inspired and guided by the Christian wisdom tradition, had come back to life. In France and especially in Germany, the liturgical movement, of which Prosper Guéranger had been the pioneer, flourished, and, together with the interest in Benedictine art, architecture, and spirituality stimulated by it, drew the attention of Catholic scholars to the monastic theology of the earlier medieval period before the rise of scholasticism. That scholarly study of the liturgy and of early medieval and patristic thought helped to prepare the ground for the liturgical and theological reforms of Vatican II.

The most potent influence in the revival of the Christian wisdom tradition, however, was the Neo-Thomist movement. Its importance grew in the first half of the century as its major representatives, both clerical and lay, made a name for themselves in Europe and America. At first, as might have been expected, these disciples of St. Thomas were content to carry on the tradition of Baroque scholasticism. Jesuits, like Pedro Descoqs or the Austrian theologians at Innsbruck, were usually followers of Suarez. Dominicans, like Ambroise Gardeil and Reginald Garrigou-Lagrange, took over and developed the Baroque scholasticism of Cajetan, as Jacques Maritain, in his early days, was also inclined to do.[24] Gradually, however, the historical research of scholars like Maurice de Wulf, Etienne Gilson, and Marie-Dominique Chenu revealed the significant difference between St. Thomas' own philosophy and the philosophies of both the Baroque scholastics and the other medieval Doctors, and, by doing so, showed that the common scholastic philosophy which Leo XIII had opposed to modern post-Cartesian philosophy did not exist. Further historical research by scholars like Cornelio Fabro also revealed that there were significant Platonic elements in St. Thomas' thought which the Baroque scholastics had failed to see.[25]

St. Thomas' own thought was more original and more complex than the earlier neo-scholastics had realized. It might also be more open to dialogue with both Kantian and post-Kantian than those neo-scholastics had thought when they attacked Rosmini on that score. Beginning with Pierre Rousselot and Joseph Maréchal, the stream of Neo-Thomist thought, from which both Karl Rahner and Bernard Lonergan emerged, took over the Cartesian subjective starting point in its philosophy and then endeavored to find its way back to objective reality through the use of Kant's transcendental method.[26] Their diversities in the interpretation of St. Thomas led to contention among the Neo-Thomists, but they also lent a vitality and rigor to Thomist thought which won for it a respected place in university philosophy.

One of the greatest services which the revived philosophy of St. Thomas rendered to the Church was its renewal of political philosophy. In the early years of the nineteenth century, European Catholics, on the whole, were sympathetic to Europe's traditional monarchies and hostile toward the anti-clerical Enlightenment liberal rationalism of the French Revolution. As Joseph de Maistre had done, continental Catholics continued to oppose the historical tradition of their national community and the established union of throne and altar to a revolutionary liberalism, based on the individual, non-historical reason of the Enlightenment. Leo XIII, however, was not convinced of the validity of that approach, and, like Taparelli and Liberatore among the nineteenth-century scholastics, he believed that a sounder basis for the Church's dialogue with contemporary society could be found in the scholastic philosophy which the Baroque theologians had used in their political philosophy. This led, as we have seen, to Leo's issuing his encyclicals *Aeterni Patris* and *Rerum Novarum*. In the last years of his pontificate, against the opposition of many French Catholics, Leo also tried to work out a reconciliation between the Church and the French Republic.

The First World War swept away the Empires of Austria, Germany, and Russia, and in the postwar years, the liberal democracies of Europe, still very much in the tradition of the Enlightenment, found themselves locked in combat with powerful anti-Christian collectivist movements—Communism, Fascism, and Nazism. In Europe's changed political climate, the crucial conflict now appeared to be the fight to the death between liberal individualist reason on one side and atheist collectivism on the other, the struggle between an artificial society, created by the independent individuals within it, and a collectivism which swallowed up the individuals and sacrificed them in the name of its own interests. Clearly, a sound middle ground between these two extremes was needed, and Catholic social thought came forward to provide it. Part of the Catholic effort on that score was made on the theoretical level and, on that level, Jacques Maritain and John Courtney Murray drew on the thought of St. Thomas in their twentieth-century defense of democracy and religious freedom. Part of the effort was also made on the level of social action justified by theoretical reflection. Apostolic movements, like Catholic Action and Young Christian Workers, were founded, and centers of instruction for Catholic workers, like Action Populaire in France or the labor schools in America, were opened. Nineteenth-century Germany and pre-war Austria already had their Catholic political parties, and after World War II, Christian Democratic parties, inspired by the political philosophy of Jacques Maritain and Luigi Sturzo, played an important role in the political life of Europe and of Latin America.[27] The revival of St. Thomas' social thought was largely responsible for that. Later in the century, the same revival and the flowering of Catholic social thought nourished by it were reflected in the documents of Vatican II, as can be seen in that Council's *Declaration on Religious Liberty* and in its *Pastoral Constitution on the Church in the Modern World*.

The challenge of collectivist ideologies, particularly in France, and the influence of the liturgical movement and popular social movements in Germany caused theologians to reflect more deeply on the dynamic and social nature of the Church. In the Baroque period, in reaction to Reformation theology, theologians like Robert Bellarmine emphasized the exterior, juridical nature of the Church, and in the individualistic climate of the Enlightenment, Catholic piety tended to become private and individual as well. The notion of the Church as an historical community enlivened by the Holy Spirit was lost to sight. Between the wars, however, that notion returned to favor, and Pius XII was favorable to it in his encyclical on the Mystical Body, *Mystici Corporis*. The work of Joseph Geiselmann in Germany brought the vital, communitarian theology of the Catholic Tübingen School back from its undeserved obscurity and focused attention once more on its great ecclesiologist, Johann Adam Moehler.[28] Thanks to Yves Congar, Moehler's communitarian vision of the Church gained popularity in France and then in England and America. The old Traditionalist vision of the Church, preserving God's revelation through its tradition and nourishing individual reason through contact with it, had been recovered. In the twentieth century, however, it could be re-incorporated into the Christian wisdom tradition in an erudite, rigorous, and convincing way.

Henri de Lubac, whose name was linked to that of Yves Congar in the "New Theology" controversy, was also troubled by the Church's failure to draw upon the richness of her tradition to counter the attraction of atheist collectivism. De Lubac's *Catholicism*, which, according to Hans Urs von Balthasar, contained the essence of de Lubac's theological agenda, returned to the patristic theology of nature, history, and community in its response to the challenge of Marxism.[30] Another of his early works, *Surnaturel*,[30] lamented the unfortunate narrowing of the Church's theological horizon in controversial Baroque scholasticism, and his later, four-volume masterpiece, *Exégèse Médiévale*,[31] revealed the richness of the older monastic allegorical interpretation of Scripture. Like Congar and the others associated with him in the "New Theology" movement, de Lubac was a Thomist. Like them, however, he had learned, from his patristic and medieval studies, that the metaphysics of nature, man, and being which underpinned the Christian wisdom tradition was not restricted, as earlier Neo-Thomists thought, to the limits of Thomistic metaphysics, particularly in its Baroque form. As a realistic metaphysics of act, form, and finality, it was clearly opposed to the mechanist, individual reason of the Enlightenment. But it had been present in patristic theology and in the monastic theology of the early Middle Ages, and it was not so alien to the vital communitarian idealism of Hegel, from which Marxism had come, that a fruitful dialogue between Catholicism and an open-minded Marxism could not take place. A broader understanding of that metaphysics, therefore, could better account for the integration of culture which the Christian wisdom tradition had achieved in the twentieth century, and it held out great promise for the future. That at least was the conviction which de Lubac and many others carried with them when they began their work at Vatican II.

A Double Collapse After Vatican II?

Despite its lasting accomplishments, the unanticipated consequences of Vatican II, at least in the short run, have dismayed a good number of Catholics. The strong and confident Church in which they grew up has gone, and in that weakened Church, the Christian wisdom tradition has lost the support which it enjoyed earlier in the century. Theology and philosophy seem to have lost their unity and focus. Questions of basic orthodoxy and fundamental method are raised today which, earlier in the century, would have seemed inconceivable. In its present state of confusion and uncertainty, theology seems to be in no condition to undertake the task of integrating Catholic culture. Indeed Catholic culture today is not easy to find. Authors, artists, and composers proud of their faith and confident in its profession have become something of a rarity. Catholic universities, we are told, are becoming increasingly secular, and for some of them at least, their Catholic identity presents a problem. Defections from the priesthood and religious life and a dearth of vocations have seriously weakened the network of Catholic schools on which the Christian wisdom tradition depended for its dissemination. Even

Catholic political philosophy, whose prospects seemed so bright after World War II, has lost its lustre and vitality. Europe's Christian Democratic parties differ little in their conduct and their approach to statecraft from their secular competitors, and with the collapse of Marxism, the justification for their existence seems less apparent. Marxism's collapse, it also would appear, has diminished the appeal of Liberation Theology for third-world Catholics. The twentieth-century revival of the Christian wisdom tradition might seem then to have run its course.

Yet, in the three decades since Vatican II, the Enlightenment reason, which challenged the Christian wisdom tradition in the seventeenth century and engaged in a running battle with it during the nineteenth and twentieth, has also fallen completely out of favor. In recent years, the Cartesian foundations of that reason have been completely undermined, and the mechanical world of Enlightenment nature is no longer the world of contemporary science and history. Present day anti-foundationalist philosophers now assert that Descartes' subjective starting point failed in its attempt to provide a certain foundation for science and philosophy through a set of basic principles or fundamental facts available to every human mind. Many linguistic philosophers indeed no longer believe that any such set of foundational truths could possibly be found. For those linguistic philosophers, truth can be no more than the warranted assertibility of a given proposition within an accepted linguistic framework. Philosophy, therefore, must restrict its work to the clarification of strictly delimited problems. Larger questions, like the meaning of the world or the goal of human life, are completely beyond its grasp. Contemporary Deconstructionists, in the tradition of Nietzsche and Derrida, are even more radical in their skepticism. From the Deconstructionist point of view, no justification can be found even for the existence of a stable knowing subject, to say nothing of a world of stable objects. Truth, for the Deconstructionist, is nothing, simply the product of the will to power. Science, culture, art, morality, and law, therefore, have no basis other than the arbitrary will of a society's oppressive dominant class. All of them can be challenged by the equally arbitrary will to power of the excluded classes. In the past thirty years, this sort of radical distrust of reason has become the dominant force in Western society. It has caused the present day crisis of meaning, the pervasive despair of finding any meaning for human life or for the world in which that life is lived. Human life and its purpose are now considered riddles to which no reasonable answer can be given. In *Fides et Ratio*, John Paul II tells us that, in his opinion, this crisis of meaning is the major challenge to the Christian faith today.[32] Before Vatican I, Enlightenment reason was the major challenge to the Catholic faith. After Vatican II, the collapse of Enlightenment reason has become that challenge.

Although *Fides et Ratio* makes no mention of the term, we could argue that the Christian wisdom tradition would be the means through which John Paul II hopes to confront the contemporary crisis of meaning. In the text of that encyclical, John Paul defends the realistic philosophy of knowledge, man, and being which, in one form or another, has structured the Christian wisdom tradition since its inception. The Pope also praises the philosophers and theologians who, in the community of the Church and under the guidance of the Holy Spirit, have preserved and explained Christian revelation in the context of a changing culture. John Paul's account of the interplay of faith and reason in the history of the Church often parallels the history of the Christian wisdom tradition adumbrated in this article.

The present pope is a philosopher, theologian, pastor and humanist. As his writings show, he is also well versed in spirituality and social theory. If he can be optimistic, then other defenders of the Christian wisdom tradition can also be. After all, they do not have to start their work from scratch as the pioneers of the nineteenth century were obliged to do. The rich heritage of the great twentieth-century philosophers, theologians, humanists, and social thinkers remains available to them. The liberal model of the university and the secularized legal system—inherited from the Enlightenment, the French Revolution, and post-Napoleonic Germany—have lost their intellectual justification. They can no longer claim, as they did in the nineteenth century, to be the unprejudiced voice of timeless universal reason. Catholics can now dispute the liberal domination of education, and they can do so as vigorously as the Deconstructionists have done. On better intellectual grounds, they can also vindicate the right of their schools and universities to integrate culture in the light of traditional Christian wisdom, provided, of course, that Catholics still possess the knowledge of their own tradition and the courage and intelligence to do so.

History can also give some encouragement to Catholics who are willing to assume that task. It will remind them that the nineteenth-century revival, far from being a mass movement, was the work of small groups. A small community of able disciples at Solesme made it possible for Guéranger to restore the liturgy and spirituality of the Benedictines. The small group assembled by Lacordaire brought Dominican theology and spirituality back to life in France and, from there, carried it to much of Europe. The number of Jesuit neo-scholastics was far from large. Newman's everyday world was limited at first to the Oriel common room and then to the Oratory at Birmingham. None of these great pioneers understood the Christian wisdom synthesis in its later fullness, but over time they managed to bring about its revival. There is no need to wait for a mass movement to begin the work of bringing the Christian wisdom tradition back to life once more. History has shown us that inspiring leaders and a group of able collaborators can do the job and, let us hope, some of those leaders may be already working at it.

Notes

1. John Paul II, *Fides et Ratio: On the Relationship between Faith and Reason* (Boston: Daughters of St. Paul, 1998).

2. *Fides et Ratio*, 89-92.

3. *Fides et Ratio*, 84-85.

4. *Fides et Ratio*, 66-67.

5. *Fides et Ratio*, 103-05.

6. For an excellent exposition of Newman's theory of liberal education, see Vincent F. Blehl, "Newman, the Fathers and Education," *Thought*, 45 (1970), 196-212.

7. For an authoritative account of medieval monastic humanism, see Jean Leclercq, *The Love of Learning and the Desire for God: A Study of Monastic Culture* (New York: Fordham University Press, 1974).

8. For the more literary theological humanism of the eleventh and twelfth centuries, see David Knowles. *The Evolution of Medieval Thought*

(New York: Vintage Books, 1964), 71-141. See also Marie-Dominique Chenu, *Nature, Man and Society in the Twelfth Century* (Chicago: University of Chicago Press, 1968).

9. Gerald A. McCool, *Nineteenth-Century Scholasticism: The Search for a Unitary Method* (New York: Fordham University Press, 1989), 158-66, 228-29.

10. See Leclercq, *The Love of Learning and the Desire for God*, 187-232; and Etienne Gilson, *The Unity of Philosophical Experience* (London: Sheed and Ward, 1955), 92-122.

11. Gerald A. McCool, "Why St. Thomas Stays Alive," *International Philosophical Quarterly*, 30 (1990), 275-87, esp. 282-83.

12. Hans Urs von Balthasar, *The Theology of Henri de Lubac* (San Francisco: Ignatius Press, 1991), 28-322.

13. Michael J. Buckley, *The Origins of Modern Atheism* (New Haven: Yale University Press, 1987), 68-144.

14. It was against the agnosticism of the "libertines" that Blaise Pascal argued in his defense of Christianity. See Paul Hazard, *The European Mind* (New York: Meridian Books, 1968), 155-79.

15. See Alisdair MacIntyre. *Three Rival Versions of Moral Inquiry* (Notre Dame: University of Notre Dame Press, 1990), 9-31.

16. For the difference between the two, see Leo Strauss, *Natural Right and History* (Chicago: University of Chicago Press, 1953).

17. See Thomas F. O'Meara, *Romantic Idealism and Roman Catholicism: Schelling and the Theologians* (Notre Dame: University of Notre Dame Press, 1982), 41, 47, 67.

18. See Wayne L. Fehr, *The Birth of the Catholic Tübingen School: The Dogmatics of Johann Sebastian Drey* (Chico, CA: Scholars Press, 1981).

19. McCool, *Nineteenth-Century Scholasticism*, 57-58.

20. Joseph R. Geiselmann, *Die katholische Tübinger Schule* (Freiburg: Herder, 1964).

21. *Fides et Ratio*, 91.

22. Bernard Lonergan has written of his debt to Newman. See Bernard Lonergan, "Insight Revisited," in *A Second Collection* (Philadelphia: Westminster Press, 1974), 263.

23. McCool, *Nineteenth-Century Scholasticism*, 213-15.

24. This is very evident in Maritain's early masterpiece, *The Degrees of Knowledge* (New York: Centenary Press, 1937, 1937).

25. Cornelio Fabro, *Participation et Causalité selon Saint Thomas d'Aquin* (Louvain: Presses Universitaires, 1961).

26. Gerald A. McCool, *The Neo-Thomists* (Milwaukee: Marquette University Press, 1994), 97-135, 160-61.

27. The most important of these parties were found in Italy and Germany.

28. For Moehler's theology, see O'Meara, *Romantic Idealism and Roman Catholicism*, 146-53. See also the splendid account of Moehler's ecclesiology in Michael J. Himes, *Ongoing Incarnation: Johann Anton Möhler and the Beginnings of Modern Ecclesiology* (New York: Crossroad, 1997).

29. Henri de Lubac, *Catholicism: Christ and the Common Destiny of Man* (San Francisco: Ignatius Press, 1988).

30. Henri de Lubac, *Surnaturel: Etudes Historiques* (Paris: Aubier, 1946).

31. Henri de Lubac, *Exégèse Médiévale*. 4 vols. (Paris: Aubier, 1959-64).

32. *Fides et Ratio*, 101-02.

CHAPTER SIX

Openness and Limit in the Catholic Encounter with Other Faith Traditions

FRANCIS X. CLOONEY

A Hindu Temple:
Encountering the Holy God, or Not?

On two of my visits to south India, I traveled to a large Hindu temple dedicated to the God Vishnu as Shrivenkateshvara, "Lord of the holy Venkatam." Venkatam is the name of a hill and the temple built on it, high above the dusty plains near Tirupati in Andhra Pradesh, the state just to the north of the large city of Chennai (Madras).[1] It is one of the most famous temples in India, and possibly the wealthiest. It is sacred to the Shrivaishnava Hindu community, those south Indians who believe that Vishnu, accompanied eternally by his consort Shri, is the supreme God who also chose in the past to descend into the world as Rama, Krishna, and in other forms, and who has also chosen even now to dwell in specific places which his presence makes holy. Traditionally, there are 108 holy places of special importance to Shrivaishnavas, 106 of them on earth. Tirupati is very old and had been already praised with great fervor in devotional songs over a thousand years ago. In the ninth century CE, a poet saint named Shatakopan sang these verses in his cycle of one hundred songs known as *Tiruvaymoli*:

For all time without end, to abide there and offer
    unfailing service,
that's what we must do,
there at holy Venkatam where cascades roar
—serving that beautiful light, my father's father's
    father.

My father, the one before my father's father's father's
    father:
at holy Venkatam where red flowers delight
the heaven-dwellers and the king of the heaven-dwellers
endlessly praise him, the beautiful great dark one.
                                    (*Tiruvaymoli* 3.3.1-2)[2]

Even today the temple is always crowded with visitors hoping
for blessings, giving praise, and seeking encounters with God.
After a long wait in outer chambers, one reaches the actual temple
and follows the line of devotees snaking their way through its
precincts, from corridor to corridor, room to room. One gradually
moves into the temple's center, and finally into a small, narrow
dark corridor about five yards long, barely high enough for one
to stand erect. It is illumined only by small oil lamps and smells
richly of a thousand years of incense and fresh flowers. At the end
of this passageway, there stands, nestled against the wall, the dark
stone image of Vishnu, Lord of the mountain. For the devotee,
this is the goal: to be here and to gain *darshan*—to see the cosmic
Lord who has taken physical form and to be seen by this Lord in
an exchange of glances that is a pure gift, as God chooses to come
near to his devotees. One can stand for a moment or two by the
image, but due to the long line of worshipers must then move
along quickly, returning again to the wider courtyard where one
can linger for as long as one wishes.[3]

Even the first time, before I had studied the devotional and
theological texts related to the temple, Tirupati already seemed to
me a very holy place. But study has deepened this sense of holiness for me and given it more intellectual weight. Tirupati and its
tradition are intellectually rich and also accessible; the body of
poetry and theological writing about the temple is abundant.

There is much to occupy the energies of scholars in Indology, the study of religion, and ritual studies, working according to the accepted academic methods by which religion is studied. Such inquiry is demanding enough, but the challenge for the religious intellectual—Catholic or of another tradition—is still more demanding because the religious questions implied by intellectual openness uncover new possibilities and therefore also new problems, objective and subjective. To take seriously both religious commitment and intellectual integrity demands a great deal, intellectually and religiously, from the person who is open to every question and yet chooses to remain willingly within the limits of faith.

In the following pages, I inquire into some of the challenges Tirupati poses to Catholic intellectuals, and on that basis sketch some key features of what and how a Catholic can or ought to think with reference to something as specific as a temple. I thereby hope also to assess more generally the resources and limitations available to Catholics as we encounter other religions in their particularity and, in turn, to examine the nature of Catholic intellectual identity, highlighting an enduring Catholic dilemma, the persistence of two basic instincts in the Catholic intellectual mentality: *openness* to what we find in religious traditions other than our own, and a sense of *limit* restricting that openness.

In choosing to focus on the example of Tirupati and to develop my thoughts in relation to one particular example, I am also choosing not to state generally the meanings of "Catholic," "intellectual," and "Catholic intellectual," but only to predict some features essential to the typical Catholic intellectual encounter with religious others. Two clarifications, though, may be helpful. First, since this volume of essays focuses on the *Catholic* Christian tradition, I keep this focus, but without prejudice to ways in which a shared, more widely Christian tradition is relevant, with common features but also viable alternative approaches.[4] Second, by "intellectual" I understand a concrete openness of mind put into action in continuing to learn, in taking questions seriously, in making judgments which assess and organize what is learned, in making sense of new knowledge for one's intellectual community, and in doing all this over a long period of time through cultivating a way of life in which faithful inquiry is central and not peripheral.

The Catholic Intellectual Tradition, Open and Bound

Once we start thinking about it, the Tirupati temple and traditional and living religious context—indicated here by some of the texts related to it—catch hold of our minds and transgress limits our Catholic faith and tradition may have presumed settled in advance. There is a temple, a holy place, understood within a sophisticated religious tradition. It is not easily disposed of as inferior to what we already believe, even though we have no good place in which to locate it. If we encounter a specific reality such as the Tirupati temple that has up until now had no place in the Christian tradition and if we seek to make sense of the encounter, we have something new to think about and to which it is necessary to respond intelligently. This intellectual activity requires us to be informed and clear as to what we are talking about and what it means, and it also expects us to be willing to enter upon a prolonged, open inquiry wherein learning leads to more learning. It tests our faith because it challenges us to articulate anew what this new learning means for believers and how our faith remains true even in this new light.

When a Catholic intellectual thinks about holy places from a Catholic perspective, he or she does not do this alone, on his or her own, but within a community which has shaped us and to which we want to remain committed. We must therefore take into account how that tradition shapes our encounter with religions. This essay is about what predictably faces Catholics who try to think seriously through and about other religions.

Catholic Openness

There is much in the traditional and contemporary Catholic consciousness which enables us to respond positively to other religious traditions in general, and also in particular instances, as when one enters a temple. Here I identify four dispositions the tradition bestows upon us. First, the Christian tradition, sharing on this issue a common heritage with the Jewish and Muslim, is *monotheistic*. There is only one all-powerful and all-knowing God, and everything is in the hands of the one true God. The world is not chaos or conflict, nor a balancing of principles of good and evil. Nor is anything merely outside of God's plan, for God's plan has no outside: everything human, including human religious striving, has a place inside God's sovereign plan for the world. When we first encounter a Hindu temple, we can presume that this too is part of God's domain and that good things happen here.

Second, according to the Catholic doctrine of *creation*, all that God has made is good. Catholics, usually and at their best, are willing to believe the world is good and humans too are good, even in their sinfulness. Sin cannot ever succeed in entirely corrupting human nature, which is the enduring gift of God. Whatever exists, inside and outside the Christian community, is fundamentally good. In some way, even in advance, we can hope and expect that the Tirupati temple is good, even if we cannot specify this hope in advance.

Third, the Catholic emphasis on the *Incarnation* as the truly divine and human event of God's coming into the world enhances and renders more deeply meaningful our appreciation of the world and human experiencing and human doing. The natural and the human constitute the place where God is to be found, and these are, in Christ, divinized, made God's own. God has chosen to live in our midst. This incarnationalism is itself enhanced and supported by a rich sense of sacramental realities within the liturgical practice of the Church and by extension among the things of everyday life—everyone's everyday life. Normatively at least, we believe that God is to be found amidst the things that we humans are and do, and temples are no exception.

Fourth, it is characteristically Catholic to believe in the value of *reasoning* and in the essential soundness of various cultural expressions of the meaning of life reasonably understood. Reason is a great and distinctive gift given by God to human beings, and it is typically Catholic to be disposed to trust the products of human reasoning as sound, good, religiously helpful, and to believe that we get quite far even in matters related to faith by thinking seriously. The history of European Catholicism has in important ways also been a history of the embrace of Greek thought by the Church in the patristic period and in grand syntheses, such as the *Summae* of Thomas Aquinas. Thoughtful Catholics will be well disposed to thinking positively about the products of natural human striving and ingenuity, and will often start out with a strong positive attitude toward what is religiously and culturally new and foreign to the Catholic tradition, expecting it to make sense. We take seriously and value as spiritually and intellectually significant both immediate religious realities—images, rites, holy temples, sacred words—and also the theoretical frameworks in which people understand and systematize those religious realities.

These four dispositions together inform a generous Catholic predisposition toward respect for the new and different, the recognition that whatever is human, even the unfamiliar and new, is profoundly a gift of God. The Catholic tradition fosters an intellectual openness which favors and fosters inquiry in all fields, including those related to religion and other peoples' religions. Tirupati need not be alien or threatening, and to dismiss it out of hand is less rather than more Christian. It is in keeping with the Catholic view of life to enter a temple with a positive expectation about what we see, what we hear, what people give themselves in devotion, and to see all this as communicating something of God, God's work in human work.

A Catholic Sense of Limits

But just as we have identified and affirmed these positive dispositions, it is also necessary to identify contrary dynamics promoted by precisely the same four factors. We are also predisposed not to take temples seriously, even if we may be benign toward them. For it should also be evident that there is much in the Catholic tradition which resists the idea that there is something positive in other religions, anything beyond noble human efforts. From the start, there is an ingrained disposition which in fact tends to preclude the possibility of our learning anything of genuine significance from the religious others we encounter, due to the same four dispositions.

First, if monotheism promotes a positive sense of the wholeness and goodness of the world in God's plan, it is also true, judging from the biblical sources where this monotheism is enunciated and where religious struggle connected with confessions of the one true God is common, that monotheism is quite compatible with religious aggression. Although biblical responses to pagan and gentile realities require a complex analysis, particularly in light of the different ways Jews and Christians are living that heritage now, there is no point in romanticizing the biblical perspective as simply irenic. In competitive situations (biblical and post-biblical), believers have marked off what belongs to God by a rejection of everything that belongs to false gods. On some occasions at least, the monotheistic impulse starkly divides the world into parts, encouraging the rejection of everything that is outside the true faith as not from God. If the biblical tradition prepares Catholics to see God at work in the world, it also prepares us to see other religions as competing centers of worship, threats to be overcome and excluded. Transmuted then into an intellectual attitude, monotheism can promote a straightforward expectation that whatever is not Christian is either in competition with the Christian, either mistaken or merely derivative or at best a sign pointing toward a superior Christian truth. The truth of the one true God offers also the security of the one correct apprehension of human truth. Nothing new can be learned from visiting a temple, because everything to be known about the one true God is available in the Bible.

Second, we have seen that the sense of the world as God's creation enables Christians to affirm its goodness. Yet in Christian theology, "creation" is a term correlated with "revelation" and "covenant," and often located as preliminary to them: God created first, but then revealed himself to his people and established his covenant with them. In more or less sophisticated ways, this ranking can serve to relegate the religious experiences and thought of the human race to the realm of the safely pre-Christian: what is natural and created may be good, but it is also "pre-covenant" and "pre-revelation." To call a Hindu temple a noble human creation may simply tell us something about Hindus and about where "we" used to be.

Third, the appreciation of the Incarnation, which allows Christians to look favorably on all that is human, bears with it also the tendency to exalt our Catholic tradition and culture above all others. Because God came in *this* way, among *us*, then *our* history is the best part of the history of God in the world. Our languages and literatures, arts and sciences, political systems and economic orders shine with the presence of God in the world. The Roman Catholic tradition (i.e., the best of a Christian humanism) is so excellent that nothing like it can exist anywhere in the world. The splendor of our culture outshines all the others. We know that no temple can match the material and spiritual glories of St. Peter's in Rome.

Fourth, reason has flourished in the Christian tradition. The confidence of faith is linked with confidence in a particular way of reasoning which applauds the clarity and good sense of the Catholic way of life. As every rational person should recognize, our theologians did get it right, and no real alternatives exist. As faith takes pride in culture, it may also become wedded to the philosophical traditions of Europe, from the Greeks to the Germans. It turns out to be most reasonable to be a Roman Catholic. The excellence of Catholic thought is mirrored in a conviction that non-Christian ways of thinking theologically can be judged deficient even in advance, lacking not only the qualifications to be called "theological" but even the right to be called "philosophical." No Hindu thinker can think or write so well as our Augustine or our Aquinas. A Catholic intellectual may be so taken with the reasonability of his or her faith that whatever is ostensibly outside it, such as the intellectual traditions developed around a Hindu temple, appears intellectually less interesting, not worth thinking about.

Monotheism, Creation, Incarnation, Reason: four dispositions foster openness, and the same four mark limits. It is most important to understand that the same values instigate both positive and negative predispositions toward what is not Christian, and instigate both at the same time. There is no question here of improvement, as if one might strive to stop being limited and cultivate openness. The intellectual who would be a Catholic—the Catholic who would genuinely believe and genuinely think— forever operates within the tension produced by this dilemma, pushed to know as much as possible and yet also assured, in advance, that nothing will unsettle truths and values already in place.

Openness and Limit in the Catholic Tradition

The preceding reflections are both brief and general, and they need to be amplified in numerous ways if they are to be useful. Here I suggest two such ways, the pattern of recent papal teaching, and the attitude of scholarly Christian missionaries. In each case, I hope to point out, merely by way of suggestion, that the paradoxical interplay of openness and limit is operative in such cases. When popes speak and missionaries think, they are inevitably saying two things at once: be open, draw a clear limit.

Example 1: Openness and Limit in Recent Papal Teaching

As a Catholic, the Catholic intellectual tends to think with a divided mind: genuine openness to the goodness of what is new, and the exclusion, in advance, of the possibility that there is something which might be reasonably and religiously true, irreducible to what Catholics already know.

Openness and limit thus mark the Catholic mind, and the teachings of Vatican II and recent papal teachings are no exception to this rule. Ecclesial openness is most famously indicated in *Nostra Aetate*, the Council document which ushered in the new era in Catholic reflection on other religions. It was very positive in its appreciation of other religions, while yet affirming the need to proclaim the Gospel:

> The Catholic Church rejects nothing of what is true and holy in these religions. She has a high regard for the manner of life and conduct, the precepts and doctrines which, although differing in many ways from her own teaching, nevertheless often reflect a ray of that truth which enlightens all men. Yet she proclaims and is in duty bound to proclaim without fail Christ who is "the way, the truth and the life" (John 14.6). In him, in whom God reconciled all things to himself (cf. 2 Corinthians 5:18-19), men find the fullness of their religious life. The Church, therefore, urges her sons to enter with prudence and charity into discussion and collaboration with members

of other religions. Let Christians, while witnessing to their own faith and way of life, acknowledge, preserve and encourage the spiritual and moral truths found among non-Christians, also their social life and culture.[5]

According to the Council, the Catholic's task is to enter into dialogue with people in other traditions, to discover and appreciate what is "true and holy," the "ray of truth" in the other religions, to select and highlight the spiritual and moral truths present in those religions. Due to the general nature of council documents, no examples are given of what is or isn't true and holy in other religions, nor is anything said to clarify what might be meant by the new collaboration, nor where the line is to be drawn between learning and Catholic fidelity.

While there have been numerous important efforts in the past thirty-five years to implement faithfully the Council's teachings, the intellectual tension between openness and total Christian confidence has not diminished. It recurs for example in the papal documents which appeal to *Nostra Aetate* in seeking to foster and guide interreligious relations. To take one early example: in an address to the Council, September 29, 1963, Paul VI urged the Council Fathers to look with respect on monotheistic traditions, which "uphold the meaning and concept of God as one, Creator, provident, most high and transcendent, that worship God with acts of sincere piety and upon whose beliefs and practices the principles of moral and social life are founded." He goes on to indicate where a line must be drawn between the erroneous and the good:

> The Catholic Church, unquestionably, and to its regret, perceives *gaps, insufficiencies and errors* in many religious expressions as those indicated, yet she cannot fail to turn her thoughts to them as well, to remind them that the Catholic religion holds in just regard all that which in them is true, good and human. (my emphasis)[6]

So too in the teaching of John Paul II. In his 1990 encyclical *Redemptoris Missio*, John Paul II cites Paul VI in highlighting the balance of openness (dialogue) and evangelization in the work of the Church:

> Interreligious dialogue is a part of the Church's evangelizing mission. Understood as a method and means of mutual knowledge and enrichment, dialogue is not in opposition to the mission *ad gentes*: indeed, it has special links with that mission and is one of its expressions. This mission, in fact, is addressed to those who do not know Christ and his Gospel, and who belong for the most part to other religions. In Christ, God calls all peoples to himself and he wishes to share with them the fullness of his revelation and love. He does not fail to make himself present in many ways, not only to individual but also to entire peoples through their spiritual riches, of which their religions are the main and essential expressions, even when they contain "gaps, insufficiencies, and errors" (Paul VI, 1963). All of this has been given ample emphasis by the Council and the subsequent Magisterium, without detracting in any way from the fact that salvation comes from Christ and that dialogue does not dispense from evangelization . . . These two elements must maintain both their intimate connection and their distinctiveness; therefore, they should not be confused, manipulated or regarded as identical, as though they were interchangeable.[7]

The key to the identification of an intellectual form of this proper and firm juxtaposition of evangelization and dialogue would have to lie in a capacity to recognize what is true and false in other religions, and to sort out the two. But here too, no examples are given to as how openness is actually to be exercised in the context of the juxtaposition. How does one act in a particular instance then? Does one visit Tirupati with an open heart and mind, while yet convinced in advance that all its devotees would be better off were Tirupati reconsecrated as a Catholic church? To do more than simply confess the faith (confession being quite enough, unless one is a theologian), one would have to be able to give good examples of ways in which the devotee would be improved by conversion.

In the 1998 encyclical *Fides et Ratio*, John Paul II reaffirms this double concern for openness and the defining of limits. In the opening section, entitled "Know yourself," he both affirms the Church's solidarity with the wider religious search for truth and makes it hard to see the solidarity as actually solid. All humans share the same great questions which found expression in the poetry and drama of the Greeks, the philosophies of the Buddha and Confucius, the prophets and wisdom teachers of Israel; and the members of the Church have the same human questions and share the same path. Yet the Church does not search, but rather chooses to accompany and aid those who seek, sharing with them the good news of Jesus Christ in "the *diakonia* of truth."[8]

In the middle of the same encyclical, the Pope insists on the integrity of cultures and reminds Catholics "to foster whatever is implicit in them to the point where it will be fully explicit in the light of truth."[9] No culture stands in a dominant position over the rest, and the Church's duties include learning from all cultures. In this context, the Pope summons Catholics to pay particular attention to India, for "it is the duty of Christians now to draw from this rich heritage the elements compatible with their faith, in order to enrich Christian thought."[10] At its end, he emphasizes the special demand placed on Catholic intellectuals in the "current ferment in philosophy . . . to discern the expectations, the points of openness and the key issues of this historical moment . . . Christian philosophers can develop a reflection which will be both comprehensible and appealing to those who do not yet grasp the full truth which divine Revelation declares.[11] Truly open—in order to understand, and to be able to converse with those genuinely seeking even the truth that has been given to us—the Catholic intellectual must be attentive to all the powerful currents of human thinking, yet without forgetting that he or she already possesses the fullness of truth.

One can imagine a Catholic inspired by the Council and papal teachings visiting Tirupati and gratefully appreciating the experience. One can also imagine a Catholic feeling assured in advance that a temple is not a place where God dwells in a special way, that it is not meritorious to visit there, and that one would do better simply to visit a Catholic shrine. The particular reason for this caution—circumscribing openness with limits—may simply be the belief that Christian faith is the only true faith, and clearly it cannot be a Catholic intellectual's place to dispute this faith claim. But it is usually also suggested, vaguely or explicitly, that there are good reasons why the cult of Vishnu at Tirupati is neither religiously nor intellectually satisfying and why the truth articulated in the Christian traditions of religious practice, philosophy, and theology are all superior to Hindu efforts at right practice, right thinking, right faith. Once this further set of claims is made, the Catholic who would be an intellectual must examine what is involved and assess the cogency of positions stated by Christian intellectuals. If evangelization rightly delimits the Christian encounter with religions, interreligious encounter rightly poses difficult questions to the evangelist, and the situation is particularly intense when we both preach the Gospel and also lay claim to the title of "Catholic intellectual."

Example 2: Openness and Limit in Catholic Missionary India[12]

Another key way of getting at the nature of the divided Catholic response to other religions is to review the history of actual encounters. As might be expected, the record shows the same mix of openness and boundary-drawing with respect to other religions that characterizes papal teaching, and some of the most remarkable missionaries exemplify what I have presented as the typical Catholic intellectual attitude, honest openness coupled with a strong sense of Christian superiority. Most missionaries work with a strong conviction that people will be better off were they to become Catholics or, more strongly, that people can be saved if they become Catholic; some of these same missionaries have also shown great respect for and interest in the religions they encountered.

Over the years, I have coupled my study of the Hindu traditions with an examination of missionary encounters, particularly involving Jesuit missionaries in the Indian context and, among those, missionaries who were particularly interested in learning about the religions they encountered, and here I mention two cases by way of example. First, Roberto de Nobili, who lived in the seventeenth century, is rightly honored as an exemplar of openness and respect for Indian culture; he learned an astonishing amount about the religious ideas and practices of south Indian Hindus, and vigorously defended Indian culture in discussion with his fellow Christians. But the limits of his openness were set, and his largely Thomistic view of religion and truth was well established before he reached India. It is a possible and good thing for an Indian to be a Christian in an Indian way, but there is nothing in his writing which conceded that Hindus, as religious persons, had anything to teach Christians. De Nobili studied Indian culture in impressive depth, but dismissed and condemned the religious practices around him in south India in each of the specific features which made them distinctively Hindu: if it is Indian, it is good, but if it is Hindu, it is not; what is Hindu is superstitious, a distortion of the Indian. De Nobili and many of his scholarly missionary successors in India took the position of intellectual judges, since they believed that they could examine religions, sort out the valuable from the superstitious, the true from the false, in order to draw on these selectively as useable created, human achievements. For de Nobili, the duty of the Catholic intellectual is to be able to make this differentiation, guided by a threefold rule which I formulate as follows: whatever is Catholic is reasonable; whatever is reasonable is conducive to the Catholic faith; whatever is non-Christian is, insofar as it is non-Christian, both unreasonable and not true.[13]

My second example, also drawn from the work of Jesuits in India, reinforces the point that missionaries who are intellectuals can nevertheless ascend to privileged intellectual positions in order to render compatible their faith and their deep knowledge of the culture they encounter. Pierre Johanns, S.J., a missionary scholar working in Calcutta in the 1920s and 1930s, followed at least implicitly in the footsteps of de Nobili as a Catholic intellectual. In a famous series of articles entitled *To Christ through Vedanta*, Johanns carefully studied in detail the ideas of great thinkers of several schools of Vedanta, one of the most important Hindu forms of Hindu theology and philosophy.[14] Studying particular themes in each school, Johanns pointed out what was good and acceptable according to Catholic theological norms and also what did not fit Catholic theology and therefore needed to be corrected.

Johanns' goal was to show how Vedanta contained possibilities which make sense in the light of Christ, and to demonstrate by scholarly analysis that until fulfillment in Christ (i.e., in Thomism, the Catholic philosophical and theological synthesis) even the best of Hindu thinking was, simply by rational standards, incomplete and defective.[15] Johanns believed that the superior truth of the Catholic system could be demonstrated by a careful study of the details of the different Vedanta positions; this study would demonstrate that the disconnected, fragmentary truths found in the Vedanta systems were moving toward an integral system in which all the pieces would fit together (i.e., toward a Catholic philosophy and dogmatic theology). Johanns' missionary agenda followed from this intellectual claim: most of what learned Hindus believed could be honored and retained by them even when they converted to Christianity which, after all, fulfilled the best aspects of their tradition; therefore, there were no intellectual bars to conversion. Like de Nobili, Johanns was a great and open-minded scholar who in principle knew in advance everything that could actually matter religiously and theologically. As a Catholic intellectual, he too worked within the strictures of the Catholic intellectual's dilemma identified above: though open to all of Indian thought, he needed nothing in fashioning the complete theological position.[16]

Thinking about Other Religions in a Catholic Way: Four Virtues in the Context of Openness and Limit

This dilemma of openness and limit has always remained operative in Catholic thinking. It has fostered legitimately high expectations regarding what is new, and at the same time set severe, prevenient limits on what the new might be allowed to mean. This Catholic intellectual dilemma has led to the consistent teaching to which both popes and missionaries have adhered: other religions should be respected as much as possible, excepting insofar as they are in error—and "error" seems to mean, "difference from what can be known from the Catholic tradition." While this twofold attitude is to be respected as a faith position, it falls short intellectually because the "non-Christian other" keeps disappearing before the "Catholic self": the Hindu is really not there, there is nothing to be thought about. If we often hear the complaint that intellectuals are not Catholic enough, it is also true that too few Catholics are intellectuals. This tension is basic to the Catholic worldview, and it is not going to go away nor be eluded by a better theological position. The dual obligation of the Catholic intellectual to be open and subject to preordained limits at the same time must then be accepted as the context for theologizing, an unsettled, unhomogenized synthesis which must be observed and negotiated by the Catholic who seeks to be an intellectual. I suggest that this is a situation without improvement or remedy, the context in which Catholic intellectuals must operate when they think about religions.

We must, therefore, now think about how a Catholic who would be an intellectual is to work within the limits of this situation. In the following pages, I will sketch the contours of an answer by clarifying features of the example of the Tirupati temple, and at the same time identifying four virtues required of the Catholic intellectual who thinks about other religions: attention to particularities; attentiveness to theological significance; honest and patient questioning even in religious matters; a willingness to make timely judgments. In doing so, I will also turn back toward the particular, looking more deeply into what Tirupati has meant for Hindus.

Attention to Particularities

Since thoughtful persons cannot settle for a generic apprehension of what is new and different, either approving of it or dismissing it, Catholic intellectuals who would venture to assess the significance of a temple such as Tirupati must think in particular, through particular words and ideas, practices, images, with attention to what people in those religious traditions have themselves thought about the things being studied. This accentuates openness and, so to speak, "limits limit." Attention to particularities, then, is the first virtue required of the Catholic intellectual who would have something intelligent to say about other religions.

For example, in Shatakopan's song about Tirupati (i.e., holy Venkatam), which we cited first at the beginning of this essay, the next verses continue to emphasize the particular beautiful features of the Lord of the temple,

> That great wondrous one with lovely red lotus eyes,
> his mouth a red ripe fruit, a dark blue gem,
> the Lord of Venkatam where clear abundant waters
> cascade,
> the only Lord of the heaven-dwellers, endlessly praised
> from of old

and his radiant beauty which transcends those features,

> If I call him "Lord of the heaven-dwellers,"
> does that glorify him who dwells in Venkatam,
> that highest radiant light, who nets lowly me
> in my emptiness?

> Is it enough to call him "light, worshipped by all the
> world, first form,"
> the ambrosia of the Veda of the Vedic scholars
> dwelling in flawless, glorious Venkatam? (3.3.3-5)

The Lord at Tirupati is a particular, lovely Lord of radiant features, the source of the world, the one praised in the eternal heavens, the vital essence of the Vedic scriptures; to approach the temple is, for the pious Hindu, to approach this Lord in particular, here and now. For Shatakopan and his tradition, the experience is vivid, and its vitality infuses ritual, song, and theology. Only in that extended particularity do they praise their God at Tirupati. It therefore seems necessary, on theological as well as broader intellectual grounds, for Catholics who would understand and assess the meaning of Tirupati to pay attention to those details.

The particularity of Tirupati is also a kind of particularity Catholics can well understand, because what is so specific is also broadly significant. Even large public temples exist as places of worship only within a framework of belief and communal articulations of meaning, and much of their meaning relies on understanding what people take them to signify. Neither generalization nor stripping it down to mere details is adequate to its meaning, which is both very particular and very universal. As we study this or other traditions, intelligence requires of us that we approach them with an expectation that there will be theological significance to what we read; it is not only our Catholic tradition which has discovered the idea that the mind must strive to understand what it believes, and to put that understanding into words. Particular names, places, images, activities all occur within intellectual contexts which give them that meaning; they belong there, and can be properly abstracted only if one is aware of the whole theological location.

Attentiveness to Theological Significance

The second virtue then, building upon respect for particularity, is attentiveness to theological significance, including a respect for our theological peers in other religious traditions. As song 3.3 from *Tiruvaymoli* shows, the cult of Vishnu at Tirupati is richly elaborated in a sacred literary canon, in the Tamil as well as Sanskrit languages. Sacred songs such as *Tiruvaymoli* and others like it form a sacred, revealed canon and are located in a commentarial tradition which we can briefly "visit" in order to understand the intellectual context of the temple.

The song itself, of course, shows the rich range of good qualities present in the Lord of Tirupati and saving deeds undertaken by him: he is our beautiful life, our father's father's father (v. 1); he is the beautiful great dark one (v. 2); he is the great wondrous one with lovely red lotus eyes, the Lord of Venkatam, Lord of the heaven-dwellers (v. 3); he is the lofty radiant light, the one called "the Lord of the heaven-dwellers" (v. 4); he is worshipped by all the world, he is the first form, ambrosia of the Veda of the Vedic scholars (v. 5); as Krishna, he lifted up a hill to protect his devotees from the cold rain; seeming to be a small dwarf, he once measured the world in three steps; he is the highest one (v. 8); he is Krishna, he is the cowherd of Venkatam who destroys disease, birth and, death (v. 9). Shatakopan is not a systematic theologian, but by amassing such claims about God even in one song, he fills out a rich sense of who the lord of Tirupati is. He also then weaves these claims into the much larger set made throughout *Tiruvaymoli*, and those are in turn woven into the canon of south Indian Shrivaishnava devotional songs and into the still broader cloth of the Shrivaishnava theological tradition.

The commentators who explained *Tiruvaymoli* elaborate the nature of the Lord of the temple in commenting on the verses. Thus, at the beginning of *Tiruvaymoli* 6.10 (which also praises Tirupati and which has received richer commentary than *Tiruvaymoli* 3.3), the great Shrivaishnava commentator Nampillai describes how Shatakopan meditated on the Lord's gracious identity, and on that basis decided to surrender to him at Tirupati:

> The Lord who is the husband of the Goddess Shri, whose every desire is satisfied, who is connected to both the heavenly and earthly realms, who is possessed of all auspicious qualities . . . who is the Lord who reveals himself to the eternal beings in the heavenly Vaikunta—this Lord thinks, "Many will lose us, since we are not able to stretch out from here a long enough arm to help them." So he descends in *avatara* as Rama, Krishna, and in other forms, shows his deeds and qualities to those living in that same time, and enables people to experience them. So that he might not be lost to those worldly beings born after that time, this Lord of desire abides on the holy mountain, holy Venkatam, along with his divine consort. The saint sees this and also the Lord's good disposition, and how one may take refuge with him without any of the requirements such as restrictions on eligibility, time, accessory aids. In this song the saint makes known his resolve to take refuge at the feet of the revered Lord of holy Venkatam, after first confessing to the great Lady that he no longer has anywhere else to go.[17]

For the tradition, Tirupati—holy Venkatam—becomes a symbol of the broader patterns of grace; the mountain becomes synonymous with divine compassion and human surrender to divine grace.

What is stated poetically in the songs and elaborated in the commentaries was at least obliquely amplified in prose theological writings. Ramanuja, the most important south Indian Shrivaishnava theologian, does not refer to the vernacular pieties of his tradition in his Sanskrit writings, but he draws on this tradition when, for example, in introducing the Sanskrit-language *Bhagavad Gita*, he describes Vishnu as both transcendent and compassionate, accessible to his devotees. On the one hand, Lord Vishnu is entirely "auspicious and utterly opposed to everything defiling"; his "essential nature is wholly knowledge and bliss," and he is "an ocean of auspicious attributes of matchless excellence inherent in his nature." He is creator of everything, but even then he "remains with his same essential nature and is inaccessible even by such means as the meditation and worship of humans or gods like Brahma." On the other hand, he chooses to be involved in the plight of sentient beings, because he is "a shoreless ocean of compassion, gracious condescension, forgiving love and generosity," desirous of providing deliverance for all beings.[18] Holy places like Tirupati are the location of this enduring commitment, compassion, condescension, because anyone can come to these temples. Clearly Ramanuja and the commentators are seeking an intelligent theological ground on which to explain who the Lord of Tirupati is, universally, while yet not obviating the value of visiting this particular holy place: the transcendent Lord is the one who graciously comes here.

What is the Catholic intellectual to make of all this? Once we choose to move beyond a simple confession of Christian faith—Christ is Lord, Christ is the Way—onto an intellectual ground where we put ourselves forward as Catholic intellectuals and venture to give some explanation of what we believe in light of what other people believe, we must think very carefully lest we allow faith to substitute for intellectual activity. This is a strenuous activity, since it is not easy to pick out what Pope Paul VI predicted to be the "gaps, insufficiencies, and errors" found in the non-Christian and therefore too, it would seem, in the tradition connected with the Tirupati temple, *Tiruvaymoli*, its commentaries, and theologies. Given the subtlety of this Hindu intellectual tradition, there are no easy intellectual grounds, theological or otherwise, on which one can merely state the superior coherence or intelligibility of Christian theological positions. Knowledge of another tradition makes it both necessary and difficult to say what it means to charge that another theological tradition is deficient, full of gaps, or in error, unless one has again retreated to a more fundamental faith position and is simply repeating that what is not Christ-centered cannot be true. If there are errors, the intellectual must show what they are, and to do that, he or she must trace the erroneous ideas in their proper theological context. He or she must not think merely about "non-Christian religions" or "Hinduism" or "temples," but rather about what Shatakopan said, and what Nampillai said that Shatakopan meant; to judge them, the intellectual must have studied them first. Without research, there can be no credible Catholic intellectual assessment of the temple's theology as this developed in its own Hindu tradition.

But again, my basic point is not so much an appeal that we must do our homework, but rather a prediction: some Catholic intellectuals will indeed undertake such research, for the positive reasons supportive of openness suggested above, but will also be likely to draw back at certain points and not cross certain predetermined limits. Such is the dilemma of openness and limit. Of course, the situation is dynamic, since believers can fail to be intellectuals, and intellectuals can step away from their faith; the careful harmonization of Catholic ways of thinking and Catholic ways of practicing the faith is always in danger of breaking down, and the juxtaposition of "Catholic" and "intellectual" may seem either to be merely arbitrary or arbitrary in a postmodern sense, whereby openness and limit constantly and forever mutually constrain one another.[19]

Honest and Patient Questioning Even in Religious Matters

Once we become involved in thinking through an example in its particularities and its theological framework, more questions abound. Our third intellectual virtue then comes into play: honest and patient questioning, even in religious matters. The questions which arise and stretch the mind are not simply those which encompass details or theological import, since some of what we learn raises further and more difficult questions of meaning for us. The next verses from *Tiruvaymoli* 3.3 can be understood as implicitly challenging some basic Christian beliefs:

> Those who take up the task of bowing low to the
>   one who lives in Venkatam
> do good for themselves and truly destroy sharp debts
>   and the deeds of the body.

> Holy Venkatam—where the quieted heaven-dwellers
>   and the leader of the heaven-dwellers worship,
> carrying many flowers, water, lamps, and incense—
> that broad hill gives us Freedom, likeness.

> He lifted up that hill to give protection from the
>   cold rain,
> he once measured the world, the highest one:
> to worship even once his hill, holy Venkatam,
>   makes deeds perish. (3.3.6-8)

These verses affirm the saving deeds of Vishnu, lord of Tirupati. Concealed in the guise of a dwarf, Vishnu grew and "measured" the earth in three steps, taking it back from an evil king; as the cowherd Krishna, he "lifted" a mountain to shield devotees from rains sent down by angry gods. Now these gods, citizens of heaven, do nothing but worship him. Acknowledging the presence of this saving Lord in worship at Tirupati destroys sin and gives liberation, since he is the destroyer and liberator (i.e., Vishnu, Lord of Tirupati, is the savior).

In this way, we may properly see ourselves as confronted with a claim which, as Catholic intellectuals, we cannot merely accept, nor merely dismiss. One cannot casually go to a temple of Vishnu to worship, since there are stark and simple differences and choices involved which have to do with acknowledging and worshiping God properly. On one level, one may simply admit that it is one thing to say, "Jesus is Lord!" and quite another to say, "Vishnu is the only refuge!" But there is more than one level to consider, once one begins to think. To draw an intellectually viable conclusion from these obvious and proper distinctions requires a further examination of how a specific starting point of faith—faith in God as I know God, as God is revealed to me—has force and how it means something outside the confines of my own faith community, either in communication with members of other religious traditions or, more commonly, in discourse about their beliefs. Of course, even believers value explanations of how their faith makes sense in a wider world. To adhere to the view that both openness and limit are legitimate characteristics of the Catholic intellectual attitude means that we are committed to both, i.e., not open some of the time, and simply resolute, adhering to the superiority of Catholic truth, at other times. Faith purifies thinking, thinking unsettles faith.

If a profession of faith is to make sense, it must bear some concreteness, and so it still seems necessary to delve deeper still into the details of the meaning of Tirupati in the wider religious context of ritual, pilgrimage and poetry, in which a poet would feel inspired in the year 800 CE or so to compose verses in honor of Tirupati, and one must also look forward and see what Shrivaishnavas have made of this claim over the centuries.

Most often, small questions are easier to start with. One might, for instance, start analyzing the verses of *Tiruvaymoli* phrase by phrase. For example, when the poet says in verse 7 that this hill "gives us freedom, likeness," perhaps this alludes to the experience of liberation (*moksa*) in which one becomes "totally like" the absolute reality, Brahman, "non-different"; this is what some Hindus believe. But the commentator Nampillai reads the words as meaning either of two possibilities. First, it could be a state of becoming one with the Lord, and therefore like him; second, it could be the gift of the state of equilibrium, wherein the person achieves the tranquillity and freedom of self-adequacy, self-realization.[20] Both interpretations, Nampillai says, are supported with Upanishadic verses (which he cites).

As for Tirupati's role, "the broad hill which gives us Freedom, likeness": the Shrivaishnavas do not want to attribute magical powers to the mountain itself, so they understand the point of the poet's making the mountain the agent of the gift of freedom to be that the mountain enables devotees—those who coming wanting freedom—to become like itself, i.e., totally dependent on the Lord, existing only for him. In other words, the tradition affirms clearly that a graced, personal relationship with God is the goal of every devotee's earthly "pilgrimage." If the issue then is not a monistic immersion in the totality or a belief in the powers of sacred mountains, but instead a theology related to specific and seemingly attractive ideas about God, self, and salvation, then the Catholic scholar is compelled to ask still more specifically where the gaps, insufficiencies, and errors might lie in the thinking of Shatakopan or Nampillai. At the least, one is faced with the prospect of exploring further issues, such as what Shrivaishnavas mean by "freedom," how one can be like God, and so on.

In the short run at least, nothing much is at stake for the Shrivaishnavas, since they do not wait upon the research of Catholic intellectuals in order to understand their faith. What is at stake more immediately has to do with us—with the possibility of a (Catholic) faithful exploration of a non-Christian religious tradition, staying with the questions that arise and not merely discarding them. This is required of one who wishes to be a Catholic intellectual when thinking about religions other than our own. If we keep taking the specifics seriously, particularly in their intellectual dimensions, and without ignoring or reducing context to something less than what we expect in the Catholic tradition, then questions will remain real, and we will need to keep asking them. A process of understanding, openly and sympathetically, is not easily brought to a halt. But this will often leave us in an ambiguous situation, where we see both the openness and limits of our Catholic tradition, and the attractive and unattractive features of the other traditions we are considering.

The idea of engaging in this patient, exploratory process may seem difficult to most readers of this essay. I myself have been to the temple at Tirupati, and I have studied its traditions a bit, but I still do not call myself an expert regarding the traditions which surround it, nor can I say that I have mastered all the Christian theological resources which need to be brought to bear on the issue of this particular religious reality which stands outside the Christian tradition. To engage in this kind of intellectual project is a very large task; since most will not undertake it, they must continue to distinguish between faith positions and intellectual claims, adhering to the former and refraining from the latter.

A Willingness to Make Timely Judgments

Insisting on the value of specific information, sensitivity to theological developments, and patience with ongoing questioning is not to postpone indefinitely the possibility of a judgment about what is true, but rather simply to point out that in the formation of a Catholic intellectual judgment, something like this extended process must be undertaken. If Catholicism makes universal claims, there must be Catholic intellectuals who can make the claims credible and work out their positions in a way that is intellectually accessible, even if not acceptable, to intellectuals who happen not to be Catholic. Postponement for the sake of more knowledge is not in itself a value.

A fourth and final virtue must also be defended, since intellectuals must eventually decide things, draw conclusions, finish researching, and finish writing (at least periodically, time and again): there must be a willingness to make timely judgments. To reflect theologically on some aspect of another tradition which is specific and theologically sophisticated is to engage in a larger intellectual task which both draws on the best of our own tradition and yet pushes us to explain anew what we believe without remythologizing the virtues of being Catholic by caricaturing other traditions' beliefs. One must remain a faithful Christian, of course, but now a clear, unencumbered sense of what another tradition is really about must infuse the context in which the affirmation of faith in Christ occurs. The challenge is to articulate a response to Tirupati which is both Catholic and also intellectual, i.e., put forward without ignoring the temple, its long-lived faith tradition, or the Hindu theology which has grown up around it.

Sometimes the judgment is a statement about who we think ourselves to be, and sometimes it occurs in response to a claim made upon us. Like visiting the temple itself, the song of

Shatakopan about it puts a challenge before listeners and readers, claiming much and asking much in return:

> All three perish, disease, birth and death,
> for those who place upon their lips and in their mind
> the fresh flowers, lovely lotus feet,
> the cowherd of holy Venkatam who destroyed disease,
>   birth and death.

> Before you weaken and your days grow short,
> before you reach the limits of the time set for you,
> go where he lies on his hooded-serpent bed,
>   to holy Venkatam
> which worships him with many flowers and ponds
>   and groves. (3.3.9-10)

No quick response, either accepting or dismissing the invitation made here, will do, if we honor the obligations imposed on us by faith and inquiry. Even if a Catholic really does not want to "go to holy Venkatam where he lies on his hooded-serpent bed," and even as she or he reaffirms commitment to Christ, he or she must remain able to be open, not contriving hasty or ill-informed judgments upon Tirupati as reasons for not going there. We must offer convincing reasons expressive of our faith, not excuses.

As a Catholic confessing the faith, one can reaffirm that Christ is the savior, the light shining on, in, and through Tirupati, and even that Vishnu, Lord of Tirupati, in some way reflects the light of Christ. One can maintain that the pilgrims who ascend to the temple of Lord Shrivenkateshvara will be better off, finding what they seek and more, if they find it in Christ. But the task is still more difficult for the Catholic who would be an intellectual, who would claim that his or her faith stance is reasonable, that in some way it can remain plausible even in the face of actual knowledge of Tirupati and its traditions. Judgments weighted with specific reference are required, in which the particular merits of Tirupati are shown to be relativized and outweighed by some incompleteness (expressible in words which are more than sheer faith claims), or vulnerable due to gaps, insufficiencies, and errors, presumably (at least partially) in reasoning—or conversely, in which one admits that there is no evidence for such gaps, and so on. There seems to be no good reason, given the Catholic tradition of thinking about these issues, for thinking that such judgments cannot be made. But at the same time, there is no reason to assert that such judgments have been made properly so far, since the expected gaps and so on in particular Hindu theological positions have not been shown. As long as this is the case, the Catholic who believes in the overshadowing of Tirupati by Christ has not yet articulated a Catholic intellectual account of what he or she believes and hopes to be the case.

For the time being, of course, this means that we cannot offer here an answer to the simple question, "What then is the Catholic intellectual to think about Tirupati?" but have only excluded a variety of premature and facile answers. A proper answer must follow and not pre-empt the process of a serious theological engagement, comparative and dialogical, with relevant contextual information, such as the theologies which Shrivaishnava theologians have written on the basis of their faith in the Lord of Tirupati. Once informed background is in place, a Christian theologian can then move forward with responsible Christian judgments about Tirupati, regarding whether God can be encountered there in a way that does not merely replicate encounters with God in holy places familiar to the Christian tradition, and whether calling God by a new name (e.g., "Shrivenkateshvara") can be an invocation which is positive and which does not merely echo properly biblical namings of God.[21]

Tirupati remains just one example, one instance standing for all the specific sacred places of this sort, the rituals, images, texts, saints, experiences which we might encounter when we notice other religious traditions in their particularity and start paying attention to them. It presents a serious possibility and challenge for the intellectual who belongs to this Catholic tradition which is both benevolently disposed to what is new, and yet inherently ambivalent about how such "religious others" are to mean anything for Catholics. If this task of balancing Catholic openness and Catholic limits, without reducing one to the other, seems to be a timid compromise, it is not. There may be no intellectually credible Catholic position other than to affirm this "both/and" stance, if neither "Catholic" nor "intellectual" is to be emptied of meaning; nor does there seem to be an easy way of reducing the whole to a simpler whole. For now, at least, the Catholic must approach other religions with openness constrained by faith, and faith unsettled by honest thinking, and in doing so, characterize what it means to be a "Catholic intellectual."

Notes

1. Since Tirupati is the popular modern name for the temple, I will henceforth refer to Tiruvenkatam as Tirupati.

2. *Tiruvaymoli* is an interconnected set of 100 songs composed in the Tamil tradition. The author, Shatakopan, is thought by Western scholars to have lived in the ninth century. Translations of the Tamil verses of *Tiruvaymoli* are my own.

3. I refer to this temple visit also in my essay "In Ten Thousand Places, In Every Blade of Grass: Uneventful but True Confessions about Finding God in India, and Here Too," *Studies in Jesuit Spirituality* 28, no. 3 (May 1996).

4. On the general issues related to the Catholic intellectual life, I have found helpful, and recommend as a background sketch, David O'Brien, *From the Heart of the American Church: Catholic Higher Education and American Culture* (Maryknoll: Orbis, 1995), particularly chapter 9, "Catholics As Intellectuals."

5. *Nostra Aetate*, nn. 6-7; as cited in *Interreligious Dialogue: The Official Teaching of the Catholic Church (1963-1995)*, ed. Francesco Gioia (Boston: Pauline Books and Media, 1997), 38.

6. "Address by Paul VI to the Fathers of the Vatican Council II," September 29, 1963; cited in *Interreligious Dialogue*, 117. Paul VI does not seem ever to have elaborated on what he had in mind in the reference to "perceives gaps, disparities and errors." His many later statements about religions and to religious leaders of other faiths seem to indicate he has in mind primarily "incompleteness"—the religions are by definition incomplete, because they lack explicit reference to Christ as the only Savior. "Disparities" is "defectus" in the Latin; the translation of Paul VI's text in John Paul II's *Redemptoris Missio*, given below, reads "insufficiencies," which seems closer to the original.

7. *Redemptoris Missio*, n. 55; as cited in *Interreligious Dialogue*, 102.

8. *Fides et Ratio*, n. 2, as cited in the version available on the Vatican website.

9. *Fides et Ratio*, n. 71

10. *Fides et Ratio*, n. 72.

11. *Fides et Ratio*, n. 104.

12. "Missionary" here signals also my focus on foreign missionaries in India; the thinking of native Indian Christian intellectuals is a very important but distinct topic for consideration.

13. On de Nobili's way of thinking, see for instance my "Roberto de Nobili's Dialogue on Eternal Life and An Early Jesuit Evaluation of Religion in South India," in *The Jesuits: Cultures, the Sciences, and the Arts 1540-1773*, ed. John W. O'Malley, and T. Frank Kennedy (Toronto: University of Toronto Press, 1998). See also *Preaching Wisdom to the Wise: Three Treatises by Roberto de Nobili, S.J.*, translated (from Latin and Tamil) and annotated by Anand Amaladass and Francis X. Clooney (St. Louis: Institute of Jesuit Sources, 2000).

14. Recently republished in two volumes, *To Christ through the Vedanta*, compiled by Theo de Greeff (Bangalore: Union Theological College, 1996).

15. The introduction to the series of articles begins this way:

> Every Catholic student of Vedanta philosophy is soon struck by the fact that there is no important philosophical doctrine of Saint Thomas, the standard philosopher of Catholicism, which is not found in one or another of the Vedanta systems. Does it follow that Catholic philosophy and Vedanta are the same? No. Vedanta possesses our philosophical materials, but it has not worked them into one system, one consistent whole . . . But in the Thomistic system we have an organic whole. It is one harmony in which the different Vedantic systems find their proper setting . . . If the Vedanta philosophers will only bring their several positive statements into harmony, if they will only adjust and thus partially limit their assertions, they will turn disconnected doctrines into a system, and that system will be Thomism, or something akin to Thomism." (*To Christ through the Vedanta*, vol. 1, p. 6.

16. Neither de Nobili nor Johanns seem to have had positive interest in temples. They worked on a scholarly level, and were interested in what they considered to be the best and most intellectual strands of Hindu thought. Temples probably did not measure up to this standard, and perhaps they were uncomfortable too with pagan holy places. The

particularity of temples escaped their intellectual gaze, and the Hindu theology which developed in temple-related traditions was, I suspect, too closely connected with idolatry for it to be something they could actually think about.

17. This is my translation of an excerpt of Nampillai's comment introducing *Tiruvaymoli* 6.10; I have made a few clarifications in the translation itself, to avoid elaborate notes.

18. As cited in John Carman, *The Theology of Ramanuja* (New Haven: Yale University Press, 1974), 77-78.

19. Serious attention to theological context also unsettles our roles as the controlling agents of interpretation. As we learn, the Hindu categories take on at least some intellectual credibility alongside Christian categories. Particular Hindu solutions to the tension between locality and universality, divine transcendence and divine immanence, human achievement and divine grace become at least intellectually cogent, operative even in a rethinking of Christian ways of thinking about Christian realities. Intellectuals, after all, always get more than they bargain for.

20. The Tamil word *camam* (Sanskrit, *samam*) can mean "like," "the same" or, adverbially, "in an equal fashion."

21. I have addressed the related conceptual problem of the limits of the canon of revelation in "Extending the Canon: Some Implications of a Hindu Argument about Scripture," *Harvard Theological Review* 85, no. 2 (1992): 197-215.

CHAPTER SEVEN

The Catholic Intellectual Tradition:
A Gloriously Rich but Difficult Inheritance

URSULA KING

The Catholic community worldwide possesses a tremendous history and tradition of intellectual life. It is an impressive heritage of which we can be truly proud. It is a tradition marked by a great richness of ideas, by an intellectual endeavor and audacity which have often moved people and history into new fields. The Catholic intellectual tradition is linked to a chain of great teachers, a fervent dedication to learning and the transmission of knowledge to others. Such a precious inheritance is a great responsibility, for it must be cherished and handed down to future generations. But such handing down does not consist of passing on something closed, complete, and static. On the contrary, the transmission of a living tradition is always a dynamic process in which we actively participate through further intellectual reflection and production.

The rich inheritance of the past provides many resources for being a Catholic intellectual today, but it is also an ambiguous and often difficult heritage which can only be passed on and appropriated with discernment. Intellectual life cannot flourish without literacy, learning, and higher education, once provided by monasteries and the Church, which laid the foundations for the early medieval European universities.[1] Slowly these were able to work out an increasing realm of intellectual independence and autonomy, leading after many centuries of growth to the modern secular universities we know today. Much of the Catholic intellectual tradition was originally created in the medieval universities which taught and developed theology, philosophy, rhetoric, medicine, and law.

But this great intellectual world was clearly a world without women, a Christian clerical culture that laid the foundations for the quasi-monastic and patriarchal framework that characterized the rise of Western science in the modern era.[2] Women of the late twentieth century have, therefore, considerable difficulty in identifying with many aspects of the intellectual life as previously conceived. Until very recently, Catholic intellectual life, and especially theology, have been understood in an entirely androcentric way because most of this life, throughout most of the history of the Church, has been deeply embedded in a rigidly patriarchal framework.

When I consulted out of curiosity an old, but classic work on *The Intellectual Life* written many years ago by Père Sertillanges, the shocking tone of a one-sided, exclusive gender perspective was only too clear.[3] The intellectual, as defined by Sertillanges, was

> a man of wide and varied knowledge complementary to a special study thoroughly pursued; he loves the arts and natural beauty; his mind shows itself to be one in everyday occupations and in meditation: he is the same man in the presence of God, of his fellows, and of his maid, carrying within him a world of ideas and feelings that are not only written down in books and in discourses, but flow into his conversation with his friends, and guide his life.
>
> At bottom, everything is connected and everything is the same thing. Intellectuality admits of no compartments. All the objects of our thought are so many doors into the "secret garden," the "wine cellar" which is the goal of ardent research. Thoughts and activities, realities and their reflections, all have one and the same Father. Philosophy, art, travel, domestic cares, finance, poetry, and tennis can be allied with one another, and conflict only through lack of harmony.[4]

Women are certainly not included in this vision of the intellectual life. Contemporary men and women may still share the same goal as the writer of this passage in seeking the harmony and balance of intellectual life with life as a whole, but we today can no longer speak the same language and remain credible. We have to use different images and words to describe the practice of intellectual life, and this is particularly true for women.

Sharing My Personal Story

As a Catholic woman academic, who probably missed getting two university posts because of being a Catholic, I can now only approach the Catholic intellectual tradition, initially such a strong component in the making of my personal identity, with a thoroughly questioning attitude, but also an attitude tinged with humility and still filled with love. After great intimacy and familiarity with this tradition, it is rather like the experience with one's own parents when one wants to affirm the close, loving bonds but is all too aware of the gaps, the shortcomings, the narrowness of vision and limitations of achievement of another generation. How then was I led to the intellectual life, and what stages marked my journey?

In reflecting here on my intellectual growth, I must make clear that I am writing as a West European, white woman who has been studying, teaching, researching, and writing in the fields of theology and religious studies for forty years now, but originally did not come from an intellectual family at all. I cannot think of a single person in my extended family who was a teacher or pursued any other intellectual occupation. Everyone was either a small businessman, a farmer, a skilled worker, or a tradesman. Note that the occupations listed here are only those of men, for the women in our family were all housewives, and there was no tradition of learning or higher education for either women or men.

I was brought up in a traditionally Catholic rural area of Germany near to where my parents had originally come from. They had settled in the city of Cologne, with a great Catholic tradition, but during the Second World War, we were evacuated to a village, where I spent most of my childhood. I went to the local village school, and then from the age of nine to fifteen, I received my secondary education in a Catholic girls' school run by women religious. This small provincial school laid the foundations for my attraction to the intellectual life. It gave me everything not experienced at home. Suddenly windows to a wider world were opened, and I discovered a larger horizon—a world of ideas; of history and politics; of current affairs in postwar Europe with its deep scars and deprivations, and its search for a new identity; classic and modern literature, languages, the sciences, mathematics and music; and the beliefs and practices of the Catholic Church. All of it stirred in me a deep intellectual hunger, a desire to seek and find knowledge, a determination to pursue higher education. Furthermore, some of the women religious and laywomen who taught us provided me with strong female models, personalities in whom learning and intellectual independence were blended with empathy, wisdom, and compassion. This very positive experience of a world I deeply loved gave me a very strong foundation for all subsequent learning in my life. I ascribe much of its strength to the strong Catholic faith which impregnated the entire milieu of the school.

Yet today I can also see that I grew up in quite a narrow Catholic milieu, almost a kind of *Kulturkatholizismus*, where Catholicism was simply a way of life in the region where we lived. Like millions of others in the world, I was brought up in the Catholic faith whose teachings I simply took for granted at that time, especially as I knew no other. Today I am a very different person and see many things very differently, but I am still a member of the Catholic Church—a church I still love, although this love now deeply hurts and even feels absurd at times. Yet I still feel part of the worldwide web of Catholics, and I admire the rich intellectual and historical traditions of this Church. As a child, I simply took its beliefs on trust, without doubt or questioning. This came much later when, through studying and travelling, I realized how different the Catholic Church is in each European country, and how much its community life differs in the different countries and cultures of the world, and how its theologies are deeply embedded in very different socio-economic and historical contexts.

As a young woman, I experienced a genuine vocation, a deep desire and attraction to study theology, an attraction first conveyed to me by some Dominican fathers who taught me in my last years in a school in Cologne. Together with a dear philosophy teacher, they inspired a restless sense of philosophical and theological enquiry, and first led me to read St. Thomas of Aquinas. I then became determined to study theology at university, against all odds and opposition, for I was drawn by an intellectual vision and calling which proved stronger than all personal and financial obstacles. It really was a struggle, in more senses than one, but I had the freedom and luck to study theology in Germany and France, where I was taught by some outstanding theology professors of international renown—all men—and over the years, I became a trained theologian. I followed what was then the traditional theological and philosophical curriculum, which included courses from biblical languages to scriptural exegesis and hermeneutics, the history of doctrine and the church, systematic and practical theology as well as some philosophy of religion, comparative study of religions, and phenomenology. A strong tradition of dogmatic theology and many details of early, medieval, and Reformation church history were transmitted to us, but I also had the good fortune of experiencing more rarely taught courses, such as the history of Christian liturgy and art, of Christian spirituality, including Orthodox spirituality, and most unusual of all for 1962, at the Institut Catholique in Paris where I was studying then, a course of lectures on Pierre Teilhard de Chardin which sparked an intellectual fire that was to have much influence on my future research activities. But I was not to know that then.

Another determining aspect of my experience, an essential one as I see it now, was the fact that as a woman I was forever in a minority, often a minority of one, among an exclusive majority of men. Thus I learned early what it means to live at the margin, first socially and geographically in the village, then intellectually in the university where I studied something very different from what other women were studying, and where I was the permanent outsider among a large group of men studying theology and preparing for the priesthood. I simply lived in this milieu and absorbed as much as I could, and progressed with my studies successfully, and sometimes with acclaim. My critical faculties were not yet sufficiently developed to articulate in any explicit way the aim of becoming a Catholic woman intellectual or to see how this might be practically possible. Nor was I critical enough to discern the oppressive structures of the educational system or question the male exclusiveness of the Catholic Church and its teaching authority. Yet I clearly remember the exhilarating sense of liberation when I experienced at a *Semaine des Intellectuels Catholiques* in Paris the authoritative lecture of a well-known woman professor of sociology. Suddenly I realized that women could be intellectuals too, that they could speak out in public, were listened to and taken seriously. It was an important psychological experience for me, for after years of listening to male professors, I suddenly saw a woman with whom I could identify, who unknowingly affirmed me in my own powers and determination to be a female teacher passionately concerned with intellectual issues. It was like tearing down an invisible wall of silence, piercing through an incapacitating mutenes, and calling me into speech with words only found years later.

In the meantime, there were many instances of non-recognition, refusal, and exclusion on the way. How well do I remember in my early student years being refused admission to join the courses on Thomas Aquinas in a German college of Dominicans, only because I was a woman. How disappointing was the answer of an eminent British Jesuit whom I consulted about job and research opportunities when I first arrived as a young theology graduate in London; he simply said to me "I am afraid there is no place for you in England." A remark never forgotten, and a prediction proved entirely wrong when I later chaired a department of theology and religious studies for many years.

Women and the Catholic Intellectual Tradition

Yet my personal experience is less important than the scale of refusal and exclusion experienced by all women in the Catholic Church today, every day. Will Catholic women ever be fully recognized? Will they be encouraged to make their full contribution to the intellectual life of the Church or, more important still, will women become real co-equals and co-partners in shaping the Catholic intellectual tradition? Will they make any difference in the way the institutional and structural levels of the Church will be organized in the future? Will women theologians and philosophers acquire the same reputation and influence as only men held in the past? That is what will count in the end.

Yet at present we women still suffer deep pain when we experience again and again the narrowness with which Christian beliefs and practices are applied to women. How often are women treated as second-class citizens by the Church? Now that an increasing number of women are taking up theology professionally and studying up to the highest levels of academic qualification, women have acquired the necessary theological tools to engage critically and constructively with the tradition. Increasingly more and more Catholic women experience not only personal doubt about practicing their faith in a feminist and postmodern world, but they also doubt collectively and call into question many aspects of the Church's practices and teachings when examined from a critical gender perspective. From such an angle, many traditions of the Catholic Church, hitherto unquestioningly taken for granted, can be seen to possess a profoundly ambiguous nature so that serious shortcomings in the acclaimed universality of the tradition are coming to light. Women question the way in which the institutional Church developed and was shaped by alien philosophical, political, and legal ideas, incorporating teachings which considered women as less than human, as never able to speak for themselves and take on the same responsibilities as men. Women now challenge the way power has been exercised and abused in the history of the Church, power over women and children, the poor, the conquered, and the colonized, who have been exploited and abused rather than been enabled to grow and develop.

We women doubt the justice of the exclusive maleness of the institutional Church and challenge the hierarchy of its offices and functions which has enabled men to exercise their lordship over others rather than practice the ministry of service of which the Gospel speaks. We women also doubt the traditional image of God, or rather the ambiguous and one-sided way in which it has been preached and transmitted so that it has often performed an oppressive rather than a liberating function in the growth of human beings. Most of all, we doubt whether Christian beliefs and the Church, as so often presented today, can remain credible in the light of contemporary experience, especially when one becomes aware of the frequently oppressive, exploitative, or paternalistic treatment of women.

Given the pervasive "hermeneutics of suspicion" with which educated Catholic women steeped in a feminist consciousness now approach the Catholic tradition, all aspects of it are open to re-examination. It is overwhelmingly evident that in the past we women did have little part in shaping the Catholic intellectual tradition. We, therefore, now become painfully aware of the narrowness of this tradition, punctuated by women's silences and symbolic absences. And today we consider this situation as profoundly inhuman and unjust. But I do not wish to say this with reference to the Catholic tradition alone. The powers of patriarchy have been almost universally dominant and so pervasive in human societies, history, and culture that no religion is exempt from them. And no religion has explicitly promoted the literacy, learning, and higher education of women. These cultural activities, so closely connected with the areas of mind and spirit, have remained the prerogative of men everywhere until modern times. Apart from a few exceptions, women did not have access to education and higher learning, including the study of theology, until the mid-nineteenth century. The general education of women and the possibility of their access to the intellectual life is a *novum* in human history, a true change in human consciousness whose full effect we are only beginning to experience now.

Having been excluded for so long from intellectual activities does not mean that we women cannot find vital resources in the Catholic tradition to nourish. In fact, a multitude of resources exist in the tradition, which include above all the countercultural traditions provided by women themselves—by women writers, saints, and mystics in the Church. Moreover, we can also foster the intellectual strength of women today and promote their full participation in the future shaping of the Catholic intellectual tradition. There is no reason why women cannot take up and reinterpret traditional works and teachings, feel inspired by them, and adapt them to their own needs and ways of seeing the world. To return to Sertillanges quoted earlier, one can also extract nuggets of wisdom from his book and thereby feed a life utterly different in practice from the one envisaged in his work, as when he writes:

> Responsiveness of the soul to the ineffable spring, its filial and loving dispositions, lay it open to receive light after light, and ever-increasing fervor and rectitude. Truth, when loved and realized as a life, shows itself to be a first principle; one's vision is according to what one is; one participates in truth by participating in the Spirit through whom it exists . . .
>
> There is no question now of proving one's skill, of showing off the brilliance of one's power, as of a jewel; one desires to get into communion with the radiant center of light and life; one approaches this center in its unity, as it is; one adores it, and renounces what is opposed to it in order to be flooded with its glory. Is not all that something like the meaning of the famous words: "Great thoughts come from the heart"?[5]

It is this "communion with the radiant center of light and life," the participation in the Spirit and its glory which women seek as much as men. Just as some women are re-visioning the Christian spiritual tradition to provide resources for the development of Christian women's spirituality today,[6] we also need people to undertake a re-visioning of the Catholic intellectual tradition in order to provide more adequate resources for women's full intellectual development. If asked whether this is being done, I cannot think of a concerted effort anywhere in the Church to address this need in a larger, institutional setting. Of course there is much research and writing being undertaken by Christian women—there is feminist, womanist, contextual, and liberation theology; there are women philosophers and feminist philosophies of religion; there are women active in interfaith dialogue, but there is no institutional setting or initiative as such to develop Catholic women intellectuals, besides perhaps in traditional religious congregations and orders. But by and large, it has been my experience that Church personnel, whether male or female, are very little conscientized as regards the feminist turn of contemporary thought and language. The Church still preaches much too much a rather traditional image and role of women without encouraging women to be intellectuals in their own right, as is now possible in the secular sphere.

Today women are gaining a new self-understanding of their own strengths and possibilities. They are claiming a new, equal place in society and Church as full members in their own right with the opportunity to develop their full potential in every sphere of human life, and this includes the celebration of the powers of the intellect. For this, women need encouragement, but also concrete resources—time, space, money, access to education and training, job opportunities. To develop to the full also includes their potential as Christians and a clear recognition of the contribution Christian women can make to today's Church and society. To assist and promote women's stronger self-definition, I suggest we need a full acceptance in terms of equal value and treatment of all girls from childhood and school years onwards, an encouragement of the independence and self-reliance of young women, and the development of a strongly self-reflective Christian commitment. We also need to recognize the existence of a great diversity of roles for women today in order to get away from the traditional, exclusive social roles of wife and mother which the Church seems to advocate more than any others.

From the perspective of my own professional discipline—that of the study of theology and religions which is closely connected for me with the ministry of teaching, with enlarging and inspiring the critical minds of the young, and in particular with drawing out the strength of women—I also advocate strongly that equal opportunities are needed for women not only to study theology, but also to teach it at all levels. Here great inequality reigns, and in a few cases institutional violence is exercised toward women, at least in Europe, by keeping them explicitly out of university positions. This is a very unjust, and also very unhelpful, situation if one wants to encourage the self-definition of women and their full participation in intellectual life.

A Modern Catholic Intellectual

Ours is not an intellectual age in the traditional sense, but one dominated by popular culture where the role of the intellectual is often one of isolation and alienation. The figure of the intellectual is often cast as someone living in almost inner emigration or, at best, performing the function of a countercultural critic. Looking at the past, one realizes that it too possessed many social and intellectual limitations, and that the place of the intellectual was not always an unambiguous or easy one. The past is marked by oppressive patriarchal structures, frequently linked to an intellectual elitism based on social class.

If one acknowledges the ambiguity of all intellectual traditions and recognizes their power both to lead, inspire, and transform as well as to dominate and destroy, it follows that it is far from unproblematic to speak of a Catholic intellectual or give the Catholic intellectual tradition unreserved praise. The celebration of its rich inheritance notwithstanding, a discerning mind is forced to admit that the treasures of the Catholic intellectual tradition require close scrutiny and evaluation, and some of that can prove rather difficult. When I was studying at university, we were always told in our modern church history courses that Catholics in Germany had not been culturally and intellectually as productive and influential as German Protestants. It was especially the families of Protestant pastors who nurtured many of the German philosophers and writers, at least in the eighteenth and nineteenth centuries, and a similar cultural fecundity is evident in many Anglican clergy families in England. Given the celibate nature of the Catholic priesthood, the situation among Catholics is quite different, and the Catholic intellectual influence has been largely exercised through education in schools and colleges.

If one asks who is an intellectual today, it is no longer the monk or theologian of medieval times, but with the onset of modernity and now even more so with the exponential diversity of postmodernity, we can think of a variety of figures. The intellectual may be a scientist, a novelist or poet, an academic or journalist, a philosopher, psychologist, political scientist, or economist—there are so many possibilities and different professional locations. The twentieth century knows of a number of outstanding Catholic intellectuals, some of them highly regarded in the wider world while more critically assessed within the Catholic Church itself. The person who comes most to my mind here, mainly because I know his work best, is the French Jesuit and palaeontologist, Pierre Teilhard de Chardin (1881-1955). He was an outstanding intellectual and scientist, a person of deep faith with a dynamic mystical spirituality. I cannot think of anyone better suited to the words of Sertillanges that "Study is itself a divine office, an indirect divine office; it seeks out and honors the traces of the Creator, or His images, according as it investigates nature or humanity."[7]

For Teilhard, all his research was ultimately linked to worship, to the adoration of the living presence of God and of the vivifying power of the Spirit. In fact, the very last paper he wrote before his death is a short essay entitled "Research, Work and Worship."[8] It is concerned with the relationship between science and religion, the training of "scientist-priests" and "worker-priests," and the awareness that the notion of Christian life and holiness has to be revised: "We need a new theology . . . and a new approach to perfection, which must gradually be worked out in our houses of study and retreat houses, in order to meet the new needs and aspirations of the 'workers' we live among."[9] I think these "workers" are in many ways the new intellectuals who drive the world forward, but Teilhard, the priest, could still only envisage them in an ascetic and all male mode. Yet his own daring vision of the evolutionary development of what he described as the "noosphere," the living layer of knowledge, insight, wisdom, and active love, redefines the unity of body, mind and spirit, of science and religion, of the masculine and feminine modes of being in the world.

Teilhard was a great intellectual, for he had faith in the fire of the spirit, faith in the transformative power of consciousness and its effect on the world. He was deeply convinced that the human desire for knowledge was a sacred quest, given to us by God. Ultimately, the quest for knowledge, embodied in the development of science and culture, converges with the quest for the Divine, for love and union with God. Teilhard's work brings together religion, science, and mysticism, and in his person we find the integration of faith with a lifestyle of intellectual enquiry and research which I understand as truly catholic in an inclusive, universal sense. Teilhard's world-affirming and world-transforming attitude is grounded in a powerful spiritual vision which has its life-giving roots in the deepest sources of the Catholic faith, in a profoundly incarnational and sacramental understanding of the world and of all of life. But his intellectual catholicity went far beyond the narrow orthodoxies of both traditional believers and traditional scientists. That is why he caused so much controversy, but also why his ideas influenced so many people, in many parts of the Catholic Church around the world, as well as many people who are neither Christians nor believers. It is the extraordinary breadth and depth of his intellectual synthesis, its complexity and audacity, its concern for renewal and transformation here and now, its ethical insistence on our responsibility for the planet, for life on earth and its future directions, that makes Teilhard's vision so attractive to so many.

The catholicity of Teilhard's synthesis is deeply rooted in some of the best heritage of the intellectual traditions of the Catholic Church, especially of the Jesuit order. Here we have an example of Catholic education, religious formation, and cultural creativity at its best and most fertile. His intellectual *oeuvre* consists of a large corpus of scientific, religious, and spiritual writings permeated by ideas steeped in Catholic imagination, culture, worldview, and lived practice.[10] Yet Teilhard, the global traveller and citizen, forever engaged in scientific research and philosophical debate, meeting individuals from many different lands and cultures, and making friends with people from many faiths and none, developed an amazing openness and catholicity which made him far transcend the narrow frontiers of his family and cultural background.[11]

But is such catholicity not welcomed in the Catholic Church? Why was Teilhard so maligned by the Church during his lifetime, and so little recognized after his death? Why does the Church not hold him up as an example of the strength and power of the Catholic faith in the modern world? Many have retold the trials and vicissitudes of his life, but the lack of recognition among

Catholics is poignantly summed up by a little anecdote told in Julian Huxley's autobiography.[12] As a great twentieth-century scientific thinker, Huxley was himself an intellectual giant who exercised an immense influence on his contemporaries. When he was director of UNESCO in Paris, he met Teilhard on several occasions and was much taken by him. He admired him greatly and felt they both were "in almost general agreement over the essential facts of cultural and organic evolution," although Huxley did not share Teilhard's religious beliefs and acknowledged their "ineradicable divergence of approach." After Teilhard's death, Huxley agreed to write the well-known preface to the English edition of *The Phenomenon of Man,* but was bitterly attacked by some of his rationalist friends "for supporting a religious (and not fully scientific) work!"[13] Huxley tells us that in 1955, shortly after Teilhard's death, the French Catholic University in Montreal, Canada, organized a public event, chaired by the vice-chancellor and announced as an "unbiased enquiry" into the theological and scientific aspects of Teilhard's work. Huxley and his wife were among the packed audience in the Magna Aula of the university and Huxley's *Memories* include the following description of what happened:

> The rostrum was occupied by a long table at which were sitting five lay professors and several clerical theologians, including a grim and majestic Dominican Abbé in beautiful white robes . . .
>
> One by one, the theologians and the professors got up and said their piece. Was Père Teilhard a good scientist? No, he was not. Was he a competent philosopher? No, he was not. Was he a sound methodologist? No, he was not. People call him a geologist, but he was only an amateur. People call him a theologian—but was he? Finally, the Dominican rose to sum up. He spoke in beautiful French and went through all the arguments. The audience sat spellbound. The Abbé in his sculptural white robes studied all the faces turned towards him, awaiting his verdict. He raised his hand from the ample folds of his cassock: Père Teilhard, he said, was a poet. "Ses paroles somptueuses sont un

piège. Prenez garde de ne pas y tomber." He sat down in profound silence. Teilhard and all his works had been condemned.[14]

This is an extraordinary testimony to the fact that in spite of almost all his religious works still being unpublished in 1955, Teilhard's name and ideas were sufficiently well-known among a French-speaking public to attract wide public attention, but also cause fear and a defensive attitude among traditional Roman Catholics. It is interesting to note how Huxley reacted to this experience, especially when the vice-chancellor invited him to speak as someone who had known Teilhard personally. Huxley's account continues:

> I accepted, and walked up to the rostrum. Turning to face the audience, I explained that, from my personal knowledge, Père Teilhard was a completely sincere man, an excellent palaeontologist, and that although I did not agree with him on all points, I considered that his reconciliation of scientific fact and religious belief along evolutionary lines was enlightened and helpful. There was a burst of spontaneous applause from the audience, as of great tension released. The clapping continued for several minutes, while the panel of assessors looked glum. As I went out of the hall, happy to have done something to vindicate my old friend, I was besieged by eager young questioners.[15]

Is this account of an occurrence in the mid-1950s perhaps indicative of the fact that Teilhard may be better understood and more acknowledged by non-believers than Christians, especially Roman Catholics? More generally speaking, are Catholics perhaps so wedded to a traditional understanding of their heritage that it is impossible for a truly modern intellectual to be accepted in their own midst? Much of the Catholic intellectual tradition in the narrow sense of the word is perhaps still too overshadowed by a strong ascetic, androcentric, and elitist legacy of the past. Yet at the same time, many fresh beginnings and creative transformations in the wider understanding of catholicity can be noted around the world. There is a genuine openness, an honest search for life-enhancing and holistic possibilities, a sincerity of critical self-questioning and a healthy experimentation with new ways of being catholic and ecumenical, a less certain but more humble way of living one's faith in a more personal, individual way, but also in search of living in a community that accepts genuine differences. And this includes very diverse approaches to the ideals of intellectuality which in turn call for a re-visioning of the Catholic intellectual tradition as hitherto understood.

Re-visioning the Catholic Intellectual Tradition

The millennium is a time for renewal and reawakening, a time for rejoicing, for celebrating our heritage, but also for its critical resifting for future generations. The intellectual world—the world of knowledge and ideas—has grown immensely, and consequently no faith tradition can any longer fully embrace it or hold a monopoly over it. To remain true to its own catholicity, its inclusive universality, the Catholic intellectual tradition must now be much more open, more in dialogue with others and with secular culture. It must become more pluralistic and abandon some of the monolithic, eurocentric features of its own self-understanding. I learnt this first not from Teilhard de Chardin, but from living in India for five years, where I was challenged to the core by the existence of other faiths and cultures which had created different intellectual and spiritual traditions of equal greatness and splendour to that of Catholicism.

Renewal is linked to *metanoia*. It is ultimately a spiritual event—and Teilhard de Chardin articulated more clearly than most that our epic journey of hominization must be one of growing spiritualization—but such change in consciousness is not only marked by a change of soul; it is embedded in a process of dynamic transformation, of a conscientisation which I see closely dependent on the multi-layered, creative use of and access to education at all levels, for all people. A postmodern secular society needs more and more intellectuals, and so does the Church, but such intellectuals are not born, they are produced by society. It is therefore essential that we create the necessary conditions which make it possible to nurture responsible intellectuals with an independence of mind as well as an integrity of soul, and a moral consciousness that is accountable to their sisters and brothers around the world.

I want to argue that the affirmation and renewal of the Catholic intellectual tradition is dependent on meeting three challenges: (1) the global challenge; (2) the gender challenge; (3) the spiritual challenge.

The Global Challenge

The *global challenge* relates to a variety of issues. It includes our consciousness of the world and the destiny of its peoples as one; our global interdependence in material and spiritual matters; the sense of the planetary, and the need for a planetary or world theology (in a pluralistic, not monolithic sense, for in reality there can only be theologies in the plural as theological truth is always mediated through different experiences, discourses, and world-views); the acknowledgement of the decisive contributions of the peoples of Asia, Africa, Latin America, and other parts of the non-Western world to the common heritage of humanity and to the shaping of our human future; the sense of the cosmic arising from the new story of the universe in which we are all immersed; a sense of reverence, wonder, and awe toward the great abundance of life, and the global responsibility we share for the ecological balance and harmony of our world. For the Catholic Church, the global challenge is closely bound up with the challenge of both Christian and global ecumenism, linked to the encounter and dialogue between different world faiths.

At a practical level, the Church is already deeply involved with issues of justice, peace, and development around the globe, helping to promote social, educational, and at times also political, transformations in different countries of the world. Also important in this context is the encouragement of interfaith dialogue, and the collaboration of members of different faiths to abolish poverty and violence, and work for ecological balance and sustainability. Besides much practical work at the grassroots level, there are also many Catholic intellectuals, women as well as men, who are deeply committed to these issues and are reformulating theological thinking on these matters.[16] Ever since the Declaration of the 1993 Parliament of the World's Religions on "A Global Ethic," there exist challenging programs in quite a few places to develop, according to the four directives of this Declaration: a global culture of "non-violence and respect for life," "solidarity and a just economic order," "tolerance and a life of truthfulness," "equal rights and partnership between men and women."[17] Here the gender challenge comes up, but little has been done so far by the religions to pursue that. More efforts are going into formulations of an "earth charter" from the perspective of different faiths, and efforts to work for peace in the world. But good will alone is not enough here. Much practical and intellectual work is needed to develop the Church's resources for peace-making—and that includes a reconsideration of the theological thinking on the just war theory, as well as deep repentance for past injustices and acts of inhumanity.

The Gender Challenge

The *gender challenge* is about the realization of the full humanity of women and men, with all the equality and justice this implies. It is about the deconstruction of traditional, fixed gender roles and the harm they have done to both women and men, but especially to women. The current understanding of human sexual differentiation, the Christian teaching about all humans being created equal and in the image of God, the validation, affirmation, and empowerment of women, and the potential for gender balance and reconciliation beyond gender differences open up exciting new theological perspectives and promise possibilities for new creative turns in the Catholic intellectual tradition. It is regrettable that the Catholic Church did not take part in the World Council of Churches "Decade of the Churches in Solidarity with Women" (1988-98). This program produced much good work among Christian women around the world in terms of practical workshops, conferences, and publications which helped to shape a new consciousness and solidarity among Christian women. Quite a few Catholic women took part in these activities, but the Church did not officially participate in raising Christian awareness about gender issues and their challenging implications. There exists a great deal of ignorance about these matters in high church circles, and many pronouncements from the Vatican cannot be understood as anything other than a reaction based on fear. If only the Church would make an effort to enter into genuine dialogue with Catholic women rather than go on making ill-informed pronouncements about women in general. Such dialogue is especially urgently needed with women intellectuals at the cutting edge of contemporary theological thinking but, as far as I can see, the position of a Catholic intellectual in the Catholic Church officially still belongs firmly to the male of the human species. In view of this, it is rather surprising, if not provocative, that so many internationally well-known feminist theologians come from a Roman Catholic background.

I am firmly convinced that Catholic women around the world must strongly aspire to leading intellectual roles in all areas of human inquiry, and must be encouraged in achieving this role in every possible way. Education to the highest possible level in every field is an indispensable condition for this, and it would be a valuable piece of research to find out how many practicing women Roman Catholics are in higher education today. It is important to document women's achievements, in the past as well as in the present, and to provide young women with strong role models and examples to emulate. In the USA, there exists in Washington the National Museum of Women in the Arts, the only one in the world, and in England, it has just been announced that a National Library of Women will be built in London, another unique phenomenon.[18] As this announcement was made while I was writing this essay, it inspired me to dream what a wonderful achievement it would be if somewhere in the world there could be a place to create a library of the works of Catholic women writers and intellectuals through the ages. This could provide such a strong focus of empowerment for Catholic women today, and it could in turn become a contributory factor in the creative and transformative re-visioning of the Catholic intellectual tradition.

The Spiritual Challenge

The *spiritual challenge* is the greatest of all and embraces the other two, for a balanced approach to global and gender questions can only grow out of a spiritually sound human life. The spiritual challenge is also the most urgent, for our culture is in a profound spiritual crisis, and the Catholic Church is by no means exempt from this. Much of the spiritual search today is evident from the growth in retreats, prayer, and meditation meetings. It is also visible in the tremendous growth of publications on spirituality, for example the texts published in the series *The Classics of Western Spirituality*, or the series on *World Spirituality*. Catholic intellectuals have made an essential contribution to the production of each of these series, now so widely used. Also important is the fact that many universities in the U.S. and elsewhere now offer courses on spirituality, and that there exists a "Society for the Study of Christian Spirituality" which is ecumenical, but has many Roman Catholic professors as members. Among women, and especially women with a feminist consciousness, there exists a large interest in spirituality of a holistic and integral kind which can bring about personal and social wholeness. The great tradition of Christian saints and mystics includes an extraordinarily large number of "women of spirit" who can provide an empowering paradigm for Christian living and are of considerable importance in the contemporary women's movement.[19] Some of these women have also made an important contribution to the Catholic intellectual tradition, if one does not dualistically separate mystical theology from other, more abstract forms of theology. I am thinking here of Hildegard of Bingen, for example, or Teresa of Avila and Catherine of Siena who, as declared "Doctors of the Church," truly belong to the rich Catholic intellectual tradition, although they represent much else besides.

The great contemporary interest in different forms of mysticism, whether in Christianity or other religions, reflects the hunger and thirst for spirituality, for direction, meaning and purpose. This deep longing, expressed in many different forms far beyond the traditional boundaries of faith communities, is also a cry addressed to the Catholic intellectual tradition. As articulated through its theological formulations, this tradition has become increasingly conceptual, abstract, and rationalistic, so much so that some feminist theologians speak of "the violence of abstraction" found in Christian theology. It is a tradition often alienated from the body, from the earth, from life, and from a God who is truly alive as the all-encompassing, all-sustaining, all-inspiring fire of divine love.

An intellectual tradition that fully embodies the incarnational heritage of Catholicism cannot be true to itself if it is falsely intellectualist and rationalistic. On the contrary, it must give full embodiment and articulate a critically reflexive evaluation for the entire range of human experiences. Only then can it be truly catholic in the wider sense. And only then can it be spiritually nourishing and help people find their own center and thereby discover their connection with the greater center that is God.

The task of an intellectual always involves taking up a critical position, to sift and question data, to interrogate and reflect thoughtfully, imaginatively, and critically on ideas, problems, and situations. Such a critical position also encompasses an ethical stance, for the intellectual has responsibilities to the wider society, and in our case this includes a responsibility toward the Church as the community of the people of God. At the present threshold of time, moving from one millennium to another, it is important to critically reflect on the Catholic intellectual tradition, take stock of its opportunities and challenges, realize its incompleteness and shortcomings, ask how it is being challenged, and suggest in what way it might be renewed.

Challenges are always needed, for they produce new growth. If the Catholic intellectual tradition can meet the challenges I have signalled here, and others too, there will be further strength and growth. We possess a gloriously rich intellectual inheritance in Catholicism, but Catholics will have to wrestle with decisive new challenges during the next millennium—the tradition cannot remain intact without some profound changes. Yet it has the resources to respond to the new circumstances and contexts of a new era. Let us hope that the Catholic intellectual tradition will remain a truly living inheritance that continues to thrive, and to inspire women and men to work together in solidarity and community for a great human task and noble intellectual vocation. Only then will the Catholic tradition shine like a bright light in a new season.

Notes

1. I have discussed the importance of education for women within the context of different religious traditions in my article "Education and Literacy" in Serinity Young, ed., *Encyclopedia of Women and World Religion* (New York: Macmillan Reference, 1998), 291-94.

2. See the fascinating study by David F. Noble, *A World Without Women: The Christian Clerical Culture of Western Science* (New York: Oxford University Press, 1992). The author convincingly demonstrates how the experimental practices of modern science are marked by a quasi-monastic asceticism, and points out how the ascetic, anti-woman attitudes of Christian monasticism have also helped to shape the process of militarization. It is a very thought-provoking book which raises many questions about the inherently ambivalent nature of many traditional Christian intellectual activities.

3. A.D. Sertillanges, *The Intellectual Life: Its Spirit, Conditions, Methods* (1920; rpt. Cork: Mercier Press, 1962).

4. Sertillanges, *The Intellectual Life*, 241f.

5. Sertillanges, *The Intellectual Life*, 24. The quotation is from Pascal's *Pensées*.

6. See Joann Wolski Conn, ed., *Women's Spirituality. Resources for Christian Development*, 2nd ed. (New York: Paulist Press, 1996).

7. Sertillanges, *The Intellectual Life*, 28-29.

8. In Pierre Teilhard de Chardin, *Science and Christ* (New York: Harper and Row, 1968), 214-20. The original title in French is "Recherche, Travail et Adoration."

9. Teilhard de Chardin, *Science and Christ*, 220.

10. This is especially true of his intimate and great love of the living Christ, and his lifelong devotion to the Sacred Heart, which took on a new, cosmic meaning in his works, which has so far been little studied, not even by Jesuits who write at length about the devotion to the Sacred Heart.

11. I cannot discuss his seminal ideas or the inspiring example of his spirituality here. For more information, see my Bampton Lectures, *Christ in All Things: Exploring Spirituality with Teilhard de Chardin* (Maryknoll, NY: Orbis Books, 1997) or the illustrated, introductory biography, *Spirit*

of Fire: The Life and Vision of Teilhard de Chardin (Maryknoll, NY: Orbis Books, 1996).

12. See especially the detailed account given by one of Teilhard's Jesuit superiors, René d'Ouince, *Un prophète en procès,* particularly vol. I, *Teilhard de Chardin dans l'Église de son temps* (Paris: Aubier, 1970).

13. Julian Huxley, *Memories II* (London: George Allen and Unwin, 1973), 29, 28.

14. Huxley, *Memories II,* 29.

15. Huxley, *Memories II,* 30.

16. The bibliographical references are large and consists mostly of Christian ecumenical sources. To quote just two examples: see the contributions in David G. Hallman, ed., *Ecotheology: Voices from South and North* (Maryknoll, NY: Orbis Books, 1994), and the study by Paul F. Knitter, *One Earth, Many Religions: Multifaith Dialogue and Global Responsibility* (Maryknoll, NY: Orbis Books, 1995).

17. See Hans Küng and Karl-Josef Kuschel, ed., *A Global Ethic: The Declaration of the Parliament of the World's Religions* (London: SCM Press, 1993).

18. The National Museum of Women in the Arts in Washington only covers the period since the Renaissance and therefore it unfortunately does not include the rich artistic heritage of medieval women who all belong to the Catholic tradition. Nor does it include any artistic achievements from women of non-Western cultures.

19. See my illustrated book on *Christian Mystics: The Spiritual Heart of the Christian Tradition* (New York: Simon and Schuster, 1998), where I have given special attention to some of these women.

CHAPTER EIGHT

"The Open-Ended Mystery of Matter": Readings of the Catholic Imagination

JOHN B. BRESLIN

Back in the mid-1980s, I was asked by a religion editor at a large New York publisher to put together a collection of short fiction by contemporary Catholic writers to replace one edited in the 1940s. The task turned out to be good fun, tracking down literary magazines, checking out annual collections of "best stories," calling up authors to talk about their stories and get permissions at fees that wouldn't bankrupt my meager fund.

But the challenging part was deciding what makes a story "Catholic": author's religious profession? narrative content? use of symbols? theological slant? Usually it turned out to be a combination of these, with a bias toward stories that dealt explicitly with Catholic experience.

Since then I have been teaching courses and giving occasional lectures at my own university and elsewhere on "Catholic fiction," expanding the range beyond the short-story anthology itself. What has emerged as an organizing principle is a series of interrelated theological themes that echo across several decades of writing as well as across several continents. What makes the stories and novels fascinating, of course, is the way each author orchestrates the themes and variations.

First of all, however, a double caveat. I do not believe that fiction—or art of any sort, for that matter—will serve as a substitute for authentic religious experience. The Romantic belief in salvation through art has long since proved bankrupt, inflating the aesthetic currency beyond our means. The burden of having to reinvent Sacred Writ in each generation has done artists no favor; it has only created a proliferating tribe of ever more ingenious scribes to interpret, or deconstruct, their texts. But a literal-minded Christian attitude that denies any connection between literature and the Bible, between metaphor and revelation, has been no more helpful. It distorts the very message it claims to serve by severing the divine and the human, pretending that God's Word could come to us in any way other than through human words.

Of all the Christian traditions, Catholicism has most consistently maintained and celebrated word and image as vehicles of divine revelation, often in the face of powerful opposition. One thinks of the myriad icons destroyed during the iconoclastic excesses of the Byzantine Church and the sad remnants of religious sculpture that still decorate English cathedrals once purged by Cromwell and his followers, all in the service of the invisible Godhead. Against this purifying drive, Catholicism has trumpeted all the implications of incarnation. For if God chose to take on our humanity, not as a garment or a disguise, but as integral to the personhood of the Second Member of the Trinity, then all Christians should be able to claim for themselves, in its deepest sense, the humanistic sentiment of the pagan playwright Terence: *Homo sum et humani nil a me alienum puto.*

What then are some of the characteristics of the Catholic imagination that inform its art, and more specifically, its literary art? How might contemporary Catholic writers reveal their conscious awareness of the divine stamp implicit in human creation and re-creation? Is there a peculiar tone, perspective, habit of thought that subtly reveals a Catholic sensibility? I would answer "yes" to all of these questions, though a particular writer may be more or less self-conscious about it, and some authors may possess it without being "dues-paying" Catholics. Let me name three such characteristics of the Catholic imagination as I shall examine it in this essay: 1) It takes the Incarnation as a starting point; 2) fosters a consequent awareness of paradox and irony as constituent of our existence as ensouled bodies or incarnate spirits;

and 3) dramatically presents the continuing struggle between grace and sin for our ultimate allegiance.

I

The first and most general theme that runs through Catholic fiction is, not surprisingly, its incarnational bias: that the physical and the spiritual are inextricably bound up with one another, that our composite nature is the truest thing about us, and that all attempts to deny the body its intrinsic place in the human scheme run the risk of Gnosticism. Put most broadly, this incarnational strain prejudices Catholic writers in favor of inclusivity over exclusivity, of the "both/and" option over the Protestant "either/or," most famously expressed in modern times by Kierkegaard. To which one can oppose James Joyce's reputed description of Catholicism: "Here comes everybody!"

Catholicism is a highly sensate religion, even more so perhaps in its pre-Vatican II liturgy, where the smell of incense and the sound of Gregorian chant were a regular feature of every high mass, whether funereal or festal. Ritual has always been important because of a fundamental fascination with the senses as instruments of evangelization. *Dinglichkeit*, as the German has it, permeates the Catholic imagination. Put into a formula, this fascination might read as follows: the physical world in all its beauty *and* imperfection transformed by ritual into prayer, that is to say, sacrament. A contemporary writer, André Dubus, exemplifies this process most persuasively in what is perhaps his best known short work, "A Father's Story."

The narrator and central character, Luke Ripley, a not particularly pious individual in the popular sense, is describing one of his own daily rituals, attendance at an early morning mass, celebrated by Father Paul, who is also his closest friend:

> Do not think of me as a spiritual man whose every thought during those twenty-five minutes is at one with the words of the Mass. Each morning I try, each morning I fail, and know that always I will be a creature who, looking at Father Paul and the altar, and uttering prayers, will be distracted by scrambled eggs, horses, the weather, and memories and

daydreams that have nothing to do with the sacrament I am about to receive. I can receive, though: the Eucharist, and also, at Mass and at other times, moments and even minutes of contemplation. But I cannot achieve contemplation, as some can; and so, having to face and forgive my own failures, I have learned from them both the necessity and wonder of ritual. For ritual allows those who cannot will themselves out of the secular to perform the spiritual, as dancing allows the tongue-tied man a ceremony of love.[1]

For Luke, the prime analogate for religious experience is sacramental. It is the moment of communion, the receiving and placing of the host on his tongue, that concentrates his mind and his senses on God:

There is . . . a feeling I am thankful I have not lost in the forty-eight years since my first Communion. At its center is excitement; spreading out from it is the peace of certainty. Or the certainty of peace. One night Father Paul and I talked about faith. It was long ago, and all I remember is him saying: Belief is believing in God; faith is believing that God believes in you. That is the excitement, and the peace; then the Mass is over, and I go into the sacristy and we have a cigarette and chat, the mystery ends, we are two men talking like any two men on a morning in America, about baseball, plane crashes, presidents, governors, murders, the sun, the clouds. Then I go to the horse and ride back to the life people see, the one in which I move and talk, and most days I enjoy it.[2]

Religious experience is extraordinary but grows out of the ordinary and depends on the ordinary things of life (the taste of a bread wafer) for its transforming experiences. In Luke's case, the experience is specifically sacramental and circumscribed by ritual; once the Mass ends, he and Father Paul happily return to the ordinary: the news of the day and the ride back to his stables. But the ritual is repeatable, and so the sacramental transformation (not elimination) of experience remains regularly available, even at the end of this father's tale of covering up an accident and sinning against others to preserve his daughter's safety. The ending also elicits from Dubus a remarkable passage of dialogue with God in which Luke attempts to justify what he has done by carrying the "scandal of the particular," which is at the heart of Catholic sacramentalism, to its outermost boundaries:

> I do not feel the peace I once did, not with God, nor the earth, or anyone on it. . . . Now in the mornings . . . I say to Him: I would do it again. For when she knocked on my door, then called me, she woke what had flowed dormant in my blood since her birth so that what rose from the bed was not a stable owner, or a Catholic or any other Luke Ripley I had lived with for a long time, but the father of a girl.
> And He says: I am a Father too.
> Yes, I say, as You are a Son Whom this morning I will receive; unless You kill me on the way to church, then I trust You will receive me. And as a Son You made your plea.
> Yes, He says, but I would not lift the cup.
> True, and I don't want you to lift it from me either. And if one of my sons had come to me that night, I would have phoned the police and told them to meet us with an ambulance at the top of the hill.
> Why? Do you love them less?
> I tell him No, it is not that I love them less, but that I could bear the pain of watching and knowing my sons' pain, could bear it with pride as they took the whip and nails. But You never had a daughter and, if You had, You could not have borne her passion.
> So, He says, you love her more than you love Me.
> I love her more than I love truth.
> Then you love in weakness, He says.
> As You love me, I say, and I go with an apple or carrot out to the barn.[3]

At one level, of course, this is not very precise theology, but as an empathetic argument it strikes home, at least with a number of Catholic fathers and daughters (and some mothers and sons) I have surveyed. It is also a remarkably daring way to end a short story, risking a mix of the banal and the sublime. Why do I think it works? Because the rest of the story prepares us for such a dialogue by locating it within an understanding of Luke Ripley that encompasses all those characterizations of himself that did *not* rise from bed on that fateful night as well as the one that did.

In other words, Dubus has so intertwined the strands of Luke's character, including his faith, that these final sentences seem to come naturally from his mouth and, even more remarkably, from God's as well. And so this story represents for me a triumphant example of the Catholic imagination at work, stretching toward the sacred while never loosening its tether to the human.

II

A certain fascination with "Dinglichkeit," the sheer stuff of the world—for example, in Ignatius Loyola's "application of the senses" to gospel narratives—elucidates one aspect of the incarnational principle. The ritual impulse serves to order that fascination and give it a social dimension by turning things into signs without evacuating their physicality. But there is another side to incarnation as well, the strain put on the human reason to conceive a union of the divine and human so complete that the one person Jesus Christ can be acknowledged as fully human and fully divine without confusion or contradiction of either identity. The early Christological debates, with their careful Greek distinctions, "solved" the problem in one sense but left the mystery untouched and therefore endlessly available for artists and writers to explore within the conceptual framework erected by the Church.

Out of this imaginative tension arise a fondness for paradox and an attention to irony which are hardly unique to writers within the Christian tradition (witness Socrates and Sophocles, not to mention the masters of Zen), but which acquire a certain urgency and achieve a definite prominence in their writing. That the infinite might choose to become finite, the creator a creature, is a theme sounded as early as St. Paul's letters, especially in the even more ancient paschal hymn he quotes in Philippians 2:5-11, where the emphasis is on the emptying out (*kenosis*) of God in Christ, followed by glorification. With the inclusion of the nativity accounts in the gospel narrative, the way was opened for a more tender play of paradox on infinity in bonds, as well as a set of reflections on the "scandal of the particular."

Both of these "spinoffs" of incarnation are important, for they reflect two rather different effects of this doctrine: first, an often sentimental embrace of the infant Jesus as the image of a God who cancels out human suffering in the interests of universal good feeling; and conversely, Christ's appearance among us seen as an arbitrary intervention of God into human experience that upsets all our categories and challenges with his suffering and death our secular certainties about progress and the good life.

Flannery O'Connor is an American twentieth-century writer who has wrestled with this incarnational dilemma and opted for a non-sentimental Christian vision in her fiction. What distinguishes O'Connor is that she reflected at some length on her writing in essays and letters, not so much interpreting her fictions as giving them a broader philosophical and theological context. Thus she offers us a way of approaching not only her own work but that of many other authors whose Catholic instincts have shaped their attempts to diagnose the ills of the age. What tools are available to the writer of fiction for this task of discernment? Faced with a complacent Christendom (of whatever stripe) and a revived paganism, O'Connor's fellow Southern Catholic novelist, Walker Percy, recommends that the writer must be

> as cunning and devious as Joyce advised—more cunning even than Joyce, for he is working with a prostituted vocabulary which must be either discarded or somehow miraculously rejuvenated. The stance which comes most naturally to him is not that of edification but rather that of challenge, offense, shock, attack, subversion. With the best of intentions, he subverts both the Christendom and the paganism of his culture and he does so cheerfully and in good heart, because as a creature of the culture he is subverting himself, first, last, and always.[4]

Irony and paradox thus become basic tools of the demolition process, much as they often are in the parables of Jesus, for in both cases the storyteller is confronting a complacent audience, secure in its prejudices, which seem the only defense against a hostile world and a meddlesome divinity. But there is a deeper theological reason for their importance, as suggested above: they take a divine stamp from the central Christian mysteries of Incarnation and Redemption. They assert, respectively, that the Creator has become a part of creation so that the Almighty can be found in a human infant, the weakest of creatures; and that the absoluteness of death is only overcome by entering into it in its most brutal form.

The misunderstandings of the title story of her first collection, "A Good Man is Hard to Find," based on its brutality, particularly vexed Flannery O'Connor because they revealed a failure to see that the violence of the ending was neither the point of the story nor merely gratuitous. For all the self-deceit and banality that the grandmother reveals in the first half of the story as she ungraciously sets off with her family on their trek to Florida, she reacts as most of us would in the face of catastrophe and terror. When their car overturns in an accident for which she is largely responsible, and they are suddenly confronted by the escaped convicts led by the Misfit, she tries to placate him by offering unfelt sympathy and understanding: " 'I just know you're a good man,' she said desperately. 'You're not a bit common.' "[5] But the Misfit knows better; his problem cuts deeper than the social niceties. For him the only issue is whether Jesus raised the dead; believe that and you have no choice but to "throw away everything and follow Him, and if He didn't, then it's nothing for you to do but enjoy the few minutes you got left the best way you can—by killing somebody or burning down his house or doing some other meanness to him. No pleasure but meanness" (*CW*, 152).

One could hardly put the alternatives of belief more starkly; both secular humanism and conventional church-going piety are simply burned away in the heat of the Misfit's passion. And what happens next only heightens the paradox, for in a moment of recognition that both redeems and kills her, the grandmother reaches out to the Misfit in his anguish at not knowing Jesus' power over death: "Why, you're one of my babies. You're one of my own children!" That moment of grace is balanced by the Misfit's benediction over her dead body: "she would of been a good woman if it had been somebody there to shoot her every minute of her life" (*CW*, 153).

Speaking at Georgetown University in 1963, O'Connor complained, "the reader wants his grace warm and binding, not dark and disruptive." She clearly chose the latter pair in response to a superficial and skeptical society that could not appreciate goodness because it refused to acknowledge evil. "Instead of reflecting a balance from the world around him, the novelist now has to *achieve* one by being a counterweight to the prevailing heresy" (*CW*, 862). And that heresy for O'Connor is precisely what the Misfit points to, forgetting what Dietrich Bonhoeffer defined out of his own extremity as "the cost of discipleship," or in O'Connor's words, "the *price* of restoration . . . the cost of truth, even in fiction" (*CW*, 863).

How high does that "cost," that "price" come? In O'Connor's fictional world, it often requires losing life in order to save it. The grandmother and her family are only the first of a series of corpses that punctuate the ends of her stories. In one of her last, "The Lame Shall Enter First," the victim is a young child named Norton, who takes religious metaphors quite literally in a world where they have been drained of any meaning whatsoever. Norton's widowed father, Sheppard, is hell-bent on doing good in the best social activist fashion: counseling at a reformatory, coaching Little League, attending city council meetings.

Rather than grieve his wife's loss and console his son, he has focused his energies on Rufus, a satanically clever delinquent who scorns his reforming efforts and discovers a willing disciple for his literalist doctrines of heaven and hell in the vulnerable Norton. Sheppard buys the boys—really Rufus—a telescope to instruct them in the promises of science and space exploration, but Rufus uses it to convince Norton that his mother is in the heavens "but you got to be dead to get there. You can't go in no space ship" (*CW*, 612). Only at the end of the story, when he finally realizes how Rufus has consistently played him for a chump, does Sheppard begin to understand the enormity of his crime against Norton: "He had stuffed his own emptiness with good works like a glutton. He had ignored his own child to feed his vision of himself. He saw the clear-eyed Devil, the sounder of hearts, leering at him from the eyes of [Rufus] Johnson" (*CW*, 632). But the revelation comes too late to save Norton, who has taken Rufus' directions quite literally and, with the aid of a rope, has "launched his flight into space" from the attic beam in a desperate attempt to reach his mother.

O'Connor expressed reservations about the story because she felt little sympathy with Sheppard, and there is perhaps a whiff of caricature about him. But the clear link between Sheppard's blind sentimentality about Rufus and his willful cruelty toward Norton reminds us of Percy's remark that these fatal twins have presided over the worst evils of our century, from world wars to genocide. And for his part, Rufus knows enough to reject Sheppard's messianic pretensions ("that big tin Jesus"); Rufus may be going to hell, but it won't be for any sin of idolatry ("When I get ready to be saved, Jesus'll save me, not that lying stinking atheist . . .") As in "A Good Man," O'Connor insists on the reality of evil and the dangers of denying its existence; in her view, Rufus and the Misfit are closer to the Kingdom of God than Sheppard, though at the end his posture of despair, like the grandmother's maternal gesture, may signal a possible redemption: "His image of himself shriveled until everything was black before him. He sat there paralyzed, aghast" (*CW*, 630-32). For O'Connor this is where Sheppard—and the reader—touches on the true "horror" of the story; the image of Norton hanging in the attic is shocking but anticlimactic.

In another story from her final collection, O'Connor took a more "comic" but no less astringent viewpoint on the blindness of the age. Ruby Turpin, the "heroine" of "Revelation," has no doubts about the existence of God and few about her own place in the divine scheme of things; she sees herself and her husband Claud securely situated in a social hierarchy that runs from "no account niggers" at the bottom to rich white folks with lots of land and money at the top. But when she tries to align this socioeconomic scale with a moral one ("common" rich folks), she finds "all of the classes . . . moiling and rolling around in her head, and she would dream they were all crammed in together in a box car, being ridden off to be put in a gas oven" (*CW*, 636). An unsettling image, to say the least, but one Ruby can live with. What finally unsettles her is a direct attack from a plain looking young college student named Mary Grace, who gets so infuriated with Ruby's garrulous self-satisfaction that in a fit of apoplexy she hurls a textbook (titled *Human Development*) at her head. But more searing than the injury is Mary Grace's "message" for Ruby: "Go back to hell where you came from, you old wart hog" (*CW*, 646). It is a message Ruby cannot ignore, for it bears all the marks of direct prophecy. Indeed, the rest of the story is Ruby's attempt to square her own sense of being "saved" with this divine admonition; and in true Old Testament fashion, she presents her complaint to God in no uncertain terms: "How am I a hog and me both? How am I saved and from hell too?" And in a final paroxysm of anger, like an unquiet Job, she roars out the ultimate challenge, "Who do you think you are?" (*CW*, 652-53).

The words trigger a vision in the twilight sky, and caught up in an ecstasy, Ruby beholds the company of the saved marching into Jerusalem led by

> whole companies of white-trash, clean for the first time in their lives, and bands of black niggers in white robes, and battalions of freaks and lunatics shouting and clapping and leaping like frogs. And bringing up the end of the procession was a tribe of people whom she recognized at once as those who, like herself and Claud, had always had a little of everything and the God-given wit to use it right. She leaned forward to observe them closer. They were marching behind the others with great dignity, accountable as they had always been for good order and common sense and respectable behavior. They alone were on key. Yet she could see by their shocked and altered faces that even their virtues were being burned away. (*CW*, 654)

What will come of this "revelation"? All we're told is that, when it ends, Ruby's "eyes [are] small but fixed unblinkingly on what lay ahead." The process of burning away her virtues has already begun, and with them her blindness. Like Asbury Fox with his vision of the Holy Ghost descending upon him in ice at the end of another "comic" story, "The Enduring Chill," the price they both must pay for vision is the stripping away of all self-delusion, that is, a radical honesty which translates into humility, what Jesus called allowing the seed to fall into the ground, pruning the vine—to produce a richer harvest. Another kind of death.

III

As Flannery O'Connor's hard-edged prose makes clear, no aspect of the human condition reveals human cussedness and resistance to grace more dramatically than the reality of sin. By declaring as a matter of faith that the Virgin Mary was the only human conceived without original sin, the Catholic Church has both affirmed the universal reality of sin and insisted at the same time that the human and the sinful are not, in principle, coterminous. One can be human and sinless, as Jesus was, of course, in an altogether unique way; but Mary's sinlessness is exceptional in the literal sense—the only human case. For the rest of us, however, sin colors the atmosphere in which we live and infects our innermost life as well. Catholic authors have in general not shied away from depicting sin in action; indeed a writer like Graham Greene has sometimes been accused of reveling in it. And nowhere does sin show itself more human and more various than in his masterwork, *The Power and the Glory*. Over the past ten years, I have taught this novel at least a dozen times and am always (happily) surprised at how readily college students take to it, even past its fiftieth anniversary. Much of the background is ancient history now, though the peasant rising that continues in Chiapas reveals how little things have changed politically and economically in that area. The central character, the otherwise nameless Whisky Priest, hangs on as the last active priest in his province, constantly in danger of betrayal and arrest. His nemesis, the equally nameless Lieutenant, is determined to stamp out all vestiges of the oppressive Catholicism of his childhood to free his people for a more prosperous atheism. They are well matched in their passions, and when they finally meet face to face near the end of the novel, it becomes clear that they are opponents who should be brothers.

The priest has broken all of his vows, fathered a child he desperately loves, and become an alcoholic. And yet he keeps traveling from village to village offering what sacramental consolation he can, even as the net gets tighter. Arrested at one point for possessing whisky (also banned by the puritanical state), he spends a night in a crowded, stinking prison cell, expecting at any moment to be turned in by his fellows for the substantial reward. The narrator comments: "This place was very like the world: overcrowded with lust and crime and unhappy love, it stank to heaven; but he realized that after all it was possible to find peace there, when you knew for certain that the time was short."[6] In fact, the only prisoner unsympathetic to him is a pious woman in whom he sees mirrored his own past when he was an ambitious village pastor whose gloved hands were regularly kissed by just such as her. When he is finally released, he sees on the jail wall his "Wanted" picture from that past and realizes how his venial sins then ("impatience . . . pride, a neglected opportunity") cut him off "from grace more completely than the worst sins of all."

It is a "mystery" to him, since it seems to violate all the principles of moral theology, but he has tested it on his pulses and knows it to be true. Such an insight also calls up similar moments of revelation in Catholic fiction, like the dramatic scene between the curé (also unnamed) and the comtesse in Georges Bernanos' *Diary of a Country Priest*. The bumbling young priest gathers up all his courage to confront the formidable mistress of the local chateau about her daughter's deeply troubled state. To his initial horror, he discovers himself way over his head in the middle of a sordid domestic scene where the comtesse rightly considers herself the wronged party. But for all her outward piety and valid grounds for complaint, it slowly becomes clear to the priest that it is *her* soul that is in most danger. Relying on an intuition and a strength of character that at first shocks and then astounds her—and himself—the curé strips away layer after layer of self-righteousness from the poor woman until she finally admits that she has hated God every day of her life since her infant son died.

To his insistence that she resign herself to God, open her heart to Him, she flings back:

> "Well then—what? I go to mass. I make my Easter. I might have given up going to church altogether—I did think of it at one time. But I considered that sort of thing beneath me."
>
> "Madame, no blasphemy you could utter would be as bad as what you've just said! Your words have all the callousness of hell in them." She stared at the wall and did not answer. "How dare you treat God in such a way. You close your heart against Him and you—"
>
> "At least I've lived in peace—and I might have died in it—"
>
> "That's no longer possible."
>
> She reared like a viper: "I've ceased to bother about God. When you've forced me to admit that I hate Him, will you be any better off, you idiot?"
>
> "You no longer hate Him. Hate is indifference and contempt. Now at least you're face to face with Him."[7]

Beneath the outward piety and appearance of calm control, a glacier had been building for years, powerful enough to sweep all before it, and surely this insignificant curé. But it is precisely his lack of stature, his bumbling manner, that makes him the one person God can use to touch her heart, offer her conversion:

> "All right then: Thy kingdom come." She looked up at me and I met her eyes. So we remained for a few seconds, and then she said: "It's to you I surrender."
>
> "To me!"
>
> "Yes, to you. I've sinned against God. I must have hated Him. Yes, I know now that I should have died with this hate still in my heart, but I won't surrender—except to you."
>
> "I'm too stupid and insignificant. It's as though you were to put a gold coin in a pierced hand."
>
> "An hour ago my life seemed so perfectly arranged,

everything in its proper place. And you've left nothing
standing, nothing at all."

"Give it to God, just as it is!"

"I'll either give Him all or nothing. My people are
made that way."

"Give everything."

"Oh, you don't understand! You think you've managed
to make me docile. The dregs of my pride would still be
enough to send you to hell."

"Give your pride with all the rest! Give everything!"[8]

After a final dramatic gesture by the comtesse, the priest blesses
her and leaves. The following night she dies in her sleep, leaving
the curé to deal in vowed silence with the rumors that swirl
around their encounter, fueled by the distorted story the daughter
reports from her eavesdropping.

Bernanos' comprehension of the subtleties of sin and grace is
even finer than Greene's, but they both share an awareness of the
tortuous ways of the human heart and its skill at deception. Like
the pious woman the whisky priest encounters in the jail, the
comtesse is in far greater danger than she can imagine, and for
precisely the same reason the priest was before he became a drunken
outcast: their pride is monumental and only bolstered by their
outwardly blameless lives. It is in this sense that (apparently) venial
sins—and even (apparent) acts of virtue—can put our souls in more
danger than do our spectacular failings which can't be ignored.

A wonderful image for this paradox comes from another
European Catholic, the German novelist Heinrich Böll, in a short
story entitled "Candles for the Madonna." Through no obvious
fault of his own, the (once again) nameless hero has proved a
failure in his business dealings as a maker and seller of candles in
postwar Germany. Discouraged after one last futile effort to
unload them, he stays overnight in a *pensione* where he encounters
a young, apparently unmarried couple embarrassedly seeking a
night's lodging. The next morning he comes upon them again in
a nearby church, waiting to go to confession. He is inspired to
confess himself but is distressed to discover he can't recall any sin
worth confessing, even after seven years:

I felt unclean, full of things that needed to be washed away, but nowhere was there actually anything that in coarse, rough, sharp, clear terms could have been called sin . . .

I was like a pail of water that has remained exposed to the air for a long time. It looks clean, a casual glance reveals nothing in it: nobody has thrown stones, dirt, or garbage into it; it has been standing in the hallway or basement of a well-kept, respectable house; the bottom appears to be immaculate; all is clear and still, yet, when you dip your hand into the water, there runs through your fingers an intangible repulsive fine dirt that seems to be without shape, without form, almost without dimension. You just know it is there. And on reaching deeper into this immaculate pail, you find at the bottom a thick indisputable layer of this fine disgusting formless muck to which you cannot put a name; a dense, leaden sediment made up from those infinitesimal particles of dirt abstracted from the air of respectability.[9]

After the young man follows the girl into the box to make his confession, our hero does the same, but to no effect. By the time he emerges, the young couple has left and he is again alone in the old and shabby church. He approaches "an old stone Madonna standing on a bare, disused altar" before which the girl had said her penance:

The Virgin's face was coarse-featured but smiling, a piece of her nose was missing, the blue paint of her robe had flaked off, and the gold stars on it were no more than lighter spots; her scepter was broken, and of the Child in her arms only the back of the head and part of the feet were still visible. The center part, the torso, had fallen out, and she was smilingly holding this fragment in her arms. A poor monastic order, evidently, that owned this church.[10]

Before this unpromising image, he unloads all of his remaining sample candles and begins to light them one by one and affix them in their own wax to the cold plinth until it is "covered with restless flickering lights and my suitcase was empty":

I left it where it was, seized my hat, genuflected once more, and left: it was as if I were running away.

And now at last, as I walked slowly to the station, I recalled all my sins and my heart was lighter than it had been for a long time . . .[11]

Compare this to the final words of the note the comtesse sends to the curé, thanking him for restoring hope to her heart:

"This hope is the flesh of my flesh. I can't express it. I should have to speak as a little child.

I wanted you to know all this tonight. I had to tell you. And don't let's mention it ever again. Never again! How peaceful that sounds! Never. I'm saying it under my breath as I write—and it seems to express miraculously, ineffably, the peace you've given me."[12]

A final example, this time from Asia, makes even greater use of another half-destroyed image of the Virgin to convey a bass note of sorrow that flows into a similar peace. Shusaku Endo, who died in 1996, was one of Japan's most respected and popular novelists; he was also a Catholic who could never completely reconcile his Christian faith and his Japanese identity. Baptized at his mother's urging when he was eleven, Endo spent the rest of his life struggling with what he described as a "ready-made suit" or "arranged marriage" he could neither adjust to comfortably nor entirely throw off. Out of that struggle he fashioned fictions that ranged back and forth between the early seventeenth-century persecutions and contemporary Japan, always probing the viability of the Gospel in a Japanese culture he often referred to as a "mud swamp."

In "Mothers," one of his longest and most powerful short stories, he takes up again that central question. The unnamed narrator is, not surprisingly, a Japanese Catholic novelist who has written about the early days of Christian persecution and developed a fascination with the *kakure* Japanese converts who apostatized under torture but secretly continued to maintain Christian rituals and passed them along to succeeding generations, even down to the present. Priestless, they elected leaders who baptized children and carried on prayer rituals and instruction. Even when Japan reopened to the West a century ago and missionaries returned, many of the *kakure* refused to recognize them, contending that they alone had maintained the true faith.

The story opens with the writer arriving on a small off-shore island in order to meet with a group of *kakure* who remain isolated in the mountains. He is welcomed by the local Catholic priest, who reveres him as a Catholic intellectual but cannot fathom why he would want to meet with these backward folk who are a source of some embarrassment to contemporary Japanese Catholics. But apart from his stated historical interests, the narrator also has his own personal reasons which only emerge in the course of the story.

The story itself falls neatly into a series of doublets, one part of which takes place on the island while the other takes the author back into his past, more specifically, to his troubled relationship with his mother, whom he constantly disappointed as an adolescent. His memories and haunting dreams of her coalesce around a battered statue she prized of the Mother of Sorrows; indeed the two faces have become one in his dreams:

> . . . a figure of my mother with her hands joined in front of her, watching me from behind with a look of gentle sorrow in her eyes.
>
> I must have built up that image of my mother within myself, the way a translucent pearl is gradually formed inside an oyster shell. For I have no concrete memory of ever seeing my mother look at me with that weary, plaintive expression.
>
> I now know how that image came to be formed. I superimposed on her face that of a statue of "Mater Dolorosa," the holy ˙Mother of Sorrows, which my mother used to own.[13]

After his mother's death, the narrator kept the statue, moving it from place to place, and recovering it after it had been severely burned in an air-raid in 1945. When facing major surgery, he took the statue with him to the hospital:

At night beneath the dim lights, I would often stare from my bed at the face of the Holy Mother. For some reason her face seemed sad, and she appeared to be returning my gaze. It was unlike any Western sculpture of the Mother of God I had ever seen . . . where the face had once been, only sorrow remained.

At some point I must have blended together the look on my mother's face and the expression on that statue. At times the face of the Holy Mother of Sorrows seemed to resemble my mother's face when she died. I still remember clearly how she looked laid out on top of her quilt, with that shadow of pain etched into her brow.[14]

The narrator, then a teenager, had missed her death, hanging out with a school friend who specialized in pornographic cards and movies.

This personal revelation occurs just before the writer is taken to meet the leader of the *kakure*, who is polite but initially suspicious of this outsider whose Catholic guides make little effort to hide their contempt for these yokels. They sing some of their melodies, all addressed to the merciful Mother: "Turn eyes filled with mercy upon us."

But the narrator wants to see their "altar icons," a Buddhist phrase used as code for Christian images. Reluctantly, the leader agrees, taking the group into an inner room and drawing the curtain and revealing:

A drawing of the Holy Mother cradling the Christ child—no, it was a picture of a farm woman holding a nursing baby. . . . The farm woman's kimono was open, exposing her breast. Her obi was knotted at the front, adding to the impression that she was dressed in the rustic apparel of a worker in the fields. The face was like that of every woman on the island.[15]

For all its crudeness, the narrator cannot tear his eyes away from that face. He feels all the generations of *kakure* prayers offered up before such an image, pleading, always, for mercy:

Many long years ago, missionaries had crossed the seas to bring the teachings of God the Father to this land. But when the missionaries had been expelled and the churches demolished, the Japanese *kakure*, over the space of many years, stripped away all those parts of the religion that they could not embrace, and the teachings of God the Father were gradually replaced by a yearning after a Mother—a yearning which lies at the very heart of Japanese religion. I thought of my own mother. She stood again at my side [as she had done in his island dreams], an ashen-coloured shadow. . . . Her hands were joined in front of her, and she stood gazing at me with a touch of sorrow in her eyes.[16]

As he leaves with his guides—and to their consternation—the writer, the sophisticated intellectual from Tokyo, begins to hum the melody of the *kakure* prayer he had just heard and "muttered the supplication that the *kakure* continually intoned: 'In this vale of tears, intercede for us; and turn eyes filled with mercy upon us.' " Battered statue, primitive drawing, sorrowing mother, and Mother of Sorrows all coalesce in the author's prayerful communion with the despised *kakure*, whom he resembles in their need for forgiveness and in their isolation from conventional Japanese Catholics.

"The Still, Sad Music of Humanity"

I have tried in this essay to limn the contours of the Catholic imagination as it reveals itself in selected examples of twentieth-century fiction. At its heart lies a deep commitment to the human in all its dimensions as the privileged locus for God's active presence in our world (*verbum caro factum est*). But that Incarnate God also suffered and died, and so the dark side of our condition demands the writer's attention. A sinless literature, as John Henry Newman famously commented, would thus be a contradiction in terms. The same could be said for a literature without irony or paradox, and that is certainly a charge no one could lay against Graham Greene, Flannery O'Connor, or any of the other authors discussed here. The whole human experience, graced and sinful, forms the ture arena of Catholic literature.

For all the intensity of religious experience in Luke Ripley's sacramental life, the rest of it mirrors the confusion and uncertainty of the modern age inhabited by our international cast of troubled characters. In his final effort to preserve intact a primordial innocence already lost, Luke Ripley testifies to the brokenness of the human condition while trusting boldly in a redemption wrought only through weakness—"As You love me," he says to God and ends the story's concluding dialogue. In this we find the aesthetic link that joins sacrament, paradox, and sin, as in the tuneless hymn of the *kakure* that strangely consoles Endo's narrator. These epiphanies are no less charged with divine revelation and human meaning for being chastening rather than ecstatic. Like the mystery of incarnation they echo, these contemporary Catholic authors sound the depths of human experience and find as much to mourn as to celebrate, but they leave us finally hopeful because they believe with Hopkins that "the Holy Ghost over the bent / World broods with warm breast and with ah! bright wings."[17]

Notes

1. André Dubus, "A Father's Story,," in *The Substance of Things Hoped For*, ed. John B. Breslin (New York: Doubleday, 1987), 152.

2. Dubus, 152-53.

3. Dubus, 166-67.

4. Walker Percy, *Signposts in a Strange Land*, ed. Patrick Samway (New York: Farrar Strauss, 1991), 181.

5. Flannery O'Connor, "A Good Man is Hard to Find," in *Collected Works of Flannery O'Connor* (New York: Library of America, 1988), 148. Hereafter cited internally as *CW*, followed by page numbers.

6. Graham Greene, *The Power and the Glory* (New York: Penguin, 1977), 125.

7. Georges Bernanos, *The Diary of a Country Priest* (New York: Doubleday Image), 130.

8. Bernanos, 134.

9. Heinrich Böll, "Candles for the Madonna" in *The Substance of Things*, 205-06.

10. Böll, 206.

11. Böll, 208.

12. Bernanos, 136.

13. Shusaku Endo, "Mothers," in *The Substance of Things*, 190-91.

14. Endo, 191-92.

15. Endo, 195.

16. Endo, 196.

17. Gerard Manley Hopkins, *Poems*, ed. W.H. Gardner and N.H. MacKenzie, 4th ed. (Oxford: Oxford University Press, 1970), 66.

CHAPTER NINE

The Catholic "Intellectual": An Empirical Investigation

ANDREW M. GREELEY

What is a Catholic intellectual? The perennial debate about that question has always provided great cocktail and dinner party conversation for Catholics who are either intellectuals or would like to think they are. The beauty of discussions on the subject is that they can go on forever, since they are thinly disguised arguments about either first principles or definitions. You derive your definition of the Catholic intellectual from your basic assumptions and then dispute the basic assumptions of others. Inevitably such exchanges will lead only to repeated statements of the primary assumptions, which in their very nature are not subject to reexamination. It is the nature of the argument about Catholic intellectualism that no one can possibly change her mind about the subject. The argument never advances and never ends. But, if you're an intellectual, banging your head against a brick wall of this sort provides a decent and inexpensive evening's entertainment. Moreover, you can return home confident that you have won the argument, even though the others present are not perceptive enough to realize it or honest enough to admit it.

The same argument can be repeated at the next dinner party on the related subject of what is a Catholic university.

Thus one hears it said, with the same *ex cathedra* confidence of a papal statement, that Catholic intellectuals are no different from any other intellectuals, that it is the function of the Catholic intellectual to defend the traditional body of Catholic teaching as proposed by the *Magisterium*, that Catholic intellectuals are bound by the obligation to dissent, that the Catholic intellectual must be critical of the society and culture of which he is a part, that the Catholic intellectual must demonstrate that one can be a good Catholic and a good scholar at the same time, even though this often seems impossible, and that the Catholic intellectual must always be on the side of the poor against the rich.

I am reasonably confident that these arguments or ones similar to them will appear elsewhere in this volume. They are, as I have said, fun. But they are also a waste of time. Moreover, they imply the obligation of those who have some claim to be Catholic and intellectual to modify their attitudes and behavior to fit the definition being proposed. If you really want to be a Catholic intellectual, you must do what we say or you have no legitimate claim to the title. It is of the very nature of an intellectual to reject out of hand such an authoritarian demand, whether it comes from the Vatican or from another intellectual (or would-be intellectual).

My modest goal in this paper is to avoid such enjoyable but bootless arguments and address the empirical question of what Catholic intellectuals in fact are. Those who enjoy debating over theory and definitions will abhor this approach. They have made up their minds and do not want to be bothered by data. They will assert that truth is not gained by counting noses. They will brush aside my statistics as irrelevant. Who cares what people really are?

Nonetheless, because I am a hard-nosed and (to change the cliché) died-in-the-wool empiricist (and was long before I became a sociologist), I will persist in my heresy. I want to know more about what living, breathing, practicing Catholic intellectuals are like. In truth, I think that most of the theories that are propounded in the debate are rubbish because they represent only the experience of those Catholic intellectuals (or would-be intellectuals) who write about such matters and that these are not necessarily a representative sample.

I will address two sets of questions: 1) Are those Catholics who are engaged in academic pursuits discernibly Catholic? Do they differ in any important ways from intellectuals who are not

Catholic? 2) What is the nature of their relationship to the Catholic Church? Are they alienated from the Church? Or, to be more precise in the present Catholic context, are they more alienated than anyone else?

The first of the two sets of questions focuses on the issue of whether there is any such thing as a Catholic "sensibility"—a way of looking at reality from a Catholic viewpoint which may persist after someone has rejected the formal Catholic teaching and the authority of Church leaders. Shaughnessy raises this question in his study of the impact of Eugene O'Neill's Catholic background on his work. Even though he had left the Church and rejected all formal belief, Shaughnessy asks, was O'Neill still influenced by his Catholic heritage?

Shaughnessy makes his own the definition of "sensibility" proposed by Edward Cady:

> Deeper in the psyche than ideas, perhaps a source for them, certainly a major determinant of our choice of one possible idea in favor of another, sensibility is more than "feelings," emotion. It connotes tact, a feeling for life, a way of taking events and making experience, a ground for life-style and at last for morality.

"Sensibility," Shaughnessy goes on, "suggests a personal response, an individual's own psychological experience in receiving the worldview and the established values of the group." He concludes in his study that O'Neill was influenced in his work by his Catholic experience, even if he had departed from the Church. One must ask, therefore, whether intellectuals with a Catholic background bring a distinctly Catholic sensibility to their work, whatever may be their formal relationship with the Church.

Secondly, one must ask whether the Catholic intellectuals in the contemporary world find that they too must follow O'Neill's path and reject the Catholic heritage and the Catholic Church, even if they still view reality with a distinctively Catholic sensibility, or whether now they are able to combine their heritage and the institutional affiliation with their intellectual vocation.

Data and Theory

The data for this analysis (and for the six graphs illustrated herein) comes from the pooled General Social Survey, a study that the National Opinion Research Center has conducted for the last quarter-century. Of the approximately 32,000 respondents, a little less than 2% work in occupations that can fairly be described as "intellectual"[1]—some 636 individuals, of whom 172 are Catholics. Their occupations are based on the three-digit Census occupational code with which all General Social Survey respondents are categorized. Seven percent of the "intellectuals" are in the physical or life sciences, 18% in the social sciences, 28% are college or university teachers, and 55% are artists, journalists, musicians, composers, painters, sculptors, and writers. There are no differences between Catholics in this distribution and other "intellectuals."

There are two major disadvantages in using the General Social Survey data in this analysis: 1) The data embrace not a single year but a quarter century. 2) Six hundred and thirty six respondents constitute a very small sample. However, the principle advantage of General Social Survey data is that they actually exist. Since no one is likely to fund a detailed survey of the religious attitudes and behavior of Catholic intellectuals, a data set drawn from the pooled General Social Survey sample is the best we have or are likely to have to address this question. Moreover, while ideally one might want to have more than 636 respondents, this is a sufficient number to make possible tests of statistical significance when one compares Catholic intellectuals with other intellectuals.[2] Finally, while a quarter century is a broader analytic category than one normally uses in survey analysis, logically it is as valid as a year, so long as one makes one's estimates not to the present year, but to the present quarter-century. In fact, an investigation of some of the key variables in this analysis indicates that they have not changed appreciably in the last quarter century. Thus the regular church attendance of Catholic intellectuals has in fact increased six percentage points from the first half of the General Social Survey to the second half; and, while "trust" has diminished in American society in the last quarter-century, Catholics and Catholic "intellectuals" maintain their higher scores on the "trust" item. The reader is always welcome to fund his own research on this issue if he finds my argument tenuous.

If one adds the requirement that an "intellectual" must have a graduate degree, the numbers are reduced to 213, of whom 53 are Catholic. In either case, Catholics are approximately one-quarter of the country's "intelligentsia," the same proportion as in the general population. In this analysis, I will not add the constraint of a graduate school degree so as not to diminish even more the already thin case base. However, I did attempt to replicate the findings about the larger group on the smaller group and found no changes in the pattern I will report.

Forty-one percent of "intellectuals" who are not Catholic are women, as opposed to 47% of Catholics. There was no significant difference in educational attainment. Catholics were substantially younger than others: forty-three years old as opposed to forty-eight years old. Our data do not permit us to estimate how "good" Catholic "intellectuals" are at their work. However, they do earn significantly higher incomes.

I propose to measure the presence of a Catholic "sensibility" by considering two dimensions which recent writing considers to be characteristic of Catholic culture: communalism and sacramentalism (see Tracy; Greeley). Catholics, in David Tracy's words, tend to possess "analogical" imaginations; that is to say they tend to perceive the world as a revelation of God's presence. Moreover, the Catholic imagination tends to picture human relationships with reality as communal rather than individualist (Durkheim; Weber). Catholics tend to see religion and all other activities as behavior of communities rather than of isolated individuals.

Does this imagination, both sacramental and communal, survive the training and perspective required to be an "intellectual?" Or is it eroded by the socialization and acculturation process that the intellectual life demands?

Two questions must be asked of the measures used to operationalize these dimensions of the Catholic imagination: 1) Are Catholics in fact different from other Americans on these measures? 2) Are the Catholic "intellectuals" likely to have lower scores on them than other American Catholics, or are they more likely to have similar scores to the "intellectuals" who are not Catholic?

Communalism

There are two measures of communalism: propensity to frequent sociability and propensity to trust other people. If the imagination of Catholics is shaped by a religious worldview that emphasizes community, one can expect Catholics to be more sociable and more trusting. If the Catholic imagination is diminished by "intellectual" pursuits, then Catholic "intellectuals" will score lower than other Catholics on these measures.

The first measure is a scale composed of a group of six items which measure the social interactions of respondents:

How often do you spend a social evening
   a) with relatives;
   b) with someone who lives in your neighborhood;
   c) with friends who live outside the neighborhood;
   d) with your parents;
   e) with a brother or sister;
   f) at a bar or tavern.

A scale was formed of these six items. Catholics were significantly more likely to score above the mean on this scale than were others (Figure 1). Moreover, Catholic "intellectuals" had significantly higher scores than did Catholics who were not intellectuals. Far from weakening the Catholic propensity to sociability, an intellectual occupation seems to have enhanced it.

The second measure is the response to the question, "Do you think most people can be trusted?" While the response that most people can be trusted has diminished since the early years of the General Social Survey, Catholics have always been significantly higher than other Americans in their willingness to trust other people. Figure 2 shows this higher level of trust among Catholics and a higher trust among Catholic "intellectuals" than among other Catholics. Once again Catholic "intellectuals" not only display a greater trust than do other Americans, they also show a

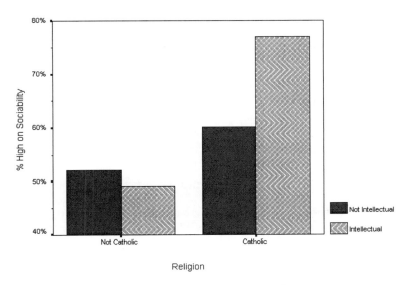

Figure 1. SOCIABILITY BY RELIGION AND OCCUPATION

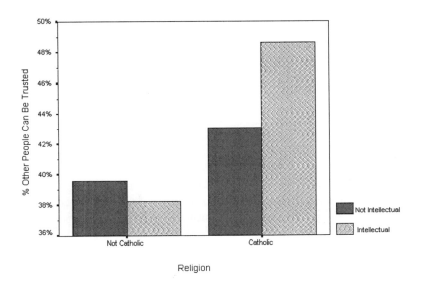

Figure 2. TRUST BY RELIGION BY OCCUPATION

greater level of trust than do other Catholics. It would have been sufficient for our contention that Catholics with an intellectual orientation in their career be no lower on the trust measure than other Catholics. In fact, however, they are higher on this measure.

We conclude from measures of sociability and trust that there is indeed a dimension of communalism in the Catholic imagination that shapes how Catholics perceive the world around them and that a career as an "intellectual" does not diminish the strength of this dimension. In fact, it would appear to sharpen it.

Sacramentality

Are Catholics, as David Tracy has argued, really more likely to have a more "analogical" worldview, more likely to see creation as reflecting a creator? A battery of items derived directly from Tracy's work was administered frequently in the General Social Survey. The question was worded as follows:

> Here is a card with sets of contrasting images. If you think that "the world is basically filled with evil and sin," you would place yourself at 1. If you think "there is much goodness in the world which hints at God's goodness," you should place yourself at 7. If you think things are somewhere between these two, you would place yourself at 2, 3, 4, 5, or 6.
>
> a) The world is basically filled with evil and sin . . . there is much goodness in the world which hints at God's goodness.
> b) The good person must be deeply involved in the problems and activities of the world . . . The good person must avoid contamination by the corruption of the world.
> c) God is almost totally removed from the sinfulness of the world . . . God reveals himself in and through the world.
> d) Human nature is basically good . . . Human nature is fundamentally perverse and corrupt.
> e) Through such things as art and music we learn more

about God . . . It is dangerous for a human to be too concerned about worldly things like art and music.

f) The world is a place of strife and disorder . . . Harmony and cooperating prevail in the world.

g) Human achievement helps to reveal God in the world . . . Most human activity is vain and foolish.

When a scale was prepared from these items and comparison made between Catholics and others (Figure 3), it became evident that Catholics were significantly more likely than others to have an analogical worldview, to see creation as good and as reflecting God. Moreover, Catholic "intellectuals" were significantly more likely than other Catholics to endorse items which reflect the analogical imagination.

A final measure of religious imagination is based on forced choices between images that come to mind when one hears the word God: Mother versus Father, Master versus Spouse, Judge versus Lover, Friend versus King. The scale which emerged from a factor analysis of these variables related positively with God as Mother, Spouse, Lover, and Friend and negatively with God as Father, Master, Judge, and King. Catholics were significantly higher than Protestants on this "Grace" scale and Catholic "intellectuals" higher than other Catholics (Figure 4).

Thus, as measured by both verbal statements and symbolic images, Catholic were more likely see the world as a sacrament of a warm and loving God and Catholic "intellectuals" even more likely than other Catholics. It was necessary for my theory only that Catholic "intellectuals" not be lower on these measures. However, it would appear that involvement in an "intellectual" occupation actually sharpens the Catholic sacramental perspective.

As one would predict from Tracy's theory of analogy and from Durkheim and Weber on the sacramental and communal aspects of Catholicism, Catholics are more likely to see the world as graced and the human community as reassuring. Catholics are different because they imagine reality differently, not completely different, but "significantly" different. Moreover, these differences have not been assimilated out of the Catholic imagination. They have not been eroded even by socialization into "intellectual"

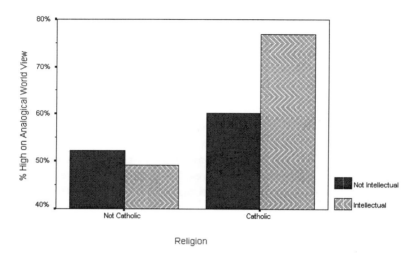

Figure 3. ANALOGICAL WORLDVIEW BY RELIGION AND OCCUPATION

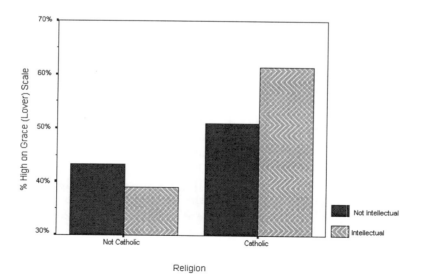

Figure 4. IMAGE OF GOD BY RELIGION AND OCCUPATION

occupations. I have argued for many years that Catholics are different, and neither theologians nor sociologists have paid any attention, worse luck for them.

Professor Robert Bellah announced recently that in America even Catholics had become Protestants. In a long career marked by foolish and undocumented statements, this one may take the prize as the most foolish and least documented. Catholics are different and Catholic intellectuals are even more different. Saying that they are just like everyone else is a social scientific and theological dogma for which there is simply no confirmation in the empirical data, and is also a gratuitous insult to American Catholics.

The Catholicism of the Catholic "intellectual," I suggest, comes from a specifically Catholic sensibility with which such a person looks at the world around her and relations between and among human persons. The "intellectual" with a Catholic sensibility tends to see the world as graceful (full of grace) and human community as supportive rather than oppressive. Will these different perspectives affect a Catholic intellectual's work? It will certainly not dictate answers to the issues which the "intellectuals" may address. If he is a sociologist, for example, it will not influence his findings on Catholic sexual attitudes. If he is a physicist, it will not affect his theories on the Big Bang or the Great Attractor.

However, imagination is important in any scholarly quest or administrative style. The questions one asks, the way one goes about answering the questions, the hints and insights one's imagination feeds to one, the instincts with which one approaches reality are all shaped by imaginative perspectives. The Catholic sensibility is different, and hence Catholic "intellectuals" tend perhaps to ask different questions, approach answers with different styles, listen to different whisperings from their creative imagination, and follow different instincts and hunches.

Is this difference "bad"? Ought all intellectuals be suspicious of too much sociability, too great trust, too much awareness of the mysterious and the revelatory, too many hints and hunches and insights that go beyond the current scholarly canons?

One can answer those questions in the affirmative only if one believes that there is no room for pluralism or variety in intellectual endeavor. The Catholic imagination, as David Tracy has so often argued, has no monopoly on truth and no inside track in the pursuit of truth. But neither is it without something important to contribute to the search for truth. Catholic intellectuals finally bring not different answers to intellectual matters but different styles.

What about social attitudes? Do Catholic intellectuals have different attitudes on such matters as Feminism?

Using the National Opinion Research Center Feminism scale (which, it must be remembered, was constructed more than twenty-five years ago) based on attitudes towards a woman president, women staying at home, and the family suffering if women work, one can see in Figure 5 that Catholics are significantly higher on pro-feminist attitudes than are other Americans. However, there is no significant difference between Catholic "intellectuals" and other intellectuals on this issue, though Catholic "intellectuals" do have higher scores on the Feminism scale than do other Catholics.

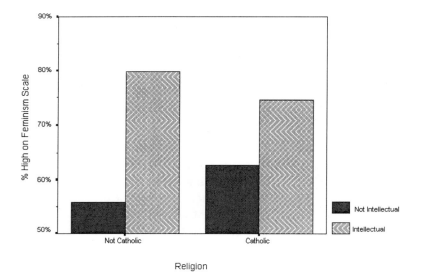

Figure 5. FEMINISM BY RELIGION AND OCCUPATION

In summary then, the answer to the first general question posed in this essay is that there is indeed a discernible difference between Catholic "intellectuals" and others in that the former imagine reality differently. Catholics do have a different sensibility. They are more likely to see the world as both communal and sacramental, as loving and trustworthy, than their secular counterparts and than do other Catholics.

Relationship to the Church

There was perhaps a time when it was hard to be an intellectual and a Catholic. Certainly there is enough autobiographical testimony and anecdotal suggestion that Catholics found it difficult to remain in the Church and at the same time pursue intellectual efforts. Is there any evidence that this is true today? Are Catholic "intellectuals" alienated from the Church? Are they less likely to be devout, more likely to reject the Church's sexual teaching, more anti-clerical, more committed to science as a religion than other Catholics? On balance the answers to these questions seem to be in the negative.

Twenty-six percent of those who are "intellectuals" today were raised Catholic, and 26% of intellectuals identify as Catholic today. Thus the Church has suffered no net losses in its "intellectuals." Eighty-nine percent of all of those who were raised Catholic are still Catholic, as are 81% of the intellectuals who were raised Catholic. Thus there has been a "leakage" of some eight percentage points more for "intellectuals" who were raised Catholic than for those in other occupations who were raised Catholic. However, this "loss" is canceled by the fact that virtually the same number of intellectuals have joined the Church. To put the matter differently, a quarter of the American intelligentsia apparently see no conflict between being a Catholic and working in an "intellectual" occupation.

It is possible that their Catholic affiliation is merely nominal. The issue is not whether all of them are devout, but rather whether Catholic "intellectuals" as a group are notably less devout than other Catholics. This does not in fact seem to be the case. In Figure 6, we observe that Catholic "intellectuals" are significantly

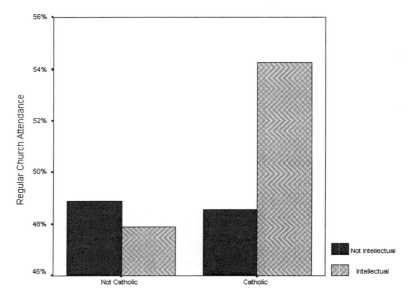

Figure 6. CHURCH ATTENDANCE BY RELIGION AND OCCUPATION

more likely to attend church services regularly (at least two or three times a month) than other Catholics.[3] Since church attendance among Catholic "intellectuals" correlates neither with education nor income, it cannot be argued that it is the "inferior" who participate frequently in religious services. A similar chart (not reproduced) shows that Catholic "intellectuals" are also more likely to pray daily than other Catholics.

However, Catholic "intellectuals" are also more likely to approve of the legality of abortion for any reason and of premarital sex than are other Catholics. It is worth noting, nonetheless, that a third of Catholics who are not "intellectuals" also support abortion for any reason and that only a fifth of Catholics who are not "intellectuals" think that premarital sex is always wrong. Thus, if there is evidence that on sexual matters Catholic "intellectuals" are alienated on these issues, they are only marginally more alienated than are other Catholics. The differences between the two groups of Catholics vanish when education, age, and gender are taken into account. Thus Catholic "intellectuals" are "softer" on abortion and premarital sex not because of their occupations but because they are younger, better educated, and more likely to be women than are Catholics in other occupations.

On the issue of abortion in cases of rape and incest, there is no difference between Catholic "intellectuals" and Catholics in other occupations: four out of five believe that it should be legal.

Science and Religion

There is no measure in the General Social Survey that makes it possible to ascertain directly whether Catholic "intellectuals" perceive a conflict between science and religion, the conflict which is supposed to have driven "intellectuals" away from the churches. However, there are two questions which enable us to construct a rough measure of such conflict. General Social Survey respondents are asked the following question: "I am going to name some institutions in this country. As far as the people running these institutions are concerned, would you say you have a great deal of confidence, only some confidence, or hardly any confidence at all in them?" Among the twelve groups proposed to the respondents for evaluation are "organized religion" and "scientific community."

Americans have much higher confidence in science leadership than in church leadership: 43% versus 31%. Catholics are significantly more likely than others to express a "a great deal of confidence" in the leaders of the scientific community and that Catholic intellectuals are significantly more likely than other Catholics to express such confidence. However, "intellectual" Catholics are less likely than other Catholics to express confidence in the church leadership, though the difference is not statistically significant. If one subtracts confidence in church leadership from confidence in scientific leadership, one may have a rough-and-ready measure of a perception of conflict between science and religion. Among "intellectuals" who are not Catholic, there is a significant difference in church attendance between those who are high on this conflict measure and those who are not. However, among Catholic intellectuals, the difference is much smaller and not statistically significant. The conflict between science and religion" affects the church attendance of other "intellectuals" but not of Catholic "intellectuals"—perhaps because they are able more easily to disregard their clergy leadership.

Therefore, to the question of whether Catholic "intellectuals" are alienated from the church (to any greater extent than other Catholics), we may answer that there is no net loss to the Church in its proportion of the American "intelligentsia"; that Catholic "intellectuals" are as likely as other Catholics to attend mass regularly and to pray daily; that they are marginally more likely to approve of abortion on demand and premarital sex than other Catholics but because of demographic reasons and not occupational ones; and that their Catholic devotion is unaffected by their perception of possible conflict between science and religion. Whatever may have been true in the time of Eugene O'Neill and James T. Farrell, it is now possible to be both an "intellectual" and a "practicing" Catholic.

Catholic "intellectuals," in sum, do bring to their work a distinctively Catholic sensibility, both communal and sacramental, and they are as likely to be active Catholics as are other Catholics.

Reflections

Some two percent of American Catholics, approximately eight hundred thousand men and women, qualify by their occupation as "intellectuals." They are for all practical purposes invisible. Most Catholic clergy do not know of their existence and could not care less about them. The Catholic "intellectuals" themselves are probably unaware that they constitute a quarter of the American "intelligentsia." Their Catholicism generally seems to be low-key. They do not deny their faith, but neither do they emphasize it, perhaps because they work in environments where they feel that their religion would put them constantly on the defensive.[4] Certainly the rest of the "intelligentsia" are serenely ignorant of the possibility that someone could be a good Catholic and simultaneously an able intellectual. They consider their Catholic colleagues who are good scholars to be happy exceptions. Anti-Catholicism continues to be the anti-Semitism of the American "intelligentsia." This prejudice is not sufficiently strong to affect hiring and promotion at state universities in this country. However, it persists in some of the great private universities.

Despite the Galileo affair (which was, be it noted, a long time ago), there is more room in the Catholic heritage for intellectual investigation and artistic exploration than there is in much of American Protestantism. Catholicism is not a fundamentalist religion. Catholic scholars need not worry about evolution or other problems of the literal interpretation of the Bible. They also attribute much less credibility to their religious leadership than do fundamentalist and evangelical Christians.

The emergence of an independent but faithful Catholic intellectual elite (and I use this word in the non-pejorative sense) is a "dirty little secret" of late twentieth-century American history that everyone wants to cover up, each for his or her own reasons.

When did the changes occur which seem to have made compatible loyalty both to the Catholic heritage and to an intellectual career? Shaugnessey suggests that the Catholic Church which emerged from the Second Vatican Council was utterly different from the Church which Eugene O'Neill knew. Certainly the Council made life easier for Catholic intellectuals. However, my research in June of 1961 showed that a Catholic intelligentsia was already emerging several years before the Council.[5] Data from the mid-fifties seem to anticipate this finding. In my own anecdotal experience as a seminarian frequently visiting the University of Chicago in the late nineteen-forties, there were already young Catholics present who were seriously devoted to both their work and their religion. The fervent campaign of the Catholic Church on Intellectual and Cultural Affairs in the late nineteen-fifties against Catholic "anti-intellectualism" (in the writings of Ellis, O'Dea, Donovan, and Weigel) was perhaps addressing a situation which no longer existed. The "big change," I would suggest, came during the "post-war" years, the era of the G.I. Bill between 1945 and 1950.

But what changed?

Were some "intellectuals-in-training" able to find priests who were sympathetic to them? Had the leaders of the Church institution mellowed somewhat because they were less defensive about the threats to the faith of their immigrant membership? Or were the third generation of Catholic Americans more likely to be confident of both themselves and their religious faith?

Perhaps the answer to all three questions is "yes." My own hunch in 1961 and today is that the emergence of the grandchildren of immigrants was a decisive phenomenon in American Catholic life, one that everyone knows about but few (especially Catholic leaders) factor into their attempts to understand Catholicism in this country. If the Second Vatican Council had not happened, American Catholicism would have had to invent something like it.

I find myself wondering how many more generations it will take before the existence of a large Catholic intelligentsia will cease to be an ugly little secret.

Notes

1. I place the word "intellectual" in quotation marks hereinafter because it is based on a nominalistic definition-occupation code. More theoretical and *a priori* definitions do not perhaps correlate with occupation. According to these definitions, a postal clerk may well be an intellectual and a person with a Ph.D. in astrophysics may not be an intellectual. Such definitions, however, cannot be measured in any meaningful fashion.

2. There are not enough cases in the sample to permit comparison between, for example, Catholic and Jewish intellectuals or Catholic and liberal Protestant intellectuals.

3. Catholic "artists" are eleven percentage points less likely to attend church than "scholars." However, the numbers on which this comparison are based are so small that the difference is not statistically significant.

4. Frequently they will tell one, "I was raised Catholic." Asked if they still go to church, they shuffle their feet and admit that they do. Occasionally, someone will acknowledge that they are on the parish council or the parish school board.

5. For which finding I was roundly denounced in a solemn high symposium in *The Commonweal*. That journal has never really forgiven me. In the last three-and-a-half decades they have routinely attack almost everything I've written. None of those who ridiculed the findings of *Religion and Career* either in the symposium or elsewhere have ever admitted that they were wrong.

Works Cited

Donovan, John D. 1964. *The Academic Man in the Catholic College*. New York: Sheed and Ward.

Ellis, John Tracy. 1958. *American Catholics and the Intellectual Life*. New York: Sheed and Ward.

Greeley, Andrew. 1964. *Religion and Career*. New York: Sheed and Ward.

_____. 1966. *Religion as Poetry*. New Brunswick, NJ: Transaction Publishing.

O'Dea, Thomas F. 1958. *American Catholic Dilemma: An Inquiry Into the Intellectual Life*. New York: Sheed and Ward.

Shaughnessy, Edward. 1997. *Down the Nights and Down the Days: Eugene O'Neill's Catholic Sensibility*. Notre Dame: Notre Dame University Press.

Weigel, Gustave. 1958. "Introduction" to O'Dea, *American Catholic Dilemma*. New York: Sheed and Ward.

CHAPTER TEN

The Catholic Intellectual Tradition: Some Characteristics, Implications, and Future Directions

ANTHONY J. CERNERA AND OLIVER J. MORGAN

As we close this first volume of essays entitled *Examining the Catholic Intellectual Tradition*, it seems appropriate to summarize and highlight some of the central themes of this "tradition," while offering some implications for Catholic higher education into the next century. In our own work in higher education over a number of years, we have come to believe deeply in the value of the Catholic intellectual tradition and Catholic higher education for our contemporary world. We have felt the challenges to both that are inherent in today's culture. Notwithstanding these challenges, we believe that a clear description of the tradition as it has matured over time and is available for continued development may be helpful in the current situation.

An important benefit to such a description is its value for the enterprise of Catholic higher education. We believe that a critical element in the crisis of identity and mission facing Catholic colleges and universities is the uncertainty, even ignorance, of many regarding the tradition. Yet today, as perhaps never before, there is a need for educated and committed Catholic leaders and scholars who can bring the values of the tradition to their essential social roles. Institutions of Catholic higher education are critical points of contact for training the next generation of such leaders.

In addition, we believe that the sense of a teaching and scholarly "vocation" that can come from an appreciation of the tradition, and the challenge to foster an integration of knowledge and spirituality on which the tradition has been based, are themes that can meet the deepest desires of many working in higher education today, faculty and staff alike.[1]

We agree with Edmund Pellegrino, who, in summarizing the views of Pope John Paul II, reviews changes in Catholic higher education over the last several decades and suggests an "urgent need" for renewal of the tradition:

> Today, more than ever, there is urgent need for educated Catholics who can fuse religious conviction and professional competence in the face of the most profound inversions of human values Western society has ever faced. At a time when their future may be more problematic than ever, the necessity for an intellectual ministry only Catholic universities can fulfill is more evident than ever. . . . It is the integration of all knowledge, new and old, with the truth of the Gospels that constitutes the unique and irreplaceable intellectual ministry of Catholic universities.[2]

An added benefit of this examination from our point of view is the contribution that a clear understanding of the tradition will make to the overall intellectual climate of society and the confidence of many Catholic scholars. We believe that this is a time of transformation for the Catholic intellectual tradition, when the achievements of the past are clear, the challenges of the present sometimes seem overwhelming, and the outlines of the future are murky at best. It is well to remind ourselves, as Gerald McCool has done earlier in this volume, that the tradition has adapted and transformed itself before; those times of transformation must have seemed equally daunting and uncertain to those experiencing them. This is to be expected in a time of radical transformation, when the old must die to make way and give birth to new forms and structures. Patience and conviction are called for in such a time. McCool reminds us that even now small groups of scholar-believers may well be at work on the process of revival. A fresh articulation of central themes and concerns of the tradition may help to offer insight and encouragement.

Finally, as Dr. Monika Hellwig, current President of the Association of Catholic Colleges and Universities (ACCU) reminds us, the many colleges and universities that make up Catholic higher education are "responsible more than any other body for the care and continuity of the Catholic intellectual tradition. . . . Most basic to the whole enterprise is respect and care for the Catholic intellectual heritage." It is incumbent on all of us who work in Catholic higher education to explore and familiarize ourselves with the core aspects of the tradition that is uniquely interrelated with our enterprise. The tradition gave birth to great texts and works of art that are part and parcel of our civilization and educational task, as well as to the great European universities that are the cultural ancestors of our own institutions of learning. It nourished the formative education of many generations of Catholic scholars and students. In turn, the Catholic colleges and universities have become privileged places for the transmission and development of the tradition. This dual task—faithful transmission and ongoing development—makes a claim on scholars and others responsible for the tradition into the next century.

A Basic Typology

Hellwig's "typology" of the tradition offers an apt starting point. There is a Catholic *heritage* of intellectual, religious, and aesthetic works that is an essential part of the tradition. These are the classic treasury and library, the honor roll of hallowed names that characterize the tradition in its fullness. From the great treatises of the patristic writers, such as Clement, Origen, and Gregory, to the works of the Doctors of the Church, such as Bonaventure, Theresa, and Catherine of Sienna; from Augustine's *Confessions* to Pope John XXIII's *Journal of a Soul* and Thomas Merton's *Seven Storey Mountain*; from the philosophical theologies of Thomas Aquinas and Duns Scotus to the more contemporary theologies of Karl Rahner, Bernard Lonergan, and Hans Urs von Balthasar, the tradition is rich in reflections on human living from a Catholic viewpoint. From the religious poetry of John Donne and Denise Levertov, to literary works like *The Divine Comedy, Canterbury Tales* and *The Brothers Karamazov,* even up to the more modern literary writings of C.S. Lewis, Walker Percy, Flannery O'Connor, Georges Bernanos, and James Joyce, there is a full library of penetrating insight into the vagaries of human living. From the soaring beauty of medieval chant to the musical gifts of Bach and the pictorial art of Michelangelo and the architectural treasures of the great cathedrals, the Catholic tradition has inspired a wealth of imaginative works in praise of God and the human spirit. All these and so much more are part of the heritage of the Catholic tradition.

A second element of the tradition (and one more important for our essay here) is the *way of proceeding* of the Catholic intellectual tradition, what Hellwig calls its "way of doing things." Andrew Greeley, in his essay on Catholic intellectuals, speaks of a uniquely Catholic "sensibility"; John Breslin alludes to a "Catholic imagination." In separate essays McCool speaks of a "Catholic mind" and the "Christian wisdom tradition." Louis Dupré speaks lovingly about the "integrating transcendent perspective" of a Christian liberal education, while Ursula King speaks—no less lovingly but with more of a critical edge—about the need to assess the Catholic intellectual tradition as an important task at the end of the millennium.

Clearly a central task of higher education, beyond increasing students' technical and professional knowledge-base (in their majors) and familiarizing them with the great classic treasures of the past (often relegated to the general education core), is to aid them in developing a reflective habit of mind and heart, a way of learning that can last for a lifetime, a set of integrating questions and concerns that they can bring to each new endeavor. It is our belief that the Catholic intellectual tradition offers such a distinctive "way of doing things" that is at the heart of Catholic identity . . . of individuals and of institutions as well.[3]

In his provocative essay, Jeremy Driscoll helps the reader to see that an intellectual tradition of any kind, if it is to be "useful," is the catalyst for a "way of thinking" with distinctive themes and tones and is deeply connected to a "way of living." Immersing oneself in such a tradition, allowing oneself to be shaped by its concerns and sensitivities, its themes and habits of mind and heart, leads both to wisdom and to principled action. Allowing oneself to be formed by the Catholic intellectual tradition engenders several qualities or habits of thinking and living.

A Way of Thinking: A Way of Living[4]

As several writers in this volume have suggested, the formative aspect of the Catholic perspective lies in fostering an *integrative* and *contemplative* habit of thinking. Rooted in the Word of God and a lively sense of God's ongoing action in the world, the basic value of all created things and of the means for learning about them is affirmed and grounded. Nothing in creation, when viewed in relation to its rootedness and fullness in God, is foreign. In the work of redemption, which is ultimately the task of faith, the use of human means and of the various branches of learning is valued. All aspects of the human person and human development—intellectual, moral, affective, imaginative, communal—are nurtured.

The vision and values of the Catholic intellectual tradition are "world-affirming," resolutely maintaining the inestimable worth of human beings "created in the image and likeness of God" (Genesis 1:27), and the inherent goodness of the created world that is "charged with the grandeur of God,"[5] while confidently searching for the presence of God "in all things."[6] This is a deeply Catholic, *sacramental* view which integrates learning and faith, spirituality and scholarship. God is present and working in all of creation: in nature, in history, in human culture, in each human person. Because every element in creation and every valid method for learning about the created world is worthy of study, exploration, and contemplation, the impulse to a mission of education and learning is never very far from Catholic faith. The inner dynamic of Catholicism moves inevitably toward intellectual exploration and verification.

Education based on this vision values imagination and wonder as well as the desire to learn and to know, and it leads the learner to discern and act in concert with the will of the God who labors at the heart of the world:

> The entirety of Catholic liturgical life—indeed, of Catholic spiritual, intellectual, and ethical life—is geared toward producing *sacramental beholders*, people who see what is there in its full depth. That should sound familiar to educators. Is it not true in every field, whether we teach philosophy or chemistry, literature or finance, that we strive to lead people to see what is there to be seen? I am suggesting that the Catholic sacramental principle supports this with the conviction that what is there to be seen in its depth is grace. Consequently, *to teach any discipline or field is a holy activity.* . . . I suggest to you that sacramental beholders are what Catholic universities and colleges are supposed to be producing.[7]

Another quality or habit of mind that is engendered by the Catholic intellectual tradition is a move toward critical and active *engagement* in the world and human affairs. The truly Catholic perspective reveres and privileges a critical religious worldview as mutually complementary to the stance of affirmation and wonder. These are not opposed poles. "Critical" here refers to a habit of mind and an educational approach that is informed, hard-headed, reflective, and dialogical.[8]

Catholic universities are called to be privileged *loci* of dialogue between faith and culture. Engaging in this dialogue requires openness to questions of faith, openness to the struggles and values of modern culture, a willingness and the discipline to examine one's faith and the values of one's culture critically, and a commitment to search for the truth. In *Ex Corde Ecclesiae*, John Paul II underlines the need for a faith engaged this way in the affairs of the world:

> A faith that places itself on the margin of what is human, of what is therefore culture, would be a faith unfaithful to the fullness of what the word of God manifests and reveals, a decapitated faith, worse still, a faith in the

process of self-annihilation. . . . A Catholic university must become more attentive to the cultures of the world of today and to the various cultural traditions existing within the church in a way that will promote a continuous and profitable dialogue between the Gospel and modern society?

In a truly Catholic university this dialogue of faith and culture becomes a touchstone of authenticity for the mission-related, core disciplines such as theology and philosophy; it also becomes an exciting challenge for the other academic disciplines. A truly Catholic university understands that this dialogue is essential, both for the Church and for human culture:

> A Catholic university . . . is a primary and privileged place for a fruitful dialogue between the Gospel and culture. . . . Through this dialogue a Catholic university assists the church, enabling it to come to a better knowledge of diverse cultures, discern their positive and negative aspects, to receive their authentically human contributions and to develop means by which it can make the faith better understood by the men and women of a particular culture.[10]

Yet, this dialogue is only one form of engagement that the Catholic perspective envisions. The other is an active involvement in the struggle of faith and justice. The Catholic tradition, rooted as it is in biblical and religious values, shapes a vision of true human living and the world, a vision of the way human life and creation ought to be. In this way it is inseparably linked to the struggle for faith that does justice, a struggle that is central to the Kingdom of God and the mission of the church. This vision makes a claim on each of us, as believing Christians and religious institutions, to see to it that the promises of the Kingdom are made real and active in human living today. It challenges us to make compassion, care, and justice real in our own lives and particularly in the lives of those who are poor or oppressed. It confronts us, as individuals and as institutions, with the lives of the poor and summons us all to act as "neighbor" to them.

The importance of dialogue between faith and culture is perhaps more clear and concretely specified here than elsewhere. A biblically- and spiritually-based critique of modern culture is a real strength that the Christian tradition brings to scholarship about, commitment to, and work for justice. Because of its primary commitment to a more universal, religiously-based system of values and beliefs, the Catholic intellectual tradition can offer a powerful critique of cultural forces that are destructive, oppressive, and often hidden from view. An authentically "inculturated" proclamation of the Gospel will always both appreciate and critique contemporary culture, relativising its values and raising up hidden questions of value and justice.[11]

Here a Catholic institution of higher learning, rooted in its founding perspective, can be of enormous value to its culture. In a culture where many educational institutions of quality abound, such as the United States, the linkage of religious commitment, educational purpose, and concern for justice out to be highlighted as a mark of distinction. The mission and identity of an authentically committed Catholic institution of learning, linked to faith and service, can shape the imagination of its community and graduates, affect its choices and policies, and provide the focus for its research, outreach, and service to the community and culture that surround it. Ignacio Ellacuria, S.J., the martyred Jesuit rector of the University of Central America (El Salvador) puts this task succinctly:

A Christian university must take into account the gospel preference for the poor. This does not mean that only the poor study at the university; it does not mean that the university should abdicate its mission of academic excellence—excellence needed in order to solve complex social problems. It does mean that the university should be present intellectually where it is needed: to provide science for those who have no science; to provide skills for the unskilled; to be a voice for those who have no voice; to give intellectual support for those who do not possess the academic qualifications to promote and legitimate their rights.[12]

Finally, the Catholic intellectual tradition, rooted in a faith nurtured in community and tradition, seeks to be fully *collaborative.* This is one of the deep impulses signaled in the dynamic of Vatican Council II, particularly in its Pastoral Constitution on the Church in the Modern World (*Gaudium et Spes*):

> The joy and hope, the grief and anguish of the men of our time, especially of those who are poor or afflicted in any way, are the joy and hope, the grief and anguish of the followers of Christ as well. Nothing that is genuinely human fails to find an echo in their hearts. . . .
>
> In wonder at their own discoveries and their own might men are today troubled and perplexed by questions about current trends in the world, about their place and their role in the universe, about the meaning of individual and collective endeavor, and finally about the destiny of nature and of men. And so the Council, as witness and guide to the faith of the whole people of God, gathered together by Christ, can find no more eloquent expression of its solidarity and respectful affection for the whole human family, to which it belongs, than to enter into dialogue with it about all these different problems. . . . It is man himself who must be saved: it is mankind that must be renewed. It is man, therefore, who is the key to this discussion, man considered whole and entire, with body and soul, heart and conscience, mind and will.[13]

This stance of solidarity with humanity and collaboration with persons of good will, with their knowledge, values, and commitments, is eminently practical today. With the information explosion and our understanding of the complexity of problems in our time, it is difficult to imagine any individual scholar having the depth and breadth of knowledge required for a real contribution. Rather, the paradigm today is "teams" of scholar-learners, working collaboratively toward solving common problems and investigating areas of need.[14]

Catholic universities can best serve their cultures by providing an intellectual context and resources for such collaboration, while encouraging the connectedness of scholars and their branches of knowledge. In helping to create this climate of collaboration, the Church and its institutions of higher learning foster communication and dialogue that allows for its own values, commitments, and religious identity to become part of the search for truth.

These habits of mind and heart—integrative, contemplative, engaged, collaborative—are important results of exposure to the Catholic intellectual tradition, when all goes well. Scholars and leaders shaped by this tradition seek to incorporate these qualities into their lives and work.

Next, we turn our attention to several hallmarks of the tradition which characterize it as distinctively Catholic. In doing so, we will try to lay out some implications of the tradition as an intellectual tradition with a view to the context of higher education.

The Catholic Intellectual Tradition: Characteristics and Implications

What are the major themes and concerns of the Catholic intellectual tradition? What are some of its essential characteristics? And, what are the implications of these themes for higher education?

We suggest that as a living tradition of faith and intellect, the Catholic intellectual tradition is characterized by several distinctive themes: a) a unique theological anthropology, b) a sacramental view of creation, c) a conviction about the unity (continuity) of faith, reason and the search for truth, d) and a view of Catholicism as *Katholikos*. As the reader will note, many of the chapter authors in this volume have addressed these themes in their essays.[15]

Theological Anthropology

As *Gaudium et Spes* states, the "key" to a Catholic approach to life in our time is humanity itself.[16] It is not surprising to us then that John Paul II, an acute observer of modern life, has highlighted themes of human nature and dignity in many of the encyclicals of his pontificate.[17] "Man is the way for the Church," as John Paul suggests, and we would add, for the Catholic intellectual tradition as well.[18]

As it was from the outset, so too now the Catholic intellectual tradition must be rooted in a theological anthropology adequate for our times. A distinctive element of Catholicism is its understanding of human existence and what it means to be human. Human beings are made in "the image and likeness of God" (Genesis 1:26-27 and 9:6). Every human being is a spiritual creature who is alive by the breath of God which dwells in us. This is the basis of human dignity and personhood. Since each human person is an image of God (imago Dei), it can be said that, in a very real sense, every human being reflects God. The twentieth-century German theologian Karl Rahner, S.J., captured this fundamental insight of Catholic anthropology this way: "When God chooses to be what is not God, man comes to be."[19]

The Judaeo-Christian tradition affirms that persons have inherent worth and dignity before God, and are called into fullness of life and deepening relationship with God, with one another, and with all of creation. The imago Dei, that divine image that is basic to each person as created by God, is not a substance or entity, but rather a relation that specifies the peculiarly human vocation of responsible caring for one another and for all of creation, or alternatively a call to full communion with God and all creation. This core belief about human persons is one side of a Catholic theological anthropology; the other, complementary side is the astounding statement of the Incarnation.

When the Christian community gathers at the Eucharist on Sundays, those present profess in the Creed a core belief of Catholicism, indeed what some commentators would suggest is its most distinctive or defining element, namely, the Incarnation of the Word of God: "For us and for our salvation he came down from heaven; by the power of the Holy Spirit, he became incarnate of the Virgin Mary and was made man." This is not simply a vision of human existence with God "at our side"; rather, it is the unheard of statement that God became one of us, so much does God love us.

For Catholicism, as indeed for all Christian churches, the center-point of human history is that the Son of God became incarnated in Jesus of Nazareth. The eternal Word of God is made visible in the flesh. This has consequences for all of human history, both before the historical event of Jesus and into the future. God is definitively present in all of history from the beginning of time, in the present, and into the future, a future which will find its fulfillment in the final establishment of the reign of God

Rooted in these two principles of *imago Dei* and Incarnation, human existence is always graced existence. This existence, which is radically oriented toward God, is also radically social and relational. Not only do we go to God with one another, but our destiny is also fundamentally linked with all of humanity. Furthermore, there is a special connection to the poor and those who are deprived of their fundamental humanity. In the Catholic view, my humanity is diminished when the dignity and worth of another human person is damaged or destroyed. A vision of the human person and her or his fulfillment necessarily involves an active concern for justice in the world.

Several important implications emerge from this distinctively Catholic anthropology as it relates to the Catholic intellectual tradition. First and foremost, the Catholic university is the place where the deepest aspirations of the human person and the community are of utmost importance. At a Catholic university, the fundamental questions of Who am I? Whose am I? Why am I here? and, Where am I going? are of critical importance. The Catholic tradition continually raises the question "How shall we live?" as human persons with intellectual, emotional, communal, moral, and spiritual needs and desires. It privileges dialogue about faith, principled living, and concern for justice as integral to its essentially religious identity and educational mission. A Catholic institution of higher learning, shaped by this tradition, views its work as education of the imagination, individually and corporately, allowing the best in human and gospel values to shape a vision of human living and the world that is its context. Because of their effects and implications for all of us, these are not isolated concerns. They are profoundly social and deeply religious questions, and they are of ultimate significance.

Students at a Catholic university ought to be provided with ample opportunities to search for the meaning and purpose of their lives within the context of humanity's collective wisdom. In addition, the search for a more fully developed and fully integrated humanity ought to permeate the research and teaching of the faculty and provide a distinctive organizing principle for the general education program for undergraduate students.

Furthermore, it is clear from this perspective that there are always moral and spiritual dimensions to education. Education in the Catholic tradition is concerned about the whole person. A complete education assists students in their human development as persons. The end result toward which Catholic higher education strives is not simply the inculcation of knowledge or skills, valuable as these are. The Catholic educator also envisions her or his graduate as learned, virtuous, and spiritually aware, and Catholic educators commit themselves to fostering these values in their students. The goal is integration of the life of the mind with habits of the heart and right living. Thus, the Catholic university is the place where the religious and the academic are intrinsically related.

Michael Buckley captures this notion well:

> Any movement toward meaning and truth is inchoatively religious. This obviously does not suggest that quantum mechanics or geography is religion or theology; it does mean that the dynamism inherent in all inquiry and knowledge—if not inhibited—is toward ultimacy, toward a completion in which an issue or its resolution finds place in a universe that makes final sense, i.e., in the self-disclosure of God—the truth of the finite.
>
> At the same time, the tendencies of faith are inescapably toward the academic. This obviously does not suggest that all serious religion is scholarship; it does mean that the dynamism inherent in faith—if not inhibited—is toward its own understanding, toward its own self-possession in knowledge. In their full development, the religious intrinsically involves the academic, and the academic intrinsically involves the religious—granted that this development is *de facto* always imperfectly realized at best or even seriously frustrated.

To grasp the character or promise of the Catholic university, one must understand this unique institution as an organic fulfillment of the two drives for knowledge out of which it issues: the drive of inquiry toward an ultimacy or that comprehensive meaning that is the object of religion; the drive of Christian faith, i.e., of living within the self-giving of God in Christ and in the Spirit, toward the appropriation of this comprehensive experience in understanding. The inherent integrity of faith-experience moving toward intelligence and of finite intelligence moving toward completion, this mutual entailment is what a Catholic university must affirm and embody, however halting and imperfect its attempts.[20]

Creation as Sacred

Created ourselves as persons, all of us are born deeply connected to the world of created things and others. In biblical terms, the ultimate context for human living is the essential goodness of all created things, of creation as a whole (Genesis 1 and Psalm 104). God intends that all humans live in harmonious relationship with creation. The biblical-theological term for this harmony in creation is *Shalom*.

A more contemporary, ecologically-sensitive theology understands all of creation, as it comes from the hand of God, as sacred, and the role of stewardship that humans have in regard to creation as a sacred trust. That trust is given to persons as a result of their creation in the image of God. It depends upon a sacramental and contemplative sense of "the way things are." At their depth, all persons and things are rooted in God.

In an older anthropology, human creation as *imago Dei* was understood as rooted in human rationality and was characterized by themes of sovereignty, domination, and hierarchy. When seen in this partial light, creation is to be subdued and used in view of human needs and desires, whims and pleasures. This skewed view has led to such modern problems as environmental pollution, the arms race, and widespread addiction. Contemporary theologians, however, point out that the biblical notion of *imago Dei*, while viewed in terms of rationality among the Western fathers (Augustine and Aquinas, for example), can also be viewed as pointing more toward relationality on the model of the inner fellowship of the Trinity, as Orthodox theologians (for example, Gregory of Nazianzus) often did. This relational view may help to complement the theology of *imago Dei* based on the rational nature of human persons, and will be more consonant with modern sensibilities.

In this view, God intends that all humans live in harmonious relationship with creation. Humanity is entrusted with the care of creation, and persons are to act as "responsible stewards" of this gift of God. Humans are to exercise caring relationship toward the whole of creation, a task given by God for cooperative work with God and the human community. The cooperation of human and divine care maintains creation's *Shalom*.

The sacredness of creation and the Incarnation of the Word of God into history and human existence led to a sacramental principle which pervades how Catholicism engages the world. According to St. Augustine, a "sacrament" is a visible sign of an invisible reality. That invisible reality is grace or the divine presence. Pope Paul VI, in his opening address at the second session of the Second Vatican Council in 1963, expressed this classical view in a more contemporary way by referring to a sacrament as "a reality imbued with the hidden presence of God." The sacramental perspective of Catholicism maintains that one can "see" the divine in the human, the infinite in the finite, the spiritual in the material, the transcendent in the immanent, the eternal in the historical. For Catholicism, all reality is potentially sacramental. According to the Catholic understanding of things, it is in the visible, the tangible, the finite, and the historical that God can be found. All of these are actual or potential carriers of the divine presence.

As we have seen, this sacramental view can lead to a contemplative stance toward living and a sense of all creation as sacred. In Catholic colleges and universities, this translates into concrete goals and objectives for general education, major and elective courses, as well as for the other campus activities that promote the development of the whole person.

Colleges and universities are learning communities—what Rabbi David Novak hearkens back to as *universitatis magistrorum et scholarium*—intentionally "centered on knowing the great things of the world."[21] Higher education explores those things that—in the words of Parker J. Palmer, Senior Associate at the American Association of Higher Education—"reveal the world in its wonders and its terrors and its ordinariness" and they give birth to new initiates who learn the methods and disciplines—and practice the virtues—that allow them to become explorers in their own right.

Notice the metaphor here: not independent, solitary, disconnected learners (explorers), which all too often is the image for scholarly research used in the academy. We have in mind the training of explorers in the habit of collaborative and connected learning.[22] A modern scholarly community should train community-minded and collaboratively competent scholars, whose gift is the exploration of great things in interdependent ways. True research requires multiple perspectives and the cooperation of diverse inquirers. Do our classrooms, our student and faculty performance measures, our scholarly projects reflect such an ideal?

What is meant by "great things" as used above? It is important to understand this term as we use it, because we are suggesting that much of our life together in the Catholic academy should be organized around the exploration of and conversation about these "things." In keeping with what we've said so far, let us try to be clear here.[23]

We study and learn about the elegant miracles of DNA and the beautifully complex ecosystems of biology: we even apply ecosystemic models to more deeply understand human functioning in family and society. We study particles and force fields in physics, and we grow to understand that subatomic particles have the same deepest quality as newborn infants, namely, that they are hard-wired for relationship. But do we intentionally make these connections between the knowledge-base of our various disciplines and the truth about their relationship to human living and a sense of creation as grounded in divine purpose? Do we point students toward a sense of contemplation, of wonder?

We study the great works of literature and philosophy, and we come to understand that these works also study and illuminate us as spirited and sinful persons and the struggles in which we engage as part of the human condition. We study the patterns and characters of history, the claims made upon us by the law and the demands of justice; we study the economics that bind (and sometimes divide) us and the languages that allow us to reveal (and sometimes hide) ourselves; we study the artifacts left behind by other humans who have preceded us. But do we ask our students to consider how these "things" are related to them and to their lives now? Do we suggest that there might be ways to integrate the knowledge and wisdom of the past into a deep and values-rich way of thinking and living in the present? Do we speak about the yearnings of the human spirit that we might discern in our disciplines and the roots (goal) of this yearning in a desire for God?

We study more efficient and productive ways to care for one another, medically and psychologically, and we learn how to educate the young and care for the challenged and the elderly. We learn about the strengths and frailties of our human bodies and psyches. But, within this learning do we teach respect for the uniqueness of each human person and allow students to touch something of the needs of the human spirit? Do we aid students and colleagues to understand something of our divine character as "children of God," created in God's image and greatly loved?

These and other fields of study, we suggest, constitute the "great things" around which we gather as a community of scholar-learners. We gather around the "great things" of the world as God's creation.

In the face of "great things"—challenging, humbling, and mysterious as they are—there is a risk of absolutism or unbridled anarchy; there is also a risk of disconnected objectivism. Any of these can lead to what Whitehead called "inert ideas," the bane of higher education. However, when in our studies, in our labs, in our classrooms, we connect the "great things" to our own stories and to God's larger story, they come alive in our knowledge. They make a claim on our lives. They challenge us to act. Knowing, ultimately, is profoundly relational, a sacred act that leads to further action. As Palmer suggests in many of his writings, we must learn more deeply about knowing as an act of love, and love as a form of knowledge. In this way perhaps the "hidden divine" reveals itself.[24]

This task of true integration—connecting our disciplines with a wider vision, binding scholarship and spirituality—is an ongoing challenge for Catholic higher education.

Faith, Reason, and the Search for Truth

From a basic theological anthropology and theology of creation, there follows a third distinctive characteristic that is important for our reflections on the Catholic intellectual tradition. Catholicism maintains that there is a fundamental relationship of compatibility and continuity between faith and reason. Reason is fundamentally trustworthy and ultimately cannot conflict with faith. Reason can be allowed to, indeed should be encouraged to, in the words of John Paul II, "search for truth wherever analysis and evidence leads."[25]

The Catholic intellectual tradition affirms the significant role of the human intellect in the search for and discovery of truth. This search is ultimately for God, who is the source and goal of all human desire to know. The tradition affirms that human beings have the ability to grasp and understand truth through rigorous intellectual activity. Through the use of our reason, we can come to significant knowledge of the world. This includes the important task of reflection on experience and engagement in the world. Critical thinking and reflective action, as well as research, inquiry, and questioning, are cherished values of this tradition and should characterize the intellectual life of a Catholic university in all its dimensions.

For Catholicism, as in Judaism, truth has its origins in God who can "neither deceive nor be deceived." Rabbi David Novak has suggested a new role of a Catholic university in our contemporary culture. His notion is provocative, and we quote it at length:

> In earlier modernity it could be assumed that the difference between a Catholic university and a secular one was located in the proper object of the spiritual quest for truth. The quest itself was assumed to be common to all,

however. Thus it was commonly held that human persons are beings engaged in a search for truth that is proper to both their own nature and the nature of the things they seek to know (*veritas sequitur esse rerum*). Today such an assumption can no longer be made. There are large segments of the university world, especially in the humanities (which is the modern location of the study and teaching of philosophy), who do not believe that there is any real truth, either within humans or within the world, and that the search for it, by whatever means, is therefore quite futile. Human intellect, then, is simply a function of the power interests of the particular group one happens to be part of. Only power, not truth, is real and worth dealing with. In this world, there is no longer any tension between faith and intellect because there is no longer any truth over which they can even quarrel. Without the assumption of the reality of truth, neither faith nor intellect can really desire (*quaerere*) anything. The only thing left then is either at best compromise or at worst conquest. But neither compromise not conquest is an act of faith or of intellect. Thus we are left today with neither theology nor philosophy but only ideology. And, of course, in this kind of world, there is no need for a university anymore, whether a Catholic university or even a secular one.

Into this empty cultural situation both faith and intellect must forcefully reinsert and reassert themselves. That cannot be by argument, because there is nothing outside of them to argue with anymore. Instead, it must be by demonstration, by showing that human life and culture, as Aristotle said about nature, cannot stand a vacuum, in our case the intellectual vacuum that the denial of truth necessarily entails. For Catholics, this reassertion can perhaps best come through the revitalization and rededication of one of the greatest contributions your tradition has made to our civilization: the university as *universitatis magistrorum et scholarium* (community of teachers and scholars). Such a community seems to be possible only when truth is accepted from one's background and hoped for on the horizon.[26]

This principle of Catholicism forms the basis for a strong defense of academic freedom at a Catholic university. It is precisely because there is a fundamental relationship of compatibility and continuity between faith and reason that a Catholic university seeks to ensure the scholar's search for truth. Understood in this context, a denial of a professor's academic freedom would be a failure to affirm the Catholic university's conviction that the source and goal of truth is one.

This distinctive feature also relates to the idea that the Catholic university is the place where the search for truth is cherished and nourished. Since the truth is whole, there is also a fundamental unity and interconnectedness of knowledge. This conviction of the Catholic intellectual tradition is the basis of interest in interdisciplinary and collaborative approaches to learning and scholarship. In addition, it is the reason why education in a Catholic context is always interested in the synthesizing of knowledge. Learning is not complete without the students learning how to bring together what they have learned in a variety of places.

Catholicism as "Katholikos"

Towards the end of the Nicene Creed, the community professes its belief in the "one, holy, catholic, and apostolic church." The Jesuit scholar Walter Ong has noted that the early Church chose to use the Greek word *katholikos* rather than the Latin equivalent *universalis*. While both words mean universal, *universalis* carries within it the image of turning around a point, describing a circle and hence an area with boundaries. *Katholikos*, on the other hand, means throughout-the-whole. It suggests permeation, a leaven within a larger whole that expands as the larger whole expands.

As Ong pointed out,

"throughout-the-whole," *katholikos*, "catholic," does not suggest a boundary as "universal" does. It is expansive, open, growing. If the whole gets larger, what is "throughout the whole" gets larger too. This concept "throughout-the-whole" recalls Jesus' description of the kingdom of God as leaven, yeast, placed in dough. In Matthew 13.33 (echoed in Luke 13.21) we read, "The reign of God is like the yeast which a woman took and kneaded into three measures of flour. Eventually the whole mass of dough began to rise." Yeast is a plant, a fungus, and it grows. It has no limits itself, but is limited only by the limits of whatever it grows in. The Church, understood as Catholic in this way, is a limitless, growing reality.[27]

The Church is more fully catholic when it is *katholikos*. The Church gathered at the Second Vatican Council was a visible manifestation of what Walbert Buhlmann and Karl Rahner have called the "world-church." Gathered together for the first time were representatives from every continent of the planet, no longer only Europeans or North Americans representing those continents. During the twentieth century, the geographical center of Catholicism has shifted from Western Europe and North America to Latin America, Africa and Asia. Today more than 70% of the 1.1 billion members of the Catholic Church live on these continents, whereas at the beginning of the century, 90% of Catholics lived in Europe and North America.

The Second Vatican Council recognized that the twentieth century was a period of rapid and profound change. Seeking to understand better the nature and implications of this ongoing change, the Council developed a process of reflection and thinking referred to as "reading the signs of the times" (*Gaudium et Spes*). The Church recognized that it has much to learn from as well as to contribute to the world.

One would expect to find at a Catholic university in North America a commitment to serious study of the Western intellectual tradition. That tradition has been shaped and has carried the Catholic intellectual tradition for two thousand years. However, because of this last distinctive element within Catholicism, an education at a Catholic university should encourage its students to learn about cultures and traditions beyond their own. Such learning is done in ways that foster synthesis and greater understanding among people. This again calls for teaching and learning that explores the "depth" of things, that opens out from knowledge to mystery and wonder, that challenges learners to move from scholarship to contemplation.

This integrative "way of doing things" does not come naturally or easily, however. Faculty and staff must remind themselves that integration of learning is not solely the task of students; it depends in great measure on the modeling and mentoring of experienced explorers. We, faculty and staff alike, must ask the questions, demonstrate the potential paths of thinking and living that can lead to outcomes we hope for, namely, graduates with competence, compassion, and conscience.[28]

Two particular challenges face faculty and staff in realizing this ideal. First, it has been clear for some time that undergraduate students now come to Catholic colleges largely ignorant about their own Catholic faith and the intellectual tradition on which it is based. This challenge must be acknowledged and faced forthrightly. Second, it cannot be presumed on any particular Catholic campus that there is a unity of formation goals among groups that used to be more in tune with one another, for example, faculty student activities, extracurricular opportunities, campus ministry, and the like. Consequently, from the perspective of the Catholic intellectual tradition, students come to our campuses more needy and will meet an older adult community not quite so unified as before about the goals of their work.

This situation calls, we believe, for a long-term investment by Catholic institutions and for commitment by all those who work in Catholic higher education. This investment and commitment must be focused on appreciation and reappropriation of the mission of Catholic higher education. While many institutions have moved forward in developing a clearer sense of corporate identity and mission, this sense of mission must permeate into the teaching, scholarship, service, and professional identity of those who work in the enterprise. This is an ongoing and difficult challenge.

In part, this challenge is becoming the catalyst for examining hiring and promotion practices at Catholic institutions. While some have interpreted this challenge as presenting a mandate for hiring only Catholics, we do not agree with such a strategy. Many men and women of good will, and of diverse backgrounds and faiths, are willing to explore openly the themes and concerns we've laid out above. In our view, the presence of such scholars from different faiths yet open to exploring the richness of the Catholic tradition offers a real treasure to Catholic education.

However, a contemporary movement, complementary to the work on institutional identity, must also begin among faculty and staff who apply for work at Catholic institutions and intend to remain on campus. This entails a personal and professional commitment to learning about the Catholic intellectual tradition and integrating the teaching of one's discipline and conduct of one's scholarship with the concerns and sensitivities of the Catholic tradition. In order to mentor students well and to continue the development of the Catholic intellectual tradition, persons of good will who intend to allow their own vision and work to be shaped by Catholic values are needed on campuses. Persons who freely affiliate with institutions of Catholic higher education ought to be committed to this task of personal and professional integration as a matter of honesty and authenticity. Every person who works in a Catholic institution and exercises stewardship within it holds a public trust that is rooted in the institution's public stance. This entails reclaiming a sense of "vocation" or "calling" in the work of education and scholarship, nourished by the common vision offered by the Catholic intellectual tradition.

We suggest that one way in which such an endeavor of integration might occur is to follow the process of Vatican Council II, and from each person's particular discipline attempt to "read the signs of the times."[29] What are the particular challenges to human living and meaning that emerge from one's discipline? How are these addressed in one's classroom? In student projects? In one's scholarship? How might these concerns be addressed collaboratively with other scholars from relevant disciplines? How do my work, and the way I conduct myself personally and professionally, relate to the mission of the institution to which I belong?

Such an endeavor offers exciting challenges and possibilities to us all.

Conclusion

"Without vision, the people perish."
(Proverbs 29:18)

In this final chapter of the first volume of *Examining the Catholic Intellectual Tradition*, we have attempted to describe some hallmark characteristics of the tradition and some of their implications for Catholic higher education. In a sense we have now come full circle, arguing for the need for scholars, teachers, and others who are willing to pursue the hard task of integrating the concerns and themes of the Catholic intellectual tradition into their own work. And the need is genuine. Only the active presence of such scholars on our campuses—at least a critical mass of them within the larger community—will justify the designation "Catholic" college or university over the long term. In addition, it will be the contributions of such scholars that will insure the continued development of the Catholic intellectual tradition into the next century.

In Volume 2, we intend to engage in some exploration of the Catholic intellectual tradition from a variety of disciplinary perspectives. It is our hope that this second volume may help to stimulate discussion among colleagues in different disciplines within Catholic higher education.

Notes

1. A number of contemporary authors are reexamining the roles and interconnections of religious identity, spirituality, higher education, and modern academic culture. Such authors include: Philip Gleason, *Contending with Modernity: Catholic Higher Education in Twentieth-Century America* (New York: Oxford University Press, 1995); Jaroslav Pelikan, *The Idea of a University: A Reexamination* (New Haven: Yale University Press, 1992); Mark R. Schwehn, *Exiles From Eden: Religion and The Academic Vocation In America* (New York: Oxford University Press, 1993); John E. Tropman, *The Catholic Ethic in American Society* (New York: Jossey-Bass, 1995); and David J. O'Brien, *From The Heart of The American Church: Catholic Higher Education and American Culture*

(New York: Orbis, 1994). This reexamination is more positive and appreciative than the previous suspicious stance that adopted a facile anti-religious, even anti-Catholic bias in academia.

2. Edmund Pellegrino, "Catholic Universities and the Church's Intellectual Ministry: The Crises of Identity and Justification," *Thought* 57 (1982): 165-81.

3. "Distinctive," as used here, does not indicate "one of a kind," as though only the Catholic tradition offers such a perspective. Rather the term is meant to indicate "a special attention to" or "concern for" this characteristic or set of concerns.

4. Several of the ideas in this section were developed in *A University Committed to Ignatian Educatiion* (1996), the final report of the Task Force on Ignatian Identity and Mission, University of Scranton.

5. G.M. Hopkins, "God's grandeur," in W.H. Gardner, ed., *Gerard Manley Hopkins: Poems and Prose* (NY: Penguin, 1978). See also his "As kingfishers catch fire."

6. St. Ignatius Loyola captures the depths of this Catholic perspective in establishing the ideal of Jesuit spirituality as "finding God in all things," since that is precisely where God can be found. A hallmark of Ignatian spirituality and the educational vision that flows from it is this contemplative impulse to "find God in all things" and all things in God. See, for example, *The Spiritual Exercises of St. Ignatius Loyola*, #236.

7. Michael Himes, "Living Conversation: Higher Education in a Catholic Context," *Conversations* (Fall 1995), 21, 27 (emphasis added).

8. Pedro Arrupe, former Superior General of the Society of Jesus (Jesuits), often spoke of being "sympathetically critical" as a prophetic stance toward world and culture in the context of religiously-based university education. The true prophet measures human experience and culture by the values of God, understanding the sinfulness that infects human experience and the hostility to God that still resides in human culture. The "sympathetic" prophet also sees with God's eyes, loving the sinful person and hostile culture, and calling both to salvation by that love. See his *Inaugural Address to the Convention of Jesuit Academic Directors of Institutions of Higher Learning*. Rome, August 5, 1975.

9. John Paul II, *The Apostolic Constitution on Catholic Universities (Ex Corde Ecclesiae)*, in *Origins* 20, no. 17 (October 4, 1990): 266-276; see #44.

10. John Paul II, *Ex Corde Ecclesiae*, #43-45, 48-49.

11. This is a concrete example of how the Catholic intellectual tradition, and of an educational institution rooted in it, can be critically world-affirming, adopting a "sympathetically prophetic" stance even toward its own culture.

12. Ignacio Ellacuria, "The Task of a Christian University." Speech given at Santa Clara University in acceptance of an honorary doctorate (June, 1982). Quoted in Teresa Whitfield, *Paying the Price: Ignacio Ellacuria and the Murdered Jesuits of El Salvador* (Philadelphia: Temple University Press, 1995), 221, 455. In this and all subsequent quotations throughout our essay, such terms as "man," "men," and "mankind" are to be understood not as gender-specific but as references to all of humankind.

13. Ellacuria, "The Task of a Christian University," #1, 3.

14. Schwehn, *Exiles From Eden*, speaks of this as a need for "spirited inquiry" or "a communal questioning in search of the truth of important matters" (44, 65).

15. An earlier form of much of the remainder of this essay was published in Anthony J. Cernera, "The Catholic Intellectual Tradition and Sacred Heart University," *Sacred Heart University Review* 18, nos. 1 & 2 (Fall 1997 / Spring 1998): 74-84.

16. *Pastoral Constitution on the Church in the Modern World*, paragraphs #1, 3. See Austin Flannery, *Vatican Council II: The Conciliar and Post-Conciliar Documents* (Northport, NY: Costello, 1992).

17. See John O'Donnell, "Theological Anthropology in the Encyclicals of John Paul II," in *Continuity and Plurality in Catholic Theology: Essays in Honor of Gerald A, McCool, S.J.*, ed. Anthony J. Cernera (Fairfield, CT: Sacred Heart University Press, 1998).

18. *Redemptor Hominis*, #14.3. In *The Encyclicals of John Paul II*, ed. With introductions by J. Michael Miller (Huntington, IN: Our Sunday Visitor, 1996).

19. Karl Rahner, *Foundations of Christian Faith* (New York: Seabury Press, 1978), 48.

20. Michael J. Buckley, "The Catholic University and the Promise Inherent in Its Identity," in John Langan, ed., *Catholic Universities in Church and Society: A Dialogue on Ex Corde Ecclesiae* (Washington, D.C.: Georgetown University Press, 1993).

21. Parker Palmer, "Remembering the Heart of Higher Education," delivered at AAHE's National Conference on Higher Education, March 14-17, 1993, in Washington D.C.

22. See Parker Palmer, *To Know as We Are Known: Education as a Spiritual Journey* (San Francisco: Harper, 1993). See also Palmer's 1993 lecture, "Remembering the Heart of Higher Education."

23. We are indebted to the thinking of Parker Palmer and others for their contribution to these reflections, although their application within a Catholic educational context is purely our own.

24. Palmer, *To Know as We are Known.*

25. John Paul II, *Ex Corde Ecclesiae.*

26. David Novak, "Comment" on Michael Buckley's essay, "The Catholic University and the Promise Inherent in Its Identity," in Langan, ed., *Catholic Universities in Church and Society*, 99-100.

27. Walter J. Ong, "Realizing Catholicism: Faith, Learning, and the Future," Marianist Award lecture, 1989; monograph published by the University of Dayton, 1989, 8.

28. Pater-Hans Kolvenbach, current Superior General of the Jesuits, speaks of the kind of personal and professional integration that ought to characterize the graduate of Catholic higher education: "We aim to form leaders in service, in imitation of Christ Jesus, men and women of competence, conscience, and compassionate commitment." In "Themes of Jesuit University Education," an address at Georgetown University, Washington, D.C., 1989.

29. Readers are encouraged to consult the document, *Gaudium et Spes*, for a sense of how such a "reading" might be conducted.

NOTES ON CONTRIBUTORS

JOHN B. BRESLIN, S.J., is a member of the New York Province of the Society of Jesus, currently assigned as rector of the Jesuit Community at Le Moyne College, where he also teaches in the English Department. Before going to Le Moyne in 1999, he served as University Chaplain (1992-96) and director of the press (1981-91) at Georgetown University. He has also served as literary editor at *America*, the Jesuit weekly journal of opinion (1971-77), and as an editor in the religion department of Doubleday publishers (1978-80). He has published many reviews and essays, and has edited an anthology of modern Catholic fiction, *The Substance of Things Hope For* (Doubleday, 1987), which is currently distributed by Georgetown University Press.

ANTHONY J. CERNERA, PH.D., has been President of Sacred Heart University in Fairfield, Connecticut since 1988. He earned his doctoral degree in systematic theology at Fordham University and continues to teach at both the undergraduate and graduate levels. He has lectured extensively on world hunger, on justice and peace issues, on social action, and on a variety of theological topics. His articles have appeared in *Living Light, Momentum*, and *The Way*. He has edited three books: *Toward Greater Understanding* (1995), *Vatican II: The Continuing Agenda* (1997), *Continuity and Plurality in Catholic Theology* (1998), all published by the Sacred Heart University Press.

FRANCIS X. CLOONEY, S.J., is Professor of Comparative and Systematic Theology at Boston College. He is the author of *Hindu Wisdom for All God's Children* (Orbis, 1998), and editor and translator, with Anand Amaladass, of *Preaching Wisdom to the Wise: Three Treatises by Roberto de Nobili, S.J.* (Institute of Jesuit

Sources, 2000). In addition, he has started work on a new book on "the idea of God" in a comparative theological context.

JEREMY DRISCOLL, O.S.B., S.T.D., is a Benedictine monk and a priest at Mount Angel Abbey in Oregon. In addition, he is a professor of theology both at Mount Angel Seminary and at the Pontifical Athanaeum Sant' Anselmo in Rome, spending one semester each year in each school. His main fields of academic interest are patristics and liturgical theology as well as the specific contribution that monastic theology can make to the general academic discourse in theology. He also writes poetry with a view toward expressing in that genre the best insights of the Catholic spiritual tradition.

LOUIS DUPRÉ, PH.D., has been T.L. Riggs Professor of Philosophy and Religion at Yale University since 1973. Recognized as a preeminent Catholic philosopher, author, and lecturer, Dr. Dupré is a past president of the American Catholic Philosophical Association and of the Hegel Society of America. He has lectured at universities throughout the United States and Europe, including his alma mater, the University of Louvain, and participates in the biennial Colloque de Rome in Philosophy and Religion. The author of several books, including one on Marxism, his most personal book is *Transcendental Selfhood* (Seabury Press, 1976), in which he assembled evidence from a number of viewpoints for a religious conception of the person.

ANDREW M. GREELEY, PH.D., is a Roman Catholic priest, a theologian, a distinguished sociologist, a best-selling novelist with over fifteen million copies of his books in print, a newspaper columnist, and the author of many scholarly works. He is also a Research Associate at the National Opinion Research Center (NORC) at the University of Chicago and an Honorary Senior Fellow at the University of Ireland in Dublin. He divides his teaching time between the University of Chicago and the University of Arizona in Tucson.

MONIKA K. HELLWIG, PH.D., has been serving since 1996 as executive director of the Association of Catholic Colleges and

Universities (ACCU). Before that, she enjoyed a thirty-year relationship with Georgetown University, ultimately honored as Landegger Distinguished Professor of Theology. She has been a visiting professor at eleven institutions and has received more that two dozen academic honors. She has authored or co-authored nearly twenty books, contributed more than fifty chapters to other theological books, and produced more than sixty magazine or scholarly articles.

URSULA KING, PH.D., received her STL degree from the University of Paris, her M.A. from the University of Delhi, and her Ph.D. from the University of London. Since 1989 she has been a professor and the department head for the University of Bristol's Department of Theology and Religious Studies. For five years she was Visiting Lecturer in the Department of Philosophy at the University of Delhi and for eighteen years was lecturer and senior lecturer in the Department of Theology and Religious Studies at the University of Leeds. In addition, she is the author of several books, including *Women and Spirituality* (New Amsterdam Books, 1989), and the editor of several others, including *Turning Points in Religious Studies* (T & T Clark, 1991).

GERALD A. MCCOOL, S.J., Professor Emeritus at Fordham University in New York, is considered to be one of the pre-eminent scholars of Thomistic thought. His many published works include deeply influential studies of the roots of contemporary Catholic thought, such as *Catholic Theology in the Nineteenth Century* (Seabury, 1977), and his history of Thomism, *From Unity to Pluralism: The Internal Evolution of Thomism* (Fordham University Press, 1989). The collection of essays *Continuity and Plurality in Catholic Theology*, published in 1998 by the Sacred Heart University Press, honors and further elaborates on Father McCool's many contributions to examining the Catholic intellectual tradition.

OLIVER J. MORGAN, PH.D., is Associate Professor and Chair of the Department of Counseling and Human Services at the University of Scranton in Pennsylvania. He is also Co-Chair of that university's Center for Mission and Reflection. Trained as a pastoral and clinical theologian with specializations in marital and family therapy and addictionology, Dr. Morgan is a National Certified Counselor (NCC), a Diplomate in Psychotherapy (DAPA), and a Clinical Member of the American Association for Marriage and Family Therapy. He has published a number of articles and book reviews at the interface of counseling and pastoral theology in the *Journal of Religion and Health*, the *Journal of Pastoral Care*, and the *Journal of Ministry in Addiction and Recovery*, and has edited, with Merle R. Jordan, *Addiction and Spirituality: A Multidisciplinary Approach* (Chalice Press, 1999).

INDEX